D0948916

COMING THROUGH FIRE

COMING THROUGH FIRE

GEORGE ARMSTONG CUSTER
AND CHIEF BLACK KETTLE

DUANE SCHULTZ

WESTHOLME
Yardley

Facing title page: "Desperate battle between the Cheyennes and Company C Seventh U.S. Cavalry near Fort Wallace, June 26, 1867." (*Library of Congress*)

Westholme Publishing, LLC
904 Edgewood Road
Yardley, Pennsylvania 19067

ISBN: 978-1-59416-165-0

Printed in the United States of America.

Book Club Edition

CONTENTS

PROLOGUE
AND THE BAND PLAYED "GARRY OWEN"

Camp Supply, Indian Territory
December 1, 1868

The Osage scouts led the colorful procession down the hill. They were dressed as though they were going to war, and their faces were painted in bright colors and menacing designs. They galloped in circles, chanting war songs and yelling battle cries. They fired their rifles into the air as they made their way to join the blue-clad US troopers lined up at the bottom of the hill, waiting for the victory celebration to begin.

Colorful shields were slung over the warriors' shoulders, along with bows and quivers of arrows. Scalps lifted four days before, the blood dried and matted, hung from the tips of their spears. More scalps dangled from their saddles, along with strips of red and blue flannel torn from the blankets of their enemies, the Cheyenne. The scouts' long hair locks, swaying as the men rode, were decorated with silver ornaments taken from the bodies of their victims.

Only one man rode silently. Chief Little Beaver sat on his horse with dignity, heading in a straight line for the troops at the bottom of the hill while the others continued to ride in circles around him. He neither yelled nor fired his rifle; only for one brief moment did his expression become animated. "They call us Americans," he shouted. "We are Osages."

His warriors cheered in agreement. One of them, Koom-la-Manche, called Trotter by the white man, held up a scalp that was decorated more prominently than any other. He said he took it from the head of their greatest enemy, Black Kettle, chief of the Cheyenne.

It was ten o'clock on a bright Tuesday morning. And the band played "Garry Owen."

California Joe came next, leading the white scouts. A great bear of a man, he puffed on a pipe that jutted out from flaming red whiskers. A large-rimmed sombrero hung low over his eyes, and pieces of straw, dried leaves, and blades of grass littered his beard from the previous night's sleep on the bare ground. Old Joe was not the most fastidious of men, but he had spent the last forty years out West and could track an animal or an Indian better than just about anyone.

Of course he drank a lot and sometimes kept the others awake at night with his drunken yelling and cursing. And he gambled away most of his pay on poker—at least what was left after buying rotgut. But in spite of his hard living, he was a crack shot and seemed to know every trail, mountain pass, and watering hole as far south as Mexico. On he came down the hill, riding a mule, unfazed by the Osage scouts yelling and firing their rifles. Nothing much bothered California Joe. And the band played "Garry Owen."

The general came next, riding a prancing black stallion at the head of his staff. He had a beard and wore a fringed buckskin jacket and overshoes made from the hide of a buffalo with the hair on the inside for added warmth. At twenty-eight, he carried himself with a dashing, magisterial air. He was five feet ten inches tall and kept himself a trim 160 pounds, with broad shoulders, narrow waist, powerful arms and legs, and an expansive chest. His usual shoulder-length, wavy, bright blond hair was cut short today, but he remained an extremely handsome man. When he was in his late teens and teaching school, one of his female students said, "What a pretty girl he would have made."

George Armstrong Custer had always exhibited great flair and flamboyance in his appearance and manner, and he had about him something of an imperial bearing, which was certainly the way he felt that morning. And no wonder. He had once again achieved his lifelong ambition: to attain glory and fame.

"In years long numbered with the past," he wrote the year before the Battle of the Washita River in 1868, "when I was merging upon manhood, my every thought was ambitious—not to be wealthy, not to be learned, but to be great."

One year earlier, he had suffered the embarrassment of a dismal failure in his first campaign against the Indians. And then he was court-martialed and suspended from active duty for a year. Now, after his victory over Chief Black Kettle on the banks of the Washita River four days ago, he would again become the national hero he had been during the Civil War. Now he would be known as the greatest Indian fighter of them all. He had inflicted a major defeat on the Cheyenne, which had stunned all the other tribes. He had attacked the village of a major Indian chief, catching it by surprise in winter, something the tribes thought whites could never do. The defeat that the Cheyenne suffered demoralized all the other Indians of the Great Plains.

Custer had destroyed the entire wealth of the village—everything the people had acquired so diligently to last them through the long winter. He had slaughtered over seven hundred of their horses, ponies, and mules, and put to the torch everything they owned.

The Cheyenne who escaped the battle alive were destitute. They had nothing left but the meager clothes they had been wearing when the opening notes of "Garry Owen" woke them up that awful morning.

"We destroyed everything of value to the Indians," Custer wrote in his official report. Unofficially, he told his commanding officer, "We have cleaned Black Kettle and his band out so thoroughly that they can neither fight, dress, sleep, eat or ride without sponging upon their friends." He was not exaggerating. It was an unparalleled victory.

Custer "emerged from the Washita campaign a new man. Fame . . . had touched him again, feeding his hungry ego and giving him renewed purpose in life. Military success [at Washita], contrasting with his sorry performance in 1867, allowed the general to regain mastery. . . . Now he had a new identity and a new public persona, one firmly locked to the frontier West rather than the Civil War East: shrewd and skilled Indian fighter, mighty hunter, and master plainsman." And he owed it all to the man waiting for him at the bottom of the hill, the man who had given him a second chance at glory, General Philip Sheridan.

And the band played "Garry Owen" as Custer came down the hill. He had chosen it as the official regimental song when he took command of the newly formed 7th US Cavalry two years before, in 1866. One of his troopers, an Irishman, was singing the song one day after he had a bit too much to drink. Custer heard it, liked the song's cadence, and began to hum along.

The eighteenth-century Irish drinking song had a lively beat to it and reminded Custer of the "trampling and roar of a cavalry charge." It became forever associated with Custer's 7th Cavalry, and he ordered his band to play it on every important occasion.

> Let Bacchus' sons be not dismayed
> But join with me, each jovial blade
> Come, drink and sing and lend your aid
> To help me with the chorus.

> Instead of spa, we'll drink brown ale
> And pay the reckoning on the nail;
> No man for debt shall go to jail
> From Garryowen in glory.

Our hearts so stout have got us fame
For soon 'tis known from whence we came
Where 'er we go they fear the name
Of Garryowen in glory.

The Osage's prisoners came next: fifty-three women, girls, and young children—orphans and widows now—riding Indian ponies they had picked out of the herd before the troopers slaughtered all the rest. They were wrapped in brightly colored blankets, many of them scarlet, the favorite color of the Plains Indians. All of them, adults and children, were wrapped so tightly that only their eyes could be seen. They looked straight ahead or down, never to the sides at the guards forming two lines hemming them in.

A reporter for the *New York Herald*, DeBenneville Randolph Keim, described the scene:

"The mothers had their offspring mounted behind them, the papoose being visible only by its diminutive head peering over the back of its mother. As many as three were mounted on some of the ponies. Without a sigh, without a glance to the right or to the left, these remnants of the band of the once powerful Black Kettle, followed with all the submission of captives."

The older ones were terrified of what lay in store for them. They had seen what happened to captured white women and children, and they assumed the same fate was now in store for them: rape, bondage, being sold into slavery, or mutilation and death. They were so fearful that those who had been wounded in the battle and were in pain did not make a murmur or a whimper. Better not to draw attention to yourself.

Black Kettle's sister, Mahwissa, was among them. She had told Custer back at the Washita that the chief and his wife had both been killed in the opening minutes of the attack. When she last saw them they lay face down in the freezing waters of the Washita River, but at least he had escaped the indignity

and shame of being scalped. The Osage scout who held aloft
what he claimed was Black Kettle's scalp was wrong.

Black Kettle was finally dead. There was a bitter irony that
his death, of all the deaths of the Plains Indian chiefs, marked
Custer's greatest success in trying to subdue the Indians. More
than any chief of any tribe, Black Kettle had believed that
making peace with the whites was the only way for his people
to survive.

He had somehow kept believing that his people could
peacefully share the land even after growing hordes of whites
overran the country and started killing off the buffalo. And he
persisted in working for peace despite repeated violations of
treaty after treaty, each one guaranteeing peace to the Indians,
their own land from which whites would be excluded, and
annual payments of goods and supplies to keep them alive.

Not one treaty had brought peace and the promise of survival to the Indians, and yet Black Kettle continued to hope
that a just peace was possible. He had to keep believing that,
for he knew the alternative was annihilation through disease,
hunger, poverty, and more attacks from soldiers like the one
that almost took his life four years before, on November 29,
1864, at Sand Creek, in Colorado Territory. No band played
"Garry Owen" then.

Unlike his camp at the Washita River, Black Kettle's camp at
Sand Creek in Colorado Territory had not been hidden away
in some isolated wilderness where Osage and white trackers
like California Joe had to plow through deep snow for days to
find. Everyone in authority in Colorado Territory knew precisely where Black Kettle was because the army had told him
to camp there. There was no reason for him to hide back in
November 1864. He and his people were under the protection
of the US government. He even flew a large American flag over
his village so his people would know they were safe.

But that had made no difference to a zealous preacher turned soldier, Colonel John M. Chivington, and his regiment of Colorado Volunteers. They attacked the village at dawn, just as Custer would do four years later at the Washita, and they slaughtered more than one hundred Cheyenne, mostly old men, women, and children. Chivington's men engaged in an orgy of bloody, obscene butchery and mutilation that spared neither woman nor child.

Black Kettle miraculously escaped that time, and he still tried to work for peace. He saw more clearly than any Indian chief that there was no other way to even hope to survive.

Now Black Kettle was gone, the wealth of his people destroyed, many of them dead and still more homeless, while a single line of fifty-three captive women and children came slowly down the hill toward Camp Supply. Behind them, in a long column four troopers abreast, stretched the eight hundred men of the 7th Cavalry. Leading them were the sixteen men of the regimental band, with chief trumpeter Albert Piedfort in front. The band "made a colorful display; for the drummer, with his drums fastened to either side of the pommel, twirled his batons and crossed them in striking the drums, and the trumpeters flourished their brass horns between phrases of the music."

As they passed General Sheridan in formal review at the bottom of the hill, Custer's officers saluted with their sabers. Sheridan lifted his cap to return each salute. Custer later wrote that "General Sheridan said that the appearance of the troops, with the bright rays of the sun reflected from their burnished arms and equipments, as they advanced in beautiful order and precision down the slope, the band playing, the blue soldiers' uniforms slightly relieved by the gaudy colors of the Indians all combined to render the scene one of the most beautiful he remembered ever having witnessed."

It was a day of unremitting glory for George Armstrong Custer as the band played "Garry Owen"—victory, pageantry and redemption, and renewal. He would never know another day like it.

ONE

THEY WILL KEEP COMING

B lack Kettle, chief of the Southern Cheyenne, was a warrior long before George Custer was born. Not that anyone knew exactly how old he was, Black Kettle included. Indians did not describe the age of a man with precision. There was no need to, any more than there was a need to divide the passage of a day into artificial fragments such as hours and minutes. The day was defined by the passage of the sun overhead; the year measured by the phases of the moon, the presence or absence of grass for the ponies, the direction of the wind, whether creeks and rivers ran full or empty, and where the buffalo could be found. All these described the passage of time.

Some white settlers who knew Black Kettle estimated his age to be between the midforties and midfifties in the year 1861, when twenty-one-year-old Custer went to war for the first time. But those were the white man's years. What mattered to Black Kettle was not how many winters he had seen, but whether he could still ride like the wind at one with his horse, count coup on his enemies, and kill the buffalo. Those were the meaningful measures of a Cheyenne warrior's age.

As chief, Black Kettle knew he needed more than years. He also counted on wisdom and foresight to lead his people in the face of the cataclysmic changes that were accompanying the appearance of white settlers on the plains. The Cheyenne's world was changing with each wagon train and every mile of railroad track laid on the open range, with every farmhouse, town, fence, and rutted trail. Black Kettle could accept what his younger warriors could not—that there would be no future, no survival, for the Cheyenne nation unless it made some accommodation with this seemingly endless stream of people pouring in from the east. They came like the rivers in the spring overflowing their banks and flooding the land, leaving nothing standing.

Black Kettle had forced himself to put aside his days as a warrior a dozen years before the Civil War began, and he committed himself to making peace. He knew he had no choice; otherwise, his people would all die off. He believed the tale of the Cheyenne prophet, Sweet Medicine, which had been passed down from generation to generation. He learned it as a child, heard it as a fierce young warrior, and kept it in his mind as a chief, the prophecy that told of the doom of the Cheyenne. Sweet Medicine had understood, long before the first settlers came. And he told his story over and over.

Sweet Medicine, it was said, lived through four lifetimes of ordinary men. Babies were born, grew old, and died, and still Sweet Medicine lived. Every summer he appeared to be a young warrior, but when the grass dried up every fall, he began to age. When the snows of winter covered the ground, he walked slowly, bent over, old and feeble. And every spring he came to life and told his tale once more. It was a frightening story of people with oddly light-colored skin, people no

Cheyenne had ever seen, who would come among them and spread misfortune, calamity, disease, and death.

"Listen to me carefully," Sweet Medicine said. He repeated the warning three times. "Our great-grandfather spoke thus to me, repeating it four times. He said to me that he made us, but he also made others. There are all kinds of people on earth that you will meet some day, toward the sunrise, by a big river. Some are black, but some day you will meet a people who are white—good-looking people, with light hair and fair skin."

"Shall we know them when we meet them?" one of those seated around him asked.

"Yes," Sweet Medicine replied, "you will know them, for they will have long hair on their faces and will look different-ly from you. They will wear things different from you. You will talk with them. They will give you shiny things which flash the light and show you your own image, and something that looks like sand that will taste very sweet. They will wear what I have spoken of, but it will be of all colors, pretty. Perhaps they will not listen to what you say to them, but you will listen to what they say to you. They will be people who do not get tired but who will keep pushing forward. They will always try to give you things, but do not take them.

"At last I think that you will take the things that they offer you, and this will bring sickness to you. These people do not follow the way of our great-grandfather. They will travel everywhere, looking for a stone that our great-grandfather put on earth."

Sweet Medicine kept talking, even though his voice was growing weak and faint. He was so very tired, but he had much more to tell his people, more dangers to warn them about, more prophecies of doom and disaster that the white people would bring to the Cheyenne.

"Something [else] will be given to you, which, if you drink it, will make you crazy.

"There will be many of these people; so many that you can-not stand before them. On the rivers you will see things go up and down, and in these things will be people, and there will be things moving over dry land in which these people will be.

"Another animal will come, but it will not be like the buffalo. It will have long wavy hair on its neck and a long heavy tail. When these animals come, you will catch them, and you will get on their backs and they will carry you from place to place. You will become great travelers. If you see a place a long way off, you will want to get to it, so at last you will get on these animals. From that time you will act very foolishly. You will know nothing.

"These people will not listen to what you say. What they are going to do they will do. You people will change. At the end of your life in those days you will not get up early in the morning, you will never know when the day comes, you will lie in bed, you will have disease and will die suddenly. You will all die off.

"They will try to teach you their way of living. If you give up to them your children, those that they take away will never know anything. They will try to change you from your way of living to theirs and they will keep at what they try to do. They will work with their hands. They will tear up the earth, and at last you will do it with them. When you do, you will become crazy, and will forget all that I am now teaching you."

Sweet Medicine finally died, but the tale he told, the awful prophecy he left as his legacy, was told anew to each generation. Until it all came true.

Black Kettle did not heed Sweet Medicine's warnings when he was young, because he was a warrior then and had no fear of anyone. He earned great honor and glory and became the most famous of the Cheyenne chiefs, "the greatest chief the Cheyenne possessed," who "earned undying fame on the warpath."

In the Cheyenne's frequent battles with other tribes, Black Kettle was given the honor of carrying the Cheyenne Sacred

Arrows. They were considered to be the strongest and most powerful of the Cheyenne medicines. Losing them in battle to enemies would bring on great disaster. Only the most courageous could be trusted with their safety.

The Cheyenne had always been fierce and proud warriors. Every boy wanted to be like Black Kettle and fight, and, if need be, die in battle. The goal of every boy was to grow up to become the bravest of the brave. They focused so intently on courage in battle that they took bigger risks than Indians from other tribes. As a result, they came to be greatly feared.

But when back in their villages, it was a different story. "Cheyenne women ruled the camps, spurred men on to necessary duties, and checked them when unwise actions were contemplated. Although the women did not take part in tribal councils, their influence was immediate upon their husbands. Arguing, cajoling, and persuading, the Cheyenne women carried their points about tribal concerns."

Away from their villages, Cheyenne warriors ruled their own lives. They fought to gain the approval of others, but also for the sheer exuberant joy of it. War was a game to them, a great hunt, and young braves always went to war with pleasure and happiness. They needed enemies to fight in order to enjoy their lives to the fullest. As they wandered over the great empty plains of the west, it was seldom difficult to find strangers to attack. To the Cheyenne, anyone who was not a member of their own tribe was an enemy to be killed.

Whenever a party of braves saw other Indians, they stripped off their extra clothing, dropped everything they were carrying, and raced off after the strangers with a great deal of animated conversation and laughter. If the other party turned out to be friends, the braves were sorely disappointed, as though a long-anticipated party had just been canceled.

For Black Kettle and other Cheyenne warriors, there was much more to fighting than simply killing the enemy. In fact, inflicting death was not a particularly noteworthy or courageous act. Nor was the taking of a scalp, which was considered nothing more than a trophy, a way of keeping score, something to show to friends. The greatest feat of bravery for a Cheyenne warrior, the ultimate act of courage, was to count coup on the enemy (*coup* being the French word for blow or strike). To boast of counting coup, a brave had to touch his opponent with a stick, a bow, a whip, or the open palm of his hand.

Counting coup on an enemy right after killing him was considered brave enough—for the enemy might be feigning death and waiting to strike back. But the highest act of courage was to count coup on an enemy who was unhurt, and then to let him live. A Cheyenne warrior who had never counted coup on an enemy was considered to be worthless as a man. Black Kettle had counted coup many times.

Black Kettle grew up in a warrior culture. To be a valued member of the tribe, to be looked up to and covered in glory was to fight and kill and die. But the Cheyenne warrior culture was also cruel and merciless, and that created fear, loathing, and repugnance among the whites who later took over their land.

Mutilation was routinely practiced out of both tradition and habit. It was not uncommon for a Cheyenne warrior to cut off the arms of an enemy and keep the severed limbs as trophies. Strangers taken prisoner by the Cheyenne faced a gruesome fate. Some captives were stripped and spread-eagled over anthills, with their hands and feet tied to pegs driven deep into the ground. They were then abandoned, to go blind from staring at the sun, insane from hunger and thirst, and eaten by ants and wild animals. It took some victims days to die. Some captives died more quickly by having twigs and branches piled on top of them and being burned alive.

One Cheyenne brave remembered the killing of an old Shoshone man. "We cut off his hands, his feet, his head. We ripped open his breast and his belly. I stood there and looked at his heart and his liver. We tore down the lodge, built a bonfire on it and its contents and piled the remnants of the dead body upon this bonfire. We stayed there until nothing was left but ashes and coals."

Cheyenne women were as cruel and vicious as the men. A US Army captain described how, after one battle, Cheyenne squaws helped "scalp and torture the wounded, shooting arrows into their bodies and cutting off fingers and toes, even when they were alive."

The Cheyenne exhibited cruelty long before the coming of the whites. Richens Lacy Wootton, a trapper and hunter who was accepted by the Plains Indians, wrote that

> before there were whites to rob and plunder and steal from, the [Indians] robbed and stole from each other. Before there were white men in the country to kill, they killed each other. Before there were white women and children to scalp and mutilate and torture, the Indians scalped and mutilated and tortured the women and children of their enemies of their own race. They made slaves of each other when there were no palefaces to be captured and sold or held for ransom, and before they commenced lying in ambush along the trails of the white man to murder unwary travelers, the Indians of one tribe would set the same sort of death traps for the Indians of another tribe.

Fighting and killing, mutilation and torture were a normal part of everyday Cheyenne life, taught to each new generation. Violence filled their days long before the white man came. Cruelty was as accepted and expected a part of life as the belief that the sun would appear in the east and cross the sky only to die in the west each day of a man's life.

One of the most famous Indian fighters described Indians as "a race incapable of being judged by the rules or laws applicable to any other known race of man; one between which and civilization there seems to have existed from time immemorial a determined and increasing warfare—a hostility [that is] deep-seated and inbred." So wrote George Armstrong Custer in 1874, two years before he was killed by Indians.

The world of the Cheyenne, and of all the other Indian nations of the Great Plains, changed forever when one of Sweet Medicine's predictions came true. "Another animal will come," the prophet had said, "but it will not be like the buffalo." This new animal would come from the south, Sweet Medicine said, and it would have long hair on its neck, and the Cheyenne would catch it, mount it, and ride it.

Sweet Medicine was right. Horses did come from the south. They came from Mexico and were brought north by Mexican explorers in the sixteenth century. As early as 1680, Pawnee tribes to the east began capturing, taming, and riding horses, and the Cheyenne were not far behind in doing the same thing. Horses gave them the mobility and speed necessary to chase down buffalo and antelope, and to follow them on their seasonal migrations. And the animals permitted the Cheyenne to transport heavy loads, which enabled them to accumulate more possessions in the form of food, clothing, weapons, and skins for lodges. The entire Cheyenne nation was transformed by the horse into a nomadic people following the great buffalo herds on which they depended for most of the necessities of life.

The horse also gave them a new reason to go to war: to capture horses from other tribes. Horses became extremely valuable, well worth fighting for, and some Cheyenne turned to war for profit rather than solely for fun. For the first time, they killed for material gain.

The world of the Cheyenne changed even more when, as Sweet Medicine had predicted, they met white-skinned people who brought them rifles, which Sweet Medicine had called loud sticks that killed by stones. In addition to rifles, they brought glittering glass beads, shiny mirrors that showed the Cheyenne how they looked, and iron to make arrowheads with. They killed more effectively than stone arrowheads. In return for those tantalizing gifts, the Cheyenne gave their new white friends pelts and furs, which they sold in the east for huge profits.

Those early white men were not killed or tortured or mutilated by the Cheyenne, even though they were strangers, not of their own tribe. The whites were friendly, and they brought such useful gifts. If they were killed, the Cheyenne reasoned, then others bearing more gifts might not come. And besides, the settlers were small in number and killed only a few buffalo and antelope, just enough for their own needs, so they did not disrupt the Cheyenne way of life. The traders learned the Cheyenne language and customs, ate Indian food, and smoked their pipes. They did not kill warriors or try to take away their land, or threaten the Cheyenne in any way. Perhaps Sweet Medicine had been wrong about the white man.

Sweet Medicine was never wrong. After a while, some new traders started to take advantage of the Indians by offering them something they had never tasted before that made them feel like they had never felt before: whiskey. "Something will be given to you, which, if you drink it, will make you crazy," Sweet Medicine had said. It happened to the Cheyenne in 1832, when an unscrupulous trader named John Gannt built a trading post on the Arkansas River in what is now southern Colorado and gave the Indians hard liquor. They did not like the taste at first, but then Gannt mixed it with sugar—"something that looks like sand that will taste very sweet," the prophet had warned. It worked. The Cheyenne clamored for more, trading almost everything they owned for liquor. They gave away their valuable furs and skins, armloads of blankets, and horses and weapons. Soon they traded away their clothing, and then their wives and children.

By 1841, the lives of the Cheyenne and other tribes of the plains had changed completely and forever. That was the year the first wagon train of emigrants heading for Oregon and California passed along the Platte River, through what would later become Nebraska and Colorado. It was Indian country then, where before only a handful of white men had ever come: the traders with their trinkets and whiskey.

There were only ten wagons in that first train, and they carried only sixty-nine people. But the number kept increasing every year. Only two years later, one wagon train alone consisted of two hundred wagons and over one thousand people. And there were scores of such trains in long columns that seemed never ending. The Indians soon became alarmed, and with good reason: their land was being overrun and stripped bare. The Cheyenne watched them come "creeping up the North Platte valley like slow white worms eating their way along, eating up the grass and the game and the firewood and leaving a bare, dusty track behind them." The wagons carried tools for plowing, fencing, and building, tools for tearing up the earth, and tools for closing off the land to everyone else.

The people in the wagons were not like the traders. "If the traders occasionally had been hard to like, these people were impossible. They were greedy and stingy both. They took the grass and wood and used the good camping places, but they gave no gifts in return." If an Indian approached them, making peaceful signs for eating and smoking together, the emigrants would hurry on by, pretending not to see him, as though he did not exist. That was humiliating enough, but then the whites shamed any Indian who approached by driving him away with shouting and shooting. "They will keep coming," Sweet Medicine said. And they did.

In 1849, gold was discovered in California. Was this the stone Sweet Medicine had said the whites would be looking for? The streams of emigrants, already so disruptive and destructive to the Indian way of life, became a torrent, a flood, a deluge. In that year of 1849, seventy-seven thousand people crossed the plains on their way to California to strike it rich. In the next seven years, a quarter of a million more came.

In 1858, the situation became more threatening when gold was discovered at Cherry Creek in Colorado. In no more time than it took for fall to turn to winter, a settlement and then a town sprang up. It was called Denver. Now the wagon trains were no longer simply passing through the Cheyenne lands. Now the people from the east began to take over and occupy the land. Ranchers staked out huge tracts of ground. Soldiers came and built forts. Stagecoach companies built way stations every ten to twelve miles. Huge trains of giant freight wagons, each one carrying three to four tons of supplies and needing as many as ten yoke of oxen to pull them, left deep muddy ruts in the grasslands as they marked out new trails through the Indians' land.

"They will keep coming," Sweet Medicine had said, but who could have believed there would be so many of them coming day after day with no end in sight.

The large numbers of white people brought with them diseases and illnesses the Indians had never known. They had no immunity to whooping cough, measles, or even diarrhea. A cholera epidemic in 1849 killed almost half of all the Cheyenne. It was just as Sweet Medicine had warned: "you will have disease and will die suddenly."

Some Cheyenne were visiting a Kiowa camp on the Canadian River in New Mexico Territory when the cholera struck. A Kiowa dancer suddenly collapsed. An Osage sitting on the ground watching the dancer fell over dead. The Cheyenne chief rounded up his people and rode all night long to get as far away from the sickness as possible. But the disease went with them, and they soon began to die. Little Old Man, a Cheyenne warrior, put on his war clothes, mounted his horse, and charged through the camp with his lance at the ready to do battle. "If I could see this thing," he shouted, "if I knew where it came from, I would go there and fight it!" He clutched his stomach and doubled over in pain. As he fell from his horse, his wife ran to him and cradled his head in her arms. He was dead.

The Cheyenne broke camp immediately and headed north in terror. They rode hard all day and all night until they met another band of Cheyenne heading south. They, too, were trying to get away from the sickness, but there was no escaping it. "They will keep coming, coming. You will all die off."

The whites were like a plague overrunning the land, smothering everything in sight. And there would be no stopping it. In less than the span of a single lifetime, the Cheyenne and other tribes of the plains lost their food, land, independence, and pride. Bitterness and hatred grew apace with each new Conestoga wagon, each corral and fence post, and each new wooden building lining the streets of the white man's camp at Denver.

William Bent, one of the early traders, who married the daughter of a Cheyenne chief and adopted the Cheyenne ways, and who always treated them with respect, became the government agent to the tribe. In October 1850, he wrote a warning and a prophecy to the commissioner of Indian affairs in Washington: "A smothering passion for revenge agitates these Indians, perpetually fomented by the failure of food, the encircling encroachments of the white population, and the exasperating sense of decay and impending extinction with which they are surrounded. A desperate war of starvation and extinction is imminent and inevitable, unless prompt measure shall prevent it."

Black Kettle knew he had to make peace with the whites if he and his people were to have any future at all. But did the whites really want peace with the Cheyenne, or any other tribe for that matter? Or did they just want to see all the Indians gone somewhere else—anywhere—so they could have all the land to themselves? It was time to find out.

TWO

A MODEL
YOUNG
OFFICER

George Custer went to war on July 21, 1861, four weeks after graduating from the US Military Academy at West Point, New York. The Union and Confederate forces were going into battle for the first time, near a small stream called Bull Run, some thirty miles from Washington, DC. The night before the battle, Custer, a raw second lieutenant at the age of twenty-one, was placed in command of a company of cavalry. This was exactly where he wanted to be, even though in his final exams, his lowest grades had been in cavalry tactics.

Neither poor grades nor the prospect of facing the enemy in battle affected his self-confidence, although he later admitted to some nervousness when he was waiting for the charge to begin. And so he did what he had been doing all his life: he indulged in a practical joke. The target was another young officer who appeared as nervous as Custer.

As they waited for the signal to move out against the rebel troops, Lieutenant Leicester Walker asked Custer what weapon he intended to use. The saber, of course, was Custer's answer. But as the line of troopers started forward, Custer changed his mind, put the saber back in its scabbard, and pulled out his pistol. Walker did the same, which led Custer to switch weapons again. He holstered the gun and drew his saber. This went on several times. Custer later said that he had so much fun tricking Walker that he lost his own fear.

Army life had not tempered Custer's maverick nature—quite the opposite. His four years at the military academy provided him with even more rules to break. He was just as impulsive, mischievous, and eager to take chances and play pranks as he had been as a kid growing up in Ohio and Michigan.

It was that kind of approach to life that got him admitted to West Point in the first place. When Mary Holland's father learned that the seventeen-year-old Custer boy was spending too much time in his daughter's trundle bed—with Mary—he wanted to get Custer as far away from Ohio and his daughter as possible. He arranged for his local congressman to award Custer a coveted appointment to West Point. Custer had not been able to get a congressional appointment on his own, so he was quite happy with the new arrangement.

He quickly became one of the worst cadets in West Point's long history, but also one of the most popular. It was hard not to like someone so fun-loving and good-looking, who had such an irrepressible personality and delighted in openly flouting the rules. From his first day as a cadet he made it clear to everyone—faculty and fellow cadets—that he cared little for deportment, discipline, or grades. His focus was on getting through with a minimal amount of study and having the most fun he could. He succeeded at both.

He knew instinctively how far he could push the system without being expelled. "He delighted in going right to the line but never beyond it. He knew when he had to study, or behave, and he did what was necessary." And nothing beyond, which was why he graduated at the bottom of the class in grades but first in demerits. He had played by his own rules at West Point and was determined to do the same now that he was going to war.

But for a time, Custer was concerned that he might not get to war. He was under arrest and facing court-martial for neglect of duty and for conduct prejudicial to maintaining military discipline. A week after graduation and a month before the Bull Run battle, Custer was still at West Point waiting for orders. He was assigned as officer of the day, overseeing the summer camp for entering cadets. When two new cadets got into a fistfight, he did not stop it, but encouraged them to fight it out. A staff officer, Lieutenant William Hazen, saw them and placed Custer under arrest for failing to maintain order.

The court-martial proceedings began July 5, with Hazen testifying to Custer's fine character and overall good conduct as a cadet. It is not known why Hazen gave such a highly creative interpretation of Custer's behavior, but it served to help Custer's case. Also, the congressman who had appointed Custer to the academy interceded on his behalf. And given the Union Army's need for officers, Custer got off with a reprimand and was ordered to report to the War Department in Washington for his first duty assignment.

After a brief stop in New York City to purchase a uniform, a sword, and a small pocket revolver—and to have his photograph taken with his new possessions—he reported to the War Department on July 20, and he received orders to take command of a cavalry company already at Bull Run. There were rumors of a big battle coming soon. Like most northerners, Custer felt confident that the rebels did not stand a chance once they came up against the Yankees. The war was sure to be over after the Bull Run battle. Custer was grateful for the chance to be part of it.

But before he even left the War Department building, he was offered a greater opportunity. The officer who gave Custer his orders asked if he would like to meet the country's greatest living hero, General in Chief of the Army Winfield Scott. It was almost unheard of for a second lieutenant to meet this living legend.

Scott, who had led the army to victory in the Mexican War, was old and infirm by then but still carried himself like a commanding general. He shook Custer's hand with surprising strength and asked if he would prefer to serve with other West Point graduates drilling new recruits or join his outfit in the field. Custer, who was uncharacteristically nervous in Scott's presence, stammered that would rather go to the front.

The old general, clearly pleased with Custer's choice, made him an offer: if Custer could find a horse in Washington by seven o'clock that night, Scott would grant Custer the honor of personally delivering the general's dispatches to Irwin McDowell, commanding general of the troops at Bull Run.

There was only one problem: the army had already requisitioned all the horses in Washington for the battle.

Custer wandered the streets, racing from one livery stable to another, but he could not find a horse. He hated the thought of returning to General Scott and admitting failure, losing the chance to carry dispatches and meet another high-ranking officer on his first day in the war. But of course, being Custer, he did find a horse, and not just any horse. As he walked back to the War Department, he spied an enlisted man who had served at West Point. They recognized each other, and Custer mentioned his search for a horse. The man said he had ridden back from Bull Run to collect a horse his outfit had left behind. And so what came to be called "Custer's luck" was born—and the spare horse turned out to be one that Custer had often ridden at West Point. He rode off to his first battle in style.

Before the Union charge at Bull Run could begin that hot July day in 1861, hundreds of rebel soldiers suddenly appeared, surprising the Union troops. The Yankee infantry, new, untrained, and scared, turned and ran, leaving only Custer's outfit and some artillery units staying in place. He was ordered to guard the artillery, which placed him and his men perilously close to falling rebel shells. He later described his feelings when he came under rebel artillery fire for the first time. "I remember well the strange hissing and exceedingly vicious sound of the first cannon shot I heard as it whirled through the air." He had, of course, heard the sound of artillery fire as a cadet, "but a man listens with changed interest when the direction of the balls is toward rather than away from him."

Bull Run was a disaster for the Union army, a badly planned and poorly fought debacle that turned into a rout in which the Yankees ran helter-skelter all the way back to Washington. Custer's unit was one of the few to stay intact during the Union retreat. While hundreds of infantrymen left a trail of discarded weapons, flags, band instruments, canteens, and even clothes, the cavalry served as rear guard. It, too, was heading back toward Washington, but it did so in an orderly, military fashion.

At one point, Custer spied a blocked bridge ahead being shelled by Confederate artillery. He led his men along the bank of the creek until he found a spot where they could ford it and was able to bring his unit across without the loss of a man. It was a cool-headed act in the midst of so much carnage and chaos. Uncharacteristically, he never told anybody about his actions that day, but someone else apparently did, for he was mentioned for bravery in at least one report written after Bull Run was over.

When Custer returned to Washington with his outfit the next day, having been up for thirty hours straight, he promptly fell asleep in the rain. When he woke up, he decided to go to the Capitol to meet the congressman from Ohio who had given him his appointment to West Point. Congressman John Bingham had read of Custer's exploits at the bridge at Bull Run and was delighted to see the young man he now considered his protégé.

"Beautiful as Absalom with his yellow curls," Bingham wrote of Custer's visit, "he was out of breath, or had lost it from embarrassment. And he spoke with hesitation. 'Mr. Bingham, I've been in my first battle. I tried hard to do my best. I felt I ought to report to you for it's through you I got to West Point. I'm . . . '"

"I took his hand. 'I know, you're my boy Custer!'"

Life was dull for Custer for the rest of that summer and early fall. He became an aide to his brigade commander, the tough, acerbic, one-armed hero of the Mexican War, Brigadier General Philip Kearny.

Kearny was profane, bad tempered, and a strict disciplinarian who focused on training his men for battle. He sent Custer along on one training mission, a raid on a rebel picket line five miles away. It was a fiasco. The enemy saw them coming, caught them by surprise, and sent them in full retreat. It was Bull Run all over again, albeit on a smaller scale.

In early October, with the six-month-old war at a stalemate, Custer developed a mysterious illness that has never been identified, and was granted sick leave for two months. He went back to Monroe, Michigan, where he had spent part of his childhood living with his stepsister, Ann, and her husband. Even though he was clearly not sickly looking or laid up recuperating, his sick leave was extended for two more months, until February 1862. For someone eager to achieve military glory, it was a long time to be away from the war.

He was celebrated as a hero in Monroe and became the center of attention at dinners, parties, and patriotic rallies, and was much sought after by the young ladies of the town. One of the town's leading citizens, Judge Daniel Bacon, "pointed to him with pride as a true patriot, shook hands publicly on the streets where everyone could see—but did not invite him to his home." Custer may have looked handsome and dashing in his bright blue uniform, he may have been a graduate of the US

Military Academy and been fighting for the noble cause, but that did not make him a social equal to the status-conscious judge. Custer's stepsister and her husband were working-class people. And to make matters worse, they were not even Presbyterians.

And so the judge would not introduce him to his daughter Libbie, whom Custer had been attracted to ever since he was a boy. He used to walk by her house several times a day back then. Now she was a blossoming nineteen-year-old, and he was still walking by her house. One day, he and a friend walked by yelling loudly, joking, and stumbling all over the place. He had gotten drunk on applejack and was making a spectacle of himself in the most respectable part of town in broad daylight. And Libbie saw him. Even worse, her father did too.

His stepsister Ann was mightily upset at finding her beloved Autie, as his family called him, so drunk. When he returned to Washington, he wrote Ann that he had spent the evening with a classmate from West Point serenading young ladies all over town. "Everywhere," he told Ann, "we were offered fashionable wines and liquors, but *nowhere did I touch a drop*." And he apparently never touched a drop from then on.

Custer led his first cavalry charge against the enemy on March 17, 1862. He volunteered to lead a force of fifty men to attack a line of rebel pickets reported to be over the next hill about twenty miles south of Bull Run. "I took my position in front at a slow trot, so as not to tire horses and men," he wrote his parents. "About halfway I bade the men fire their revolvers. We then took the gallop, as the bullets rattled like hail." The bullets came from a force of three hundred rebel troops, which stopped the Union charge.

Custer led his men back to Union lines without a single loss. His first charge at the enemy had been an exhilarating moment for Custer, who was learning that he loved the thrill of combat. "It is said," he wrote to Ann back in Munroe, "that there is no real or perfect happiness during this life, this may be true but I often think that I am perfectly happy."

By April he was on his way with the one-hundred-thousand-man Army of the Potomac to Fortress Monroe, Virginia. That was where the York and the James rivers met to form a peninsula that led straight to Richmond. The Army of the Potomac had a new commander, General George B. McClellan, known affectionately as "Little Mac" to his men. McClellan's ambitious plan, known as the Peninsular Campaign, was to approach the enemy capital from the southeast, rather than taking the traditional route south from Washington, which had been tried unsuccessfully.

The campaign was a failure, another fiasco for the Union army, which sailed back to Washington in defeat five months later at the end of the summer. It had been soundly beaten by a combination of McClellan's own excessive caution and the audacity and tactical brilliance of the man who took command of the rebel army during the campaign, Robert E. Lee.

But while the Army of the Potomac had fared poorly again, Custer had had a glorious time. He distinguished himself with acts of bravery and daring, killed his first man, came to be noticed favorably by his senior commanders, including "Little Mac," ascended to great heights in a balloon, and spent two weeks behind enemy lines serving as the best man at the wedding of a Confederate officer. It was just the sort of thing Custer's friends from West Point had come to expect of him. And he loved every minute of it—except for the rides in the balloon.

At the beginning of the Peninsular Campaign, Custer was detailed to the staff of Brigadier General William F. "Baldy" Smith, who commanded the 2nd Division of the IV Corps. The first order Smith gave to the newest man on his staff was to take a ride in scientist and inventor Thaddeus Lowe's hydrogen-filled reconnaissance balloon and bring back information on the disposition of the rebel forces. If he came back, that is. Rebel troops had often taken potshots at the huge, three-story balloon and whoever might be in the little wicker basket suspended precariously beneath it.

Not long before Custer's ride, Brigadier General Fitz-John Porter had been high in the sky when the balloon broke free from its mooring lines and started drifting rapidly toward enemy lines. Fortunately for Porter, the wind changed direction and brought him back over the Union side. Not many people went up in Lowe's balloon willingly.

When Custer walked up to it, tethered near Baldy Smith's headquarters, he thought it looked "like a wild and untamable animal." When Lowe asked him if he wanted to go up by himself or with Lowe along, Custer wrote, "My desire, if frankly expressed, would have been not to go up at all; but if I was to go, company was certainly desirable." He later admitted that he had been quite scared that day.

The two men climbed into the fragile-looking basket, which was no more than two feet wide, four feet long, and two feet high. As the balloon ascended, Custer stayed seated in the bottom, staring at the ground below through the gaps between the willow bark strips. When he asked Lowe if the wicker basket could really hold the weight of two men, Lowe responded by vigorously jumping up and down. The floor did not break.

Custer managed to stand up when they reached a height of one thousand feet, and he was astonished at how clearly the rebel fortifications were defined through his binoculars. "I had the finest view I ever had in my life and could see both armies at once." He saw the outlines of trenches and earthworks, batteries of artillery, and clusters of tents, all of which he drew on a crude map.

General Smith was delighted with the information Custer brought him, and he sent him aloft three more times. He never did say whether he grew to like the experience, but at least it put him in good standing with Smith. That reputation was further enhanced when Smith sent Custer on his own through a tangled wilderness of a forest to verify the story told by an escaped slave of a trail the Confederates had built through the woods and across a dam.

Custer then led Brigadier General Winfield Scott Hancock's brigade on the trail through the forest and across the dam to a point where they could outflank a Confederate position. When the rebels spotted them, Custer put himself in harm's way in the thick of the fighting, which lasted all day. He captured a rebel officer, four enlisted men, and a Confederate battle flag, which brought him prominent recognition from Hancock in the form of a citation. Custer's star was rising.

Later that day, he saw a classmate from West Point, John "Gimlet" Lea, among a group of rebel prisoners. Lea had been wounded in the leg, and he broke down and cried when he saw his old friend. Hancock granted Custer permission to stay behind the advancing army to take care of his friend for two days. When Custer left him to return to the fighting, he gave Lea some money and clothes. In return, Lea wrote a note for Custer urging any Confederates who might capture him to treat him with the same kindness and consideration Custer had shown him.

"God bless you, old boy!" Lea said when they parted.

By the middle of May, the Army of the Potomac had slowly and ponderously made its way up the peninsula to within twenty miles of Richmond. Custer and about a dozen other cavalrymen, working independently, rode in advance of the army, scouting for enemy defenses and for roads and trails the army might use to outflank the rebels. At one point, Custer said he was close enough to the rebel capital to hear train whistles from the Richmond railroad stations.

It was around that time that he jumped into a river with all his clothes on. Union troops were getting close to the Chickahominy River, and McClellan needed to know where they could ford it. Enemy troops were on the other side. Custer got down from his horse, plunged into the muddy river, and slowly walked across, holding his revolver over his head, all the while knowing he was a perfect target. If a rebel picket behind the thick trees on the other side took aim at him, he could hardly miss. But no shots were fired, and Custer reached the opposite shore having demonstrated that that was a good place to cross. Custer, dripping wet and disheveled, was told to report his findings immediately to McClellan in person.

He was terribly embarrassed to appear before the always meticulously neat McClellan, but he had no choice, and it turned out be another of his many lucky days. The general was highly impressed by the sopping wet young lieutenant. Fourteen years later, after Custer was killed at the Little Big Horn, McClellan wrote to his widow about that day:

"He was reported to me as having accomplished an act of desperate gallantry on the banks of the Chickahominy. I sent for him at once, and, after thanking him, asked what I could do for him. He seemed to attach no importance to what he had done, and desired nothing. I asked him if he would like to come upon my staff as Captain."

It was an incredible opportunity, and Custer eagerly accepted. He became fiercely loyal and devoted to McClellan. "I have more confidence in General McClellan than in any man living," Custer wrote to his parents. "I would forsake everything and follow him to the ends of the earth. I would lay down my life for him."

The general, in turn, became devoted to his new young aide. He described him as "simply a reckless, gallant boy, undeterred by fatigue, unconscious of fear; but his head was always clear in danger, and he always brought me clear and intelligible reports of what he saw when under the heaviest of fire. I became much attached to him."

Two weeks later, McClellan asked Custer to lead two companies of cavalry over the river where he had forded it and try to capture rebel pickets on the other side and dig in on the northern bank. He led his men across, sent the pickets scurrying, and took a few prisoners. Another mission accomplished, and with his usual gallantry and flair.

Custer's star may have been on the rise, but McClellan's was about to be considerably dimmed. On May 31, the commander of the rebel army, General Joseph Johnston, launched a massive assault at Seven Pines and Fair Oaks. The Union troops beat back the attacks, and Johnston was wounded in the battle. He was replaced by Robert E. Lee, who planned and executed new assaults so daring and daunting that McClellan decided to pull back, even though he was so close to Richmond.

McClellan kept retreating under relentless pressure from Lee and Major General Thomas Jonathan "Stonewall" Jackson, whom Lee had ordered to march from the Shenandoah Valley to make a surprise attack on McClellan's northern flank. By August, McClellan had fallen all the way back to where he had started, Fortress Monroe, Virginia, and was ready to be transported back to Washington. His much-vaunted Peninsular Campaign had been another disastrous defeat for the Union.

But through it all, Custer fought bravely and enjoyed himself immensely. When Stonewall Jackson attacked the Union's northern flank, McClellan asked Custer if there was a way to send troops across the Chickahominy River to save the embattled Northern force on the other side. Custer led two brigades across to serve as a rear guard while the main Union force crossed back over to safety. He had saved a significant portion of the Union army.

At one point, he spent four days in almost constant motion and danger, grabbing what little sleep he could—sometimes just a few minutes—and hardly stopping to eat. He had an extremely high level of energy, stamina, and endurance, and could stay in the saddle for hours and still think clearly and act decisively. He was a model young officer, clearly on his way to higher rank and responsibility.

Yet in many ways he was still the boy eager to please and finding great joy and satisfaction in the heat of combat. It was still a game to him, which was how he described the first time he killed a man. It happened in early August in the White Oak Swamp during McClellan's retreat. The general sent Custer along on a cavalry assault on a rebel position. The charge turned into a race, and Custer took off after a Confederate officer riding a

Lt. George A. Custer, right, sitting next to his friend and Confederate prisoner, Lt. J. B. Washington, after the action at Fair Oaks, Virginia, in May 1862. (*Library of Congress*)

beautiful thoroughbred horse with a black saddle and a red Moroccan leather breast strap. "I selected him as my game," he wrote to Ann.

The rebel approached a fence that Custer hoped might force him to stop, but man and horse flew over it with practiced ease. Custer took the chance and urged his horse forward, and he, too, sailed over the fence. He called twice to the rebel to surrender, but the man kept going. Custer hit him with his second shot, and the man fell to the ground dead.

Custer claimed his prizes: the magnificent horse, its beautiful saddle, and a Toledo sword with an inscription in Spanish that read, "Draw me not without cause, sheathe me not without honor." The game was over for the moment for Custer. He later wrote to Ann, "It was the officer's own fault. I called on him twice to surrender."

A few months later, he wrote to a cousin who had asked him if he would be glad to see the war come to an end. Custer replied that he would be glad to see it end for the sake of the country and for all the pain, misery, and sorrow the war was causing. But as for him, he said, "I must say that I shall regret to see the war end. I would be willing, yes, glad, to see a battle every day during my life."

There would be no more battles for Custer for a while. McClellan's army was camped in Williamsburg by the first week of August. While there, Custer went to visit Gimlet Lea, the rebel officer who was recuperating from his wound. Lea asked Custer to be the best man at his wedding and offered to get married the next day if Custer would agree. He managed to secure a brief leave from McClellan and rode back to the house where Lea was being cared for, where he charmed the pretty young ladies and was charmed in return, even though he wore the uniform of the enemy. "Cousin Maggie at the piano," a guest wrote, "warbled 'For Southern Rights, Hurrah!' challengingly, while Custer, laughing, turned the [pages]; nor did 'Dixie' seem to disturb him."

He stayed for two weeks of celebrations, including lavish dinners, parties, dancing, flirtations, and much singing of Southern patriotic songs. By the time he was ready to leave, he learned that McClellan was already in Washington, and that his entire army was at Fortress Monroe, boarding vessels to take them back north. His general and his army had left him behind while he danced, ate, and sang at a rebel's wedding. Fortunately, he managed to board a boat headed for Fortress Monroe, where he then managed to catch another going to Baltimore.

Custer's idol, McClellan, was relieved of command of the Army of the Potomac, but he was not out of power for long. His successor, General John Pope, was soundly defeated at the Second Battle of Bull Run at the end of August. President Abraham Lincoln felt he had no choice but to reappoint McClellan to head the army, which he did on September 2. Two days later, Lee began to invade Maryland, only to be stopped at Antietam on September 17, 1862, which historians have called the bloodiest day in American history. The two sides suffered a combined twenty-four thousand casualties that day, and Lee went back to Virginia.

Captain Custer managed to rejoin McClellan's staff only nine days before the battle. He was assigned to accompany the Union army's chief of cavalry, Brigadier General Alfred Pleasonton, in closing off passages through South Mountain to keep rebel forces on the other side from joining Lee's main army. He performed with daring and panache again, and captured several hundred enemy soldiers and two cannon. Pleasonton cited him for his bravery, and McClellan even went so far as to mention Custer's exploits to Lincoln.

The battle at Antietam did not go as well. While the Union army stopped Lee's advance into Maryland, it did not defeat his army. Custer watched the battle unfold while standing next to McClellan, whose indecision, uncertainty, and failure to send in reinforcements to exploit possible Union breakthroughs may have denied him a major victory. While Custer later wrote that he was appalled at the extent of Union casualties, he never faltered in his loyalty to McClellan. As far as Custer was concerned, the general could do no wrong. And Custer was not alone. The majority of the officers and men of the Army of the Potomac felt the same way.

But Abraham Lincoln did not. After unsuccessfully pressuring McClellan to go on the offensive against Lee for weeks, the president relieved "Little Mac" of his command on November 5. His replacement was Ambrose Burnside, who told the president he did not feel qualified to command the army. He proved he was right a month later in his disastrous all-day assault against rebel troops lined up four deep behind a stone wall at Fredericksburg, Virginia. The Union suffered an additional twelve thousand casualties that day.

Custer missed that battle. For the time being, he was out of a job and out of the war. As a member of McClellan's staff, he accompanied him to Trenton, New Jersey, to sit in limbo awaiting further orders, which never came for Custer's hero,

McClellan. The war was over for good for him. It was also over for Custer for the time being. He secured another leave in November and headed back to Monroe. This time he was going to engage in a different kind of battle, to win the heart and hand of Libbie Bacon, who had seen him reeling drunkenly past her gate the previous winter.

Elizabeth "Libbie" Bacon was vivacious, attractive, bright, and well-schooled in etiquette, French, literature, and the arts of entertaining, subjects in which all well-bred young ladies were expected to excel. In all respects, she was the belle of the ball in Monroe, and had no shortage of eligible male suitors. But one who was decidedly still not eligible, as far as her father, Judge Bacon, was concerned, was that Custer boy, whose family was far below the Bacons in social status and whose drunken performance the previous winter the judge had witnessed.

Captain Custer was once again celebrated in Monroe as a war hero and was formally introduced to Libbie at a party in November. It was clear to everyone, and certainly to Libbie, that he was smitten with her. It seemed that everywhere she went, he appeared. He even dutifully began attending the Presbyterian church Libbie went to, and he stared intently at her through every service. She later wrote him that "from my corner in our pew I could see a mass of handsome curls. . . . You looked *such things* at me."

He kept walking by her house, "forty times a day," Libbie said. He tried to kiss her—about four thousand times, so Libbie told a friend. She passed notes to him at church and gave him a picture of herself, but then told him she could never see him again. Her father had forbidden it, and he sent her to Toledo, Ohio, to visit a friend of the family's. When Custer appeared at the station to see her off, the judge saw him touch her elbow as he helped her aboard the train, and he admonished her in a letter for allowing such a public intimacy.

In April, after being on leave for five months, Custer received orders to report back to General McClellan in Trenton. "Little Mac" was preparing his account of his campaign in 1862, and wanted Custer's help. Before he left Monroe, Libbie, back from her time away in Toledo, agreed to see him, in defiance of her father's order. She still would not let him kiss her, though, and was confused and uncertain about her feelings toward him. She did agree, however, to maintain a kind of second-hand communication with him, in which he would write letters to a friend of Libbie's who would show them to her and then write back to Custer with Libbie's comments. That way, Libbie could still claim she was following her father's orders not to have any direct contact with him.

He had not won the war for Libbie Bacon, at least not yet, and there were no signs that he was going to be allowed back into the real war any time soon. Helping General McClellan write his report was not the way to win fame and glory.

THREE

A
CIVILIZED
AND
ENLIGHTENED
PEOPLE

Black Kettle began negotiating his first treaty with the US
government in 1860, the year before Custer went to war.
It was the same year he became one of the principal chiefs of
the Cheyenne. He took his new responsibility seriously, but for
all his earnestness and dedication to his people, he and the
other chiefs who signed this treaty were not fully aware of its
significance. They did not realize how much they were giving
up or how much of what they had been promised was not
written in the treaty at all. It was in English, so they could not
read it themselves or know how much they had been lied to.

It was not the first time the Indians had been deceived, nor
would it be the last. But Black Kettle strongly wanted peace;
he knew his people could not survive without it. He saw the
prophecies of Sweet Medicine coming true year after year, so
he believed he had no choice. It was either agree to the government treaty or be killed off. And so he made his mark on the
new treaty in 1861.

The document, the Treaty of Fort Wise, was the second peace treaty the Cheyenne and other Great Plains tribes had accepted. The first had been completed in 1851 near Fort Laramie along the Oregon Trail, in what one day became known as Wyoming. The fort was about sixty-five miles north of a tiny settlement called Cheyenne.

The treaty signing in 1851 had been a spectacular, dazzling theatrical display of pomp and ceremony on both sides. In the end, of course, it turned out to be a fraud. More than ten thousand Indians of the Cheyenne, Arapaho, Oglala, and Brule Sioux nations gathered at the site in July that year. No white person had ever seen so many Indians gathered in one place. The Indian pony herds were so huge that they ate up all the grass for miles around. Soon there was no grass left, and the treaty site had to be moved thirty-five miles south to the mouth of Horse Creek.

The pageantry began with a sight that would strike terror in the hearts of whites for years to come. As the American officials stood in front of the government's white tents, close to a thousand Sioux warriors dressed in all their finery and war paint rode toward them in a long column four abreast. One carried an old, tattered American flag, said to have been given to the Sioux forty-five years earlier by William Clark and Meriwether Lewis when their expedition passed through Sioux lands.

An equally impressive parade of Cheyenne warriors followed the Sioux. Most likely Black Kettle was with them, although no one knows for certain. But it was such a significant event that no warrior or chief of his stature would have missed it. Nor would anyone want to miss the massive distribution of gifts. The Indians were given huge quantities of calico, knives, blankets, copper pots, and glittery baubles. In addition, each chief was given the full dress uniform of a general in the US Army.

After two days of feasting and celebration, the formal meetings began. The Indians were told that each tribe would be given its own territory, which, of course, included land the tribes had roamed freely for many generations without restriction. Black Kettle's people, the Cheyenne, and their allies, the Arapaho, were assigned most of what would later become western Kansas and Colorado. The territory included a dry riverbed called Sand Creek, a name soon associated with sadness and anger.

In return for receiving a portion of land that had once been theirs, the chiefs agreed not to attack whites or other Indians and gave the American government permission to build roads and military posts, some of which were already in place. Many more were in the planning stages, but no one told the Indians that.

What the chiefs were told was that they and their people would be paid handsomely: $50,000 annually for fifty years in merchandise such as shiny trinkets, textiles, kitchenware, guns, ammunition, and food. Unfortunately for the Indians, when the US Senate finally got around to ratifying the treaty, it reduced the fifty-year term to ten. No one bothered to tell the Indians.

The treaty was signed on September 17, 1851. When the final ceremony was over, "the chiefs who had come to the council looking regal and dignified went away looking foolish and uncomfortable in their awkwardly misbuttoned [American generals'] uniforms with their swords flopping and banging around their legs." The American delegates left the treaty meetings feeling satisfied that they had negotiated a just and lasting peace. It may not have been just or fair, but peace with the Cheyenne did last, at least for five years.

It was amazing that peace lasted as long as it did following the 1851 Treaty of Fort Laramie, considering how extensively and rapidly whites encroached on the land the treaty gave to the Cheyenne. Gold had been discovered in California, and the stream of emigrants crossing what was now officially Cheyenne territory was becoming troublesome.

The Cheyenne still fought with their old enemy, the Pawnee. No words on paper could induce the young Cheyenne to resist the call to battle. But, in general, they left the whites alone, even actively avoiding them, except for normal business with traders and to collect their annual supply of goods promised by the treaty.

One day in April 1856, soldiers apparently tried to arrest some Cheyenne men who were arguing with a trader over ownership of a horse. No one knows why—perhaps the soldiers were inexperienced or fearful—but they opened fire and killed one of the braves. The Cheyenne in the nearby village, terrified they would all be killed, fled north, leaving their possessions behind. During the flight, a white trapper was killed. Two months later, a Cheyenne war party looking for Pawnees to fight killed a white settler and then, wearing their full battle regalia, approached a fort. They did not attack or even fire a shot, but the soldiers opened fire. Word spread quickly that the Cheyenne were on the warpath, out to murder whites. They were not, but the rumors fed upon themselves, creating the fear of a massive uprising where none existed.

In August 1856, another Cheyenne war party hunting Pawnees tried to flag down a stagecoach. They later claimed they only wanted to beg for tobacco, but the driver, having heard the rumors, opened fire. The Indians fired back, and the driver reached Fort Kearny with an arrow sticking out of his arm. People took that as proof that all-out war was at hand.

The cavalry rode out from the fort searching for the war party. Although it did not find them, it chanced upon a peaceful Cheyenne camp of some twenty families. These were not the Indian warriors the soldiers were looking for, but they were Indians, and that was good enough. The soldiers killed ten and wounded ten more. Now there really was a war.

Cheyenne braves went on the warpath for more than a month in retaliation, attacking wagon trains, stagecoaches, ranches, and settlements. They killed a dozen people and spread terror and the desire for revenge as far east as Saint Louis. The chiefs who had signed the Treaty of Fort Laramie went to the Upper Platte River to call on the Indian agent, Thomas Twiss, a West Point graduate who gave up his army career to live among the Indians. The chiefs told Twiss that the current unrest had been started by soldiers and that they, the chiefs, were doing all they could to persuade their young men to stop fighting.

Twiss, who wanted peace for all tribes, telegraphed his superiors at the Bureau of Indian Affairs in Washington, saying that in his opinion the fighting would soon end. But it was too late. The Bureau of Indian Affairs no longer had any influence. The army had taken over, and it wanted the Cheyenne punished for violating the terms of the 1851 treaty. They had attacked whites, and they had to be taught a lesson.

In spring 1857, Jefferson Davis, the secretary of war, ordered a military expedition against the Cheyenne, led by sixty-year-old Colonel Edwin Vose Sumner, who had fought in the Mexican War and had served in the army longer than most of his soldiers had been alive. His men called him "Old Bull," but only when they were sure he could not hear them. Some said he got that nickname because his voice was so loud. Others claimed that a musket ball had bounced off his head without doing any noticeable damage.

He was a daring and courageous soldier but not much liked by his men. "Old Sumner has had one good effect on us," one of his officers wrote. "He has taught some of us to pray, who have never prayed before, for we all put up daily petitions [to God] to get rid of him."

In late May, Sumner led a force of three hundred men out of Fort Kearny looking to kill Cheyenne. They did not find any Indians for two months, and it seemed that the mission would fail. Then on July 29, the Cheyenne found them. A line of three hundred mounted warriors suddenly stretched across the desolate landscape, a sight few people had ever seen. Even "Old Bull" must have been surprised, because in his experience, Indians rarely took on a large force of soldiers in open combat. The Cheyenne had obsolete smooth-bore rifles and were considerably outgunned by the soldiers' superior carbines. But the Cheyenne believed they were invincible; they had held a ceremony in which a magic powder was placed in their weapons. The powder, so they were told, guaranteed that every shot they fired would hit a soldier, and every bullet fired by the white men would drop from their rifles and fall harmlessly to the ground.

Sumner formed his men in a long line and ordered his bugler to sound the advance. As the troopers moved off at a slow, deliberate pace, one of "Old Bull's" Delaware Indian scouts charged toward the waiting line of Cheyenne warriors and fired at them. That was the moment Sumner had been waiting for.

"Bear witness," he yelled to one of his aides. "An Indian fired the first shot."

Sumner gave the order to pick up speed, "trot march," and the soldiers raised their carbines to the ready. At the same time, the Indians raced toward the blue-clad cavalry. Suddenly, Sumner ordered his men to draw sabers; this was to be a cavalry charge out of the pages of the field manual, the stuff of countless drills, parades, and legends.

The troopers thundered forward, the sun glistening on their raised sabers. The Cheyenne halted, then turned around and fled. The sight of the sabers had shattered their confidence. They believed that the magic powder protected them from bullets from the soldiers' carbines, but not from razor-sharp steel. Sumner and his men chased the Indians for several miles and killed nine. Two soldiers died and eleven were wounded, including a twenty-four-year-old lieutenant from Virginia who was shot in the chest. His name was Jeb Stuart, and he lived to fight another day.

After tending to the wounded, Sumner followed the Indians' trail and two days later found their abandoned village, which he burned to the ground. From there he turned south toward Bent's Fort on the Arkansas River where the Cheyenne were due to arrive to receive their annual distribution of goods, as promised in the 1851 treaty. But not this year. In retribution, the Indian agent, Robert Miller, dumped all the promised weapons and ammunition into the river and gave the rest of the supplies away to other tribes. The Cheyenne got nothing.

Cheyenne warriors went on the warpath, but not for long. They had to stop when winter settled over the plains, leaving no grass for their horses. Throughout the winter, the men stayed in their camps, bitter and resentful over the loss of valuable property and supplies.

When spring came, they did not go back to war. They deliberately avoided the white settlements, wagon trains, and isolated ranches through the summer, until it was time to return to Bent's Fort to receive the next year's distribution of supplies, which they were duly given because it was deemed that they had abided by the terms of the Treaty of 1851.

Indian agent Miller noted in his annual report to Washington that "Colonel Sumner has worked a wondrous change in [the Cheyenne's] disposition toward the whites. [They] said they had learned a lesson last summer in their fight with Colonel Sumner; that it was useless to contend against the white man."

The Cheyenne remained at peace throughout 1858, despite the Colorado gold rush that brought swarms of new settlers. They continued to avoid the whites, keeping to themselves as much as possible. One exception was the Arapaho chief Little Raven. Fascinated, even amused by the white people, he went to Denver, where "he learned to smoke cigars and to eat meat with a knife and fork. He also told the miners he was glad to see them getting gold, but reminded them that the land belonged to the Indians, and expressed the hope they would not stay around after they found all the yellow metal they needed."

Black Kettle knew the whites would never leave. They would keep coming until the plains were full and the grass and buffalo had disappeared. He saw how they increasingly violated the terms of the Treaty of Fort Laramie. The seven-year-old treaty had given the US government only a limited right of passage through Cheyenne and Arapaho lands in western Kansas and Colorado, but the whites were no longer just passing through. They were staying and taking over, annexing fields, building towns, ruining the soil. They were pushing the Cheyenne and Arapaho aside, leaving them with nothing.

Despite the daily provocations, broken promises, and growing hunger from the decimation of the once-great buffalo herds, Black Kettle and other chiefs still hoped to keep peace. Sweet Medicine had been right about the white man, and now there were too many of them to resist; it was too late to try to drive them back. Black Kettle realized that he would have to make even greater concessions if his people were to survive.

In 1859, William Bent, who knew the Cheyenne better than any other white man, told the Bureau of Indian Affairs that Black Kettle and Little Raven had acknowledged to him that they were powerless to resist the increasing encroachment on their land. They told Bent they wanted to negotiate a new treaty that would give them land all their own, a reservation where they would be protected from the white settlers. They also agreed—and this was surely the hardest concession of all— to learn to farm so they could grow their own food. "They will tear up the earth," Sweet Medicine had said, "and at last you will do it with them." But they would not even be allowed that opportunity, as degrading and humiliating as it was.

Spurred by Bent's report, the commissioner of Indian affairs, A. B. Greenwood, asked Congress for the authority to negotiate another treaty. Unless the Cheyenne and Arapaho were given separate and protected land and food, Greenwood argued, the army would have no choice but to exterminate them. And that would involve a long and bloody war. Congress agreed, and in September 1860, Greenwood met with Black Kettle and White Antelope, another Cheyenne chief, at Fort Wise, southeast of Denver. A number of lesser Cheyenne and Arapaho chiefs also attended. Greenwood told them that the "Great Father" in Washington was pleased with them for having remained at peace despite the encroachment on their land and way of life.

The chiefs asked Greenwood how they could continue to keep the peace and obey the president with so many settlers coming every day. Greenwood replied that the only way was to give up all claims to the land they had been granted in 1851, land that had been theirs to begin with. They would have to move to a reservation located in a small, inhospitable corner of the territory, an arid tract unsuitable for most kinds of farming, and lacking in game, water, and timber. It was a place where whites would not want to live. Because the reservation was so utterly barren, the Indians would be dependent on the government for food, housing, and clothing. They would finally have to abandon their traditional nomadic way of life as a proud and self-sustaining people to effectively become wards of the United States.

In return for their giving up the only way of life they had ever known, Washington would agree to protect them from their white neighbors and supply $15,000 in merchandise annually for fifteen years. In order for the Indians to become self-sustaining so that they would no longer need an annual subsidy, the government promised them cattle and farm implements, along with a sawmill, houses, interpreters, people to teach them how to farm, and forty acres of land per man.

As further inducement to the chiefs to sign the new treaty, and to demonstrate the government's generosity, Greenwood paraded before them thirteen wagons overflowing with blankets, clothing, scissors, knives, kettles, flour, bacon, sugar, coffee, and tobacco. All theirs for the taking, once they signed the treaty.

Black Kettle was the first to make his mark on the document. Little Raven of the Arapaho and other principal chiefs of both tribes also signed, but some later said they did not understand how much they were giving up. Indian agent Albert Boone, grandson of Daniel Boone, wrote that Black Kettle was the only chief who fully understood the treaty's details. Whether he actually did understand its significance or merely told Boone so is unclear.

Not all the misunderstandings about this treaty were on the Indian side, however. The government in Washington believed that the chiefs had absolute dictatorial power over their people and that whatever terms and conditions they had agreed to, the Indian nations would automatically follow. That was not the case. No Indian leader, not Black Kettle, nor Sitting Bull of the Sioux, nor Cochise of the Apache, had the authority to dictate. None had the power to compel the members of their tribes to obey unconditionally. The chiefs could advise their people on a course of action, but if their young warriors chose a different path, one that violated the terms of a treaty, there was little a peace chief like Black Kettle could do to stop them. Officials in Washington, including those in the Bureau of Indian Affairs who should have known better, failed to appreciate this point. Consequently, they relied on treaties that in reality bound only those who had signed them.

At the Fort Wise meetings in 1860, the warrior chiefs refused to sign a treaty that spelled the end of their way of life. "It was freedom of movement, the privilege of ranging far and wide seasonally that gave life meaning and dignity," wrote one military historian. "Once that freedom became threatened, his culture, his creature habits and customs, and his manner of providing for his family, all of these were imperiled. To limit him to one piece of ground that he might call his own, though it was the white man's way, must suggest to him the loss of everything that made his spirit proud. It meant living on a reservation, the very mention of which he loathed. [He] would no longer be a mounted warrior; and no longer a hunter drawing his subsistence from the migratory buffalo. Such was the stake, the forfeit for the Plains Indians that made hostilities inevitable."

Wrote Custer, "If I were an Indian, I would greatly prefer to cast my lot among those of my people adhered to the free open plains rather than submit to the confined limits of a reservation."

"Listen to me carefully," Sweet Medicine had said.

The warriors listened and resolved never to live like a white man, never to sleep in a wooden shack, never to be confined behind a fence to stare out at the open plains, and, above all, never to tear up the earth like a farmer. That was the greatest degradation of all for a warrior of the plains. The story is told that when Washakie, a chief of the Shoshone, was advised by a delegation of whites that he and his people should become farmers, he stood straight and tall and glared at them. "Goddamn a potato," he shouted.

Black Kettle's Cheyenne did not become farmers after signing the treaty of Fort Wise. For two years they continued to subsist much as they always had, although with growing feelings of hunger and desperation. The government, once again, had not kept its promises. The reservation had not been prepared for them. It had not been irrigated, no farming equipment had been provided, not even seeds, and there was no one to teach them how to till the soil, to grow and harvest food. Consequently, the Cheyenne and Arapaho felt no need to stay within the confines of that barren, desolate reservation. They freely roamed the plains and lived off the buffalo, as much in

A Cheyenne camp photographed by William S. Soule in the early 1870s.
(*National Archives*)

violation of the treaty as Washington was by failing to prepare
the reservation lands. But they did abide by one important part
of the treaty: they did not attack white settlers. As late as
1863, many more whites had been shot in saloon brawls in
Denver than in confrontations with Indians.

The Cheyenne remained at peace, even when the territory
was no longer patrolled by army troopers because of the onset
of the Civil War. Before the end of 1861, fewer than three hundred soldiers were left to patrol some two hundred thousand
square miles. If the Cheyenne wanted to go to war against the
whites, that was the best opportunity they would ever have.
Never again would they have such an overwhelming advantage in numbers over the US Army.

But they took no action. Black Kettle and the other peace
chiefs kept even the most aggressive young men under control.
Their limited contact with whites was occasional begging and
trading on the streets of Denver, driven by hunger. They may
have appeared menacing, especially to newcomers from the
East, but they did not make war.

Denver had become a magnet, attracting even more emigrants from the East. Many of the more recent arrivals had
come to avoid military service. In winter 1858–1859, Denver
had been a crude, primitive settlement of log huts and shanties

with dirt floors and mud roofs. Only a few buildings had the luxury of glass windows. By summer 1860, it had blossomed into a prosperous business community with six thousand inhabitants, two newspapers, thirty-five saloons, a few churches, a library, a school, civic groups, a well-attended theater, a US mint, banks, hotels, shops, pool halls, shooting galleries, bowling alleys, and a chess club. It had all been brought about by the dreams, hard work, cunning, and greed of ambitious men who spent $700,000 of their own money to build a city.

William Byers hauled a heavy printing press six hundred miles from Omaha, over treacherous roads, to start a newspaper he called the *Rocky Mountains News*. In the June 6, 1860, edition, he published an editorial in praise of his new city:

> Lofty buildings are rising on the business streets; solid and substantial brick edifices of which old cities might well be proud. Gorgeous saloons, with mirrors and paintings, lighted from glittering chandeliers, meet the eye of the passerby on every corner, and delicious music lures him to enter. The storehouses of our merchants groan beneath tons of goods and wares from every clime. Great trains of huge prairie freighters arrive and depart almost daily, and more than a thousand emigrant wagons arrive each week.

No wonder the Cheyenne and Arapaho were attracted to such a spectacle. One year a wilderness; the next year a place of fascination. Some of the Indians were so curious about the white man's way of life that they would ride alongside the stagecoaches—the huge, ungainly boxes that bounced over the prairie the way Sweet Medicine had foretold. Of course, the Indians seemed threatening to people from the East whose only knowledge of the natives came from lurid, often fictionalized newspaper accounts of gruesome massacres.

Some new settlers, while not afraid of the Indians, were repulsed by them. After all, the common stereotype back East was that they were dirty, thieving, shiftless, and lazy. They did not work the way honest people did, but lived on government handouts. They refused to farm all that good land the government had provided for them. What was wrong with those politicians in Washington, using tax money to support Indians to the tune of $15,000 a year? And why did the Indians have to hang around Denver bothering decent white folks?

Drawn by curiosity, the Indians went to Denver, turning up where—to the settlers' way of thinking, with their notions of privacy and personal property—they had no right to be. "Many a time in going about my household duties," wrote Susan Riley Ashley, a recent arrival from Iowa, "or sitting quietly sewing or reading, an uncanny feeling took possession of me, and looking up I would discover that one or more panes of my windows framed the stolid face of an Indian. On one occasion, having forgotten to lock my outer doors, I entered my front room to find three Indians in it. With assumed bravery I put my hands against the nearest Indian to push him out. They left without resistance and took their places at the windows." The Indians meant no harm. They walked into and out of other Indians' lodges all the time, and no one got upset about it, but entering the homes of the whites obviously annoyed the residents.

There had been no hostilities for more than a year, but the fear of Indian attacks was always present, heightened by the Indians' growing presence in the city and surrounding settlements. As a result, target practice became a common form of entertainment for the populace of Denver. Men and women became expert shots; few people—male or female, young or old—ventured far from home unarmed.

The Indians continued to trade with the whites, and beg on the streets for food and tobacco, but they also stole horses, which to the whites was a hanging offense. Again, the Indians did not think they were doing wrong. In their culture, they were achieving honor by showing their skill at acquiring other men's horses. It was a game, part of their way of life.

Another offense, however, was that growing numbers of Indians became drunk in town, which further lowered their reputation in the eyes of the settlers. Some even gave them whiskey in order to gain the upper hand in trading, or to take advantage of their women. Terrible stories appeared in the newspapers about drunken Indians selling their last buffalo robes for a bottle of whiskey, or stumbling half-naked down the street in the dead of winter.

Some responsible citizens urged restraint and compassion in dealing with the Indians. Byers published an editorial in his *Rocky Mountain News* on April 23, 1861, expressing the hope that the people of Denver would try to understand the Indians and promote friendly relations with them:

> A civilized and enlightened people can well afford to remember that the tribes by which we are surrounded are our inferiors physically, morally, mentally, and that the commission of what we call crimes, assumes with them the merit of bravery and manly action. In our dealings with these untutored barbarians, we should be governed by the greatest caution—avoiding in all cases a disposition to overreach and deceive them. They are naturally, and not without reason, suspicious of their white brethren. They feel that their rights have been invaded, their hunting grounds taken possession of, and their possessions appropriated without adequate remuneration. It should be the aim of every good citizen to conciliate the Indians, and show them by a peaceful policy that we are not committed to an aggressive and tyrannous course.

All well and good. Noble advice and generous sentiments. But keep your guns loaded and ready. The time was coming when they would be needed, and there was nothing Black Kettle could do to prevent it.

FOUR

THE BEST CAVALRY GENERAL IN THE WORLD

Custer was away from the war for six months. While others gained the fame and glory he sought, or were maimed or killed, he was in Monroe, Michigan, courting Libbie Bacon. While others fought and died at Fredericksburg and Chancellorsville, he was guest of honor at dinner parties, or back East helping General McClellan write his report on the failed Peninsular Campaign. While others earned promotions, Custer was reduced in grade from captain, his brevet rank as a general's aide, to first lieutenant. And when he finally received orders to report to the War Department, he was assigned to administrative duties. The war was not going well for someone ambitious for acclaim and recognition.

Finally, on May 6, 1863, he was ordered to rejoin the Army of the Potomac at Falmouth, Virginia, on the opposite side of the Rappahannock River from Fredericksburg. He was to be an aide again, this time to Brigadier General Alfred

Pleasonton, commanding the 1st Cavalry Division. Pleasonton had been impressed by Custer during the fighting in the Peninsular Campaign and requested him by name to serve on his staff. It was pleasant duty, and for a while, Custer enjoyed himself.

He took his meals with the general, who liked to eat well and had daily shipments of delicacies sent from Baltimore. "We have," Custer wrote, "onions, radishes, and ripe tomatoes, asparagus, fresh fish, mackerel, beef, mutton, veal, bacon, pound cake, oranges, ginger snaps, candies, peas, warm biscuits instead of hard bread, fresh milk, butter, cheese, and everything." Enlisted men in the camp at Falmouth did not eat so well; indeed, not many people in the entire country ate that well, in wartime or peace.

Custer soon grew bored, however. There was no glory to be had, no opportunities for promotion, and no chance to fight. The full table at mealtimes lost its appeal. He needed to be where the action was, but for a month there had been no fighting for the Army of the Potomac.

Then, on May 20, Pleasonton sent Custer on a commando-type raid behind enemy lines leading seventy-five troopers with their horses down the Potomac on two river steamers. Their mission was to go downriver overnight without being seen, and then to ride hard some forty miles overland to intercept a party of rebels carrying a large amount of Confederate money and important mail.

At one point, Custer took ten men in a canoe paddling fast to chase a sailboat bearing the money and papers they were sent to find. After they captured the rebel boat, Custer spotted a large house on the shore. He ventured inside, surprising a Confederate officer home on leave. He was reading a volume of Shakespeare when Custer took him prisoner.

Custer led his men on to capture more than two dozen Confederate soldiers, burn two boats and a bridge, and seize two barrels of whiskey, which, so he dutifully assured his sister in a letter, he then destroyed. He had done well without losing a single man, and he received hearty congratulations from Major General Joe Hooker, commander of the Army of the Potomac. According to a Michigan newspaper account, Hooker said about Custer, "We have not a more gallant man in the field."

In early June, there were signs that Lee's Army of Northern Virginia was on the move, heading north, perhaps toward Pennsylvania. General Hooker ordered his cavalry into action. On June 9, Pleasonton's force left Falmouth and headed thirty miles west toward Culpeper Court House, where Jeb Stuart was thought to be. Pleasonton's orders were simple: destroy the rebel force.

Pleasonton did not destroy Jeb Stuart's cavalry—no one had ever been able to do that—but in several clashes, he came close to defeating it. No Union cavalry had fought as well or as hard against Stuart before. Custer was in the thick of it.

On June 9, units of Pleasonton's cavalry, led by Custer, crossed Beverly Ford and charged Stuart's troops encamped at Brandy Station. The Yankees rode with sabers drawn among Stuart's men who were getting ready for the day. Some were still cooking breakfast, and many were taken prisoner. But as Custer led his troopers through the rebel camp, they saw ahead of them a stone wall behind which were massed hundreds of Confederates—more of Stuart's cavalry ready to charge.

The Yankees leaped over the wall but turned back because they were heavily outnumbered. Soon, however, additional Union cavalry joined the fight. The charges and counter-charges continued in what turned out to be the largest cavalry battle of the war. Custer brought back a captured rebel flag to present to General Hooker. Hundreds of men on both sides were casualties, but Custer emerged unscathed and was again singled out for gallantry.

A little over a week later, on June 17, Custer and the Union cavalry battled Jeb Stuart's men near the town of Aldie,

Virginia. As the Yankees crossed the aptly named Little River—not much more than a stream—Custer's horse fell, tumbling him into the water. He rose up soaking wet and was covered with dust blown up by the horses that settled in a thick layer on his hair and clothes. Unconcerned by his appearance and discomfort, he found another horse and joined the charge. This time his horse bolted and ran toward the rebel line. Custer could not stop it, and he rode straight through the enemy force. He wheeled around and rode back the way he had come, through the Confederate troops again.

"I was surrounded by rebels," he wrote to his sister, "and cut off from my own men, but I made my way safely, and all owing to my hat, which is a large broad brim, exactly like that worn by the rebels. Everyone tells me that I look more like a rebel than my own men."

On June 25, in a heavy rain, Pleasonton, with Custer by his side, led his cavalry across the Potomac River into Maryland. It was official, not just a rumor, that Robert E. Lee was leading his much-feared Army of Northern Virginia toward Pennsylvania. No one on the Union side knew where Lee intended to go from there. Philadelphia? Baltimore? Washington? Word that Lee was coming spread panic among residents of the eastern states, and in Lee's path, lines of refugees prepared to flee.

The president ordered the Army of the Potomac to stop Lee, but no one knew where he was. A few days later, Major General George Meade replaced Joe Hooker as commander of the Army of the Potomac. Meade's first order was for part of the army to move north toward Pennsylvania, making sure to keep troops between Lee and the cities of Baltimore and Washington. Then he met with his subordinate commanders, including his chief of cavalry, General Pleasonton, who wanted to assign new division commanders and promote some subordinates.

Custer had been inspecting the guards, disappointed because he knew that other officers had been promoted and given command of divisions while he remained a first lieutenant and a general's aide. When he finished making his rounds, he returned to the tent occupied by Pleasonton's aides. He found them in a joking mood.

"How are you, General Custer?" one man said.

"Hello, General," another greeted him.

"You're looking well, General,"

"You may laugh, boys," Custer fired back. "I will be a general yet, for all your chaff."

The aides continued their taunts, roaring with laughter until Lieutenant George Yates, a friend from Monroe who had gotten his job on Custer's recommendation, decided the joke had gone on long enough. "Look on the table, old fellow. They're not chaffing." Custer saw a large envelope addressed to Brigadier General George A. Custer, U.S. Volunteers.

"He could not speak. The mortifications, the chagrin, the emotional change from rage to supreme happiness overpowered him. He sank down in a chair and feared that he was going to cry."

Here was his chance for glory. But first he had to make sure he looked the part in a way that would distinguish him from every other general. He went to see his orderly, Private Joseph Fought, who had been with him since Bull Run, to see if he could put together a proper uniform. Fought spent most of the night scrounging for scraps and trying to find two stars to designate Custer's new rank. He also needed a needle and thread to stitch the stars, one on each collar. Finally, it was done.

"The next morning [Custer] was a full-fledged Brigadier General," Fought recalled. "He wore a velveteen jacket with five gold loops on each sleeve, and a sailor shirt with a very large blue collar that he got from a gunboat on the James. The shirt was dark blue, and with it he wore a conspicuous red tie, top boots, a soft hat—Confederate—that he had picked up on the field, and his hair was long and in curls almost to his shoulders."

Thus attired, he reached his new command on the morning of June 29, prepared to lead the 2nd Brigade of Major General Judson Kilpatrick's 3rd Division. The brigade was made up of boys from the 1st, 5th, 6th, and 7th Michigan Regiments, plus a battery of artillery. The men did not know what to make of this twenty-three-year-old officer in his outlandish costume who announced he was their new commanding officer. They joked and snickered, calling him a popinjay, a dandy, with too much swagger and "West Point conceit."

Custer knew that first impressions were vital, and that his initial actions would determine whether the men came to respect him. He was also aware that more senior officers, who were considerably older, resented his promotion over them. But if he was apprehensive about how he would be received by his troops, he did not show it. Quite the opposite.

He started off abruptly, cold and aloof, criticizing everything about the outfit. These were volunteer regiments; officers and men were used to a more relaxed style of military discipline. There were no martinets in volunteer regiments, and any officer who tried to command by the rulebook did not last long. "All those little vexatious rules, apparently so trifling, which are enforced in a regular cavalry regiment as matters of habit were unknown to them, and Custer enforced every one from the first."

He found fault with the smallest things. He insisted that saluting officers, which was not a common practice among volunteers, be rigidly enforced. He ordered that officers rise as early as the men, turn out for morning roll call, and oversee the cleaning of the horses and stables every day. For officers who had been used to sleeping late while the men got the horses ready, this was hard to take.

They all cursed Custer on his first day of command. Their resentment grew as they learned that there were even more rules and regulations to follow. Hatred continued to smolder the following morning when the Boy General led them north into Pennsylvania. Those who had maps saw that they were heading toward towns few Michigan men had heard of—Littlestown, Abbottstown, Hanover, and a place called Gettysburg.

Two days later, in the late afternoon on the second day of the battle at Gettysburg, July 2, 1863, Custer took his brigade into combat for the first time, near Hunterstown, some five miles from Gettysburg. As Custer led the Michigan brigade down a road, he saw some Confederate cavalry up ahead and others in the fields on both sides. They were Brigadier General Wade Hampton's men.

Custer made his decision in an instant. From what he observed, he concluded that the rebel force numbered probably no more than two hundred, so he quickly positioned his troopers to attack. He placed one company in the road to lead the charge, but before the company commander could order the men forward, Custer changed his mind. He rode up alongside and said, "I'll lead you this time, boys. Come on!"

The sixty men of the company shouted as they raced down the road toward the rebels, only to find, when it was too late to stop, that there were six hundred, not two hundred, as Custer had thought. Many of Custer's men were hit. Custer's horse was shot, sending him to the ground. He spied a rebel soldier a few feet away taking aim at his head, ready to pull the trigger.

One of the Michigan troops, Private Norvill Churchill, shot the Confederate soldier, pulled Custer up on his horse, and headed back to camp, followed by the survivors of the charge, with Wade Hampton's men on their heels. Of the sixty Michigan men who began the charge, fewer than half were left.

It was a serous defeat, called by one historian "the most reckless and thoughtless stunt [Custer] had ever pulled in his life. The bitterest pill he had to swallow was recognizing that he had acted like a wild staff captain and not a responsible brigadier." In Custer's defense, that critic also pointed out that Custer had been a general for only a few days and learned from that experience not to be so quick to react.

Despite the losses and defeat in their first battle under their new officer, most of the men were impressed with the vigor and valor with which Custer led them. They knew that not many generals would lead a small company into battle from the front or display such bravery when in contact with the enemy. He had proved himself such a dashing and courageous cavalry leader that his men became eager to follow him. He may have dressed like a dandy and insisted on West Point rules, but by God, he could fight!

The battle raged at Gettysburg for the next two days; Confederate and Union cavalry clashed a number of times at points several miles away. Sometimes Custer rode against Jeb Stuart's men, and other times it was Wade Hampton's. Custer found a way to be where the fighting was fierce, and he loved every minute of it. Once when the 9th Michigan was ordered to charge, Custer rode out in front, saber drawn, and shouted at them to come on. Unfortunately, the regiment ran into a stone wall, which broke up the charge, and the two sides fought a hand-to-hand battle. Union troops were twice repulsed. Custer readied a third charge, but another Confederate force attacked their flank, and he quickly led them back to safety.

Later, when the 1st Michigan was ordered to advance, Custer again placed himself out in front and led the men forward against the rebel cavalry. "So sudden and violent was the collision that many of the horses were turned end over end and crushed their riders beneath them. The clashing of sabers, the firing of pistols, the demands for surrender, and cries of the combatants, filled the air." The Yankee troopers were victorious.

In another fight with Hampton's cavalry, Custer's men met them with such brute force that an observer some distance away said it sounded like a huge tree crashing to the ground. Custer wrote in his official report, "I challenge the annals of warfare to produce a more brilliant or successful charge of a cavalry."

By the time the fighting at Gettysburg was over and Lee had retreated across the Potomac River to his beloved Virginia, Custer had the total, unquestioned allegiance of his Michigan men. Soon the entire brigade was wearing red ties like Custer's, as a gesture of pride and identification with their commander. They felt part of an elite unit and wanted everyone else, including the enemy, to know who they were. Custer had given them spirit and a greater will to fight, to be the best damn cavalry outfit in the whole United States Army.

One of his troopers described him as "a glorious fellow, full of energy, quick to plan and bold to execute." Another said Custer "was not afraid to fight like a private soldier. [He] would never ask them to go where he would not lead." General Pleasonton proclaimed Custer "the best cavalry general in the world."

Not only did he win over his men, but he had gone from a general's aide to a national hero, with more glory and fame to come. After the war Custer wrote, "In years long numbered with the past, when I was merging upon manhood, my every thought was ambitious, not to be wealthy, not to be learned, but to be great." He got precisely what he set out to achieve, and at the age of twenty-three.

"The Boy General with the Golden Locks" was how James Gordon Bennett, editor of the influential *New York Herald*, described Custer. Other newspapers just said "Boy General"— that was sufficient identification. His enormous dash, valor, flamboyance, and personal courage made him one of the most colorful and charismatic figures of the war. "He fascinated a nation," a biographer wrote, "dressed in velvet and touched with luck at the forefront of a charge."

His appearance attracted people as much as his actions on the battlefield. Nature favored him with a handsome face and manly physique, but he added his own unique features to make sure everyone recognized him. Captain James Kidd of the 6th Michigan Cavalry recalled seeing Custer for the first time:

> He was clad in a suit of black velvet, elaborately trimmed with gold lace, which ran down the outer seams of his trousers and almost covered the sleeves of his cavalry jacket. The wide collar of a blue navy shirt was turned down over the collar of his velvet jacket, and a necktie of brilliant crimson was tied in a graceful knot at the throat, the long ends falling carelessly in front. The double rows of buttons on his breast were arranged in groups of twos indicating the rank of brigadier general. A soft, black hat with wide brim adorned with a gilt cord, and rosette encircling a silver star, was worn turned down on one side giving him a rakish air. His golden hair fell in graceful luxuriance nearly or quite to his shoulders.

Custer fought no more major battles until September. He spent much of his time making sure that his men were well provisioned, with the best horses, weapons, food, and quarters. He selected his staff, picking men who were old friends but who were also diligent and conscientious in the performance of their duty. They became like a family, with everyone devoted to Custer. He formed a band that followed him everywhere; the horn players even went into battle, playing "Yankee Doodle," which he chose as the signal to charge.

He also arranged a household staff. He already had Joseph Fought as his orderly and a boy named Johnnie Cisco to care for the horses and Custer's menagerie. In addition to his dogs, Custer had acquired goats, a pet squirrel, and a raccoon that slept with him at night.

In August 1863, he found a runaway slave named Eliza Denison Brown, whom he employed as his cook. Brown was perhaps in her thirties, though no one was sure. She had escaped from a plantation in Virginia to, as she put it, "try this freedom business." She grew to command Custer's headquarters and never hesitated to scold anyone if they did not behave the way she thought was proper. She became a dominating and supporting presence, soon nicknamed "The Queen of Sheba" in the brigade. Brown would stay with Custer for the next six years.

Custer returned to Monroe in September to wage his other campaign, the one for the hand of Libbie Bacon. He had been wounded in the foot by a rebel shell that killed his horse. Custer was carried off the field, but after being tended to by a surgeon, he mounted up and rode to General Pleasonton. "Fifteen day's leave-of-absence?" he asked. "They have spoiled my boots, but they didn't gain much there, for I stole them from a Reb." Pleasonton laughed and gave him twenty days, and off Custer went to claim his prize.

He paraded around Monroe in his fancy general's uniform, as befitted a national hero whose picture had appeared in the popular magazine *Harper's Weekly*. He sat close to Libbie in church and danced the night away with her at a masquerade ball. He dressed as Louis XVI, she as a gypsy girl with a tambourine.

He proposed again, and this time she agreed to marry him, but only if he could persuade her father to consent. Judge Bacon, however, had left town when he realized that Custer wanted to ask for his daughter's hand in marriage. He returned just in time to see Custer off at the train station. They chatted about the war, and Custer added that he wanted to talk about something else; he would put it in a letter.

Custer returned in triumph to his Michigan brigade on October 8. The outfit was camped in Virginia not far from

Culpeper Court House. The men welcomed him with three rousing cheers while the band blared "Hail to the Chief." The next day, as he prepared for more battles, he wrote a surprisingly perceptive self-assessment:

> Often I think of the vast responsibility resting on me, of the many lives entrusted to my keeping, of the happiness of so many households depending on my discretion and judgment—and to think that I am just leaving my boyhood makes the responsibility appear greater. This is not due to egotism, self-conceit. I try to make no unjust pretensions. I assume nothing I know not to be true. It requires no extensive knowledge to inform me what is my duty to my country, my command. 'First be sure you're right, then go ahead!' I ask myself, 'Is it right?' Satisfied that it is so, I let nothing swerve me from my purpose.

James Kidd of the Michigan brigade, who had ample opportunity to observe Custer, wrote in 1908: "He acted like a man who made a business of his profession; who went about the work of fighting battles and winning victories, as a railroad superintendent goes about the business of running trains. When in action, his whole mind was concentrated on the duty and responsibility of the moment; in camp, he was genial and compensable, blithe as a boy. Indeed, he was a boy in years, though a man in courage and in discretion."

Two days after Custer returned, the band once again played "Yankee Doodle" as he led his Michigan men in a bloody battle at Brandy Station, Virginia. He found himself surrounded by Jeb Stuart's cavalry. Custer would have to fight his way out or face capture. Custer took a picture of Libbie out of his pocket and gazed at it for a moment, then rallied his troopers.

"Boys of Michigan," he shouted. "There are some people between us and home; I'm going home, who else goes?"

He recalled in a letter: "I gave the command 'Forward!' and I never expect to see a prettier sight. I frequently turned in my saddle to see the glittering sabers advance in the sunlight. I was riding in front. After advancing a short distance I gave the word 'Charge!' and away we went, whooping and yelling like so many demons. I had two horses shot under me within fifteen minutes."

The charge was not destined to be one studied by cadets at West Point as a model to follow. Custer led the men across an open field; they approached a ditch no one knew was there, and the horses were thrown into a great pile of confusion, which took the momentum out of the charge. But Custer spurred them on, made two more charges, and got everyone back to the safety of the Union infantry.

He had accomplished what had seemed impossible, with his usual flair and drama. His actions at Brandy Station impressed the leadership, which up to then had not seen much of him in action; he still had the reputation of being all bluster and little more than a popinjay and headline seeker. Wrote one officer, "No soldier who saw him on that day at Brandy Station ever questioned his right to wear a star or all the gold lace he felt inclined to wear. He at once became the favorite in the Army of the Potomac."

To Custer it was another glorious battle, another victory. "Oh, could you have but seen some of the charges that were made!" he wrote to a friend in Monroe. "While thinking of them I cannot but exclaim 'Glorious War!'"

And so it went, from skirmish to skirmish, battle to battle, what had come to be called "Custer's luck" never failed. He won, or at least escaped, each time, and the thrill, excitement, and passion never faded. And he also won his other war, with a moving, respectful, and persuasive letter to Judge Bacon.

George Custer and Elizabeth Bacon were married on February 9, 1864, at the First Presbyterian Church in Monroe.

He was twenty-four, she was twenty-two. They traveled east with stops in Cleveland, West Point, and New York City, where Custer had his head examined by a phrenologist. The belief that the bumps and indentations on a person's head revealed one's personality, character, and intelligence was then all the rage. The phrenologist, who had no idea who Custer was, advised him to "avoid overdoing."

When they reached the brigade headquarters in Stevensburg, Virginia, Libbie was warmly welcomed, especially by Eliza Brown, who was glad to see another woman in the camp. Libbie knew little about cooking or housekeeping, and Custer discouraged her from learning. "Day by day," Libbie wrote, "Eliza tactfully and quietly took us all in hand. It was tacitly understood that I was not to know anything" about the running of the household.

The couple often partook of General Pleasonton's six-course meals, thought to rival those of the best New York restaurants. And Libbie's means of transportation were quite comfortable. "Such style as we go in," she wrote home. "My General has a carriage with silver harness that he captured last summer, and two magnificent horses."

Libbie remained in camp with Custer whenever circumstances allowed. When the army went off to fight, she lived in a boardinghouse in Washington where she was never lonely for company. "She became the leading light of the Washington social scene. She knew all the right people, went to all the right balls, wore the right clothes, and charmed every man she met."

The first time she met the president, Abraham Lincoln stopped the reception line when he heard her name. "So you are the wife of the general who goes into battle with a whoop and a yell?" the president asked. "Well, I'm told he won't do so anymore." Libbie said she hoped he would. "Oh," Lincoln replied, "then you want to be a widow, I see." They both laughed at Lincoln's macabre humor, and Custer continued going into battle with "a whoop and a yell," and so much abandon. Being married did not change him when there was a charge to be led and a battle to be won.

A month after his wedding, Custer was shocked to learn that Pleasonton, whom he loved like a father, who had nurtured his growth as a soldier and made him a general, was being relieved of command and exiled to duty out West. Lieutenant General Ulysses S. Grant, now in command of all the Union armies, had chosen someone else to take over the cavalry of the Army of the Potomac.

The person Grant selected was a thirty-three-year-old career army man whose closest friends even described him as bull-headed, profane, and unforgiving of failure or weakness. He was gruff, plainspoken, high-strung, and given to violence on the battlefield and in his personal life. A train conductor once treated the general in what he took for a disrespectful manner. He stopped his conversation with a fellow officer, beat the conductor mercilessly, tossed him off the train, then sat back down and resumed his conversation as if nothing unusual had occurred.

"He was an unimpressive little man," a biographer wrote, "five feet five inches tall, with a large bullet-shaped head and coarse hair that looked, someone said, as though it had been painted on." Lincoln described him as "a chunky little chap, with a long body, short legs, not enough neck to hang him, and such long arms that if his ankles itch he can scratch them without stooping." His men called him, with affection, "Little Phil." The nation knew him as Major General Philip H. Sheridan.

The son of poor Irish immigrants, Sheridan had grown up in Somerset, Ohio, where his father worked at building roads and digging canals. The boy dreamed of military glory from an early age and marched other boys around town, brandishing a tin sword and drilling them like a sergeant. He also learned to fight. Other boys picked on him because of his stubby size, long arms, and strangely shaped head. But before long, he showed that he could beat up every boy in town, no matter his size. They left him alone after that.

He dropped out of school and took jobs clerking at local stores, but he still hoped for a military career. "My sole wish was to become a soldier, and my highest aspiration to go to West Point." He got his chance in 1848, when the local congressman's appointee to the Military Academy could not go because of his poor mathematics skills. Sheridan pestered the congressman until he won an appointment to enter West Point as a member of the class of 1852.

Sheridan had a hard time at the academy because of his academic deficiencies, social status, odd appearance, and belligerent nature. He was regarded as an outcast by many cadets. "Not only was he short, unattractive, argumentative, and poor, he was obviously Irish Catholic," at a time when prejudice against Catholics and the Irish was rampant.

Sheridan made it to his senior year when he came close to running a bayonet through a cadet from Virginia who offended him by his tone of voice. The next day, Sheridan, without any further provocation, hit the cadet in the head. He was arrested and sentenced to a year's suspension. Unrepentant, Sheridan went back to Ohio and his old job at the dry-goods store.

He returned to West Point the following year. After graduation he spent eight years as a second lieutenant fighting Indians in the western territories, as fearless on the battlefield as he had been in the schoolyard. Not all his relations with Indians were hostile, however. For a time he lived with an Indian woman who was the daughter of a chief. Her white friends called her Francis. Sheridan was not the only soldier to live with an Indian woman—it was quite common then—but later in life when he wrote his memoirs, he made no mention of her.

In May 1862, Sheridan was promoted to a colonel in command of a cavalry regiment. He quickly demonstrated that he was a superb fighter, distinguishing himself in a series of stunning victories in Mississippi and Kentucky, and at the Union offensive in southeastern Tennessee and northwestern Georgia (Chickamauga, Chattanooga, and Missionary Ridge). Promotions followed these successes: brigadier general in September 1862, lieutenant general in 1864, and now, in the spring of that year, commander of the cavalry of the Army of the Potomac, where one of his new generals was Custer.

The two men got along well from the outset, and Custer soon became Sheridan's favorite—his "pet," as rivals called him. In the months and years to come, Sheridan would assume an even larger role in Custer's life and career than Pleasonton had. Sheridan would lead Custer through the rest of the Civil War, where they won one victory after another, and into his postwar years as an Indian fighter. If not for Sheridan, Custer's career would have ended with his 1867 court-martial; that would have been history's final judgment of him. It would be thanks to Sheridan that Custer would regain his former glory in action along the banks of the Washita River.

On May 9, 1864, Sheridan led the ten-thousand-man Union cavalry deep into Virginia in a column that stretched thirteen miles. It took four hours for it to make its way past any given point. Its mission was to force Jeb Stuart's cavalry out and destroy it. Custer and his Michigan brigade led the way.

At Beaver Dam, Custer's men captured two trainloads of supplies bound for General Lee, including medical supplies and a million and a half food rations Lee's hungry men desperately needed. They also took custody of more than three hundred Union prisoners who were being transported to Richmond. Custer's men appropriated the food for themselves, then set fire to the rest of the supplies and fired artillery shells into the boilers of the locomotives.

Two days later, at Yellow Tavern, only two miles from the outer defenses of Richmond, they found Stuart's men. The rebels attacked first, however, catching the Union troopers in crossfire from three directions. The Yankees had been dismounted when the attack began and were trapped in a field with no cover from trees or rocks.

Custer galloped into the middle of the field with bullets whizzing all around him. He shouted to his men to lie down flat and promised that help was on the way. Custer "stayed with them, sitting coolly on his charger, while they all hugged the ground, encouraging them to hold on with his happy-go-lucky manner." Another of his Michigan regiments arrived quickly, and Custer immediately ordered a charge. "His headquarters flag of the gayest colors was flying in advance of the moving mass of glittering blades," an officer from another outfit recalled. "The shrill blast of one hundred bugles and the familiar air of 'Yankee Doddle' rang out upon the battlefield while brave men of the Michigan brigade rode boot to boot into what seemed the very jaws of death."

And of course, Custer's charge succeeded. Jeb Stuart was killed, his troops were scattered, and Custer received praise from ranks high and low. Another glorious victory. Another mission accomplished.

A month later, on June 10, Custer's forces were doing battle at Trevilian Station, Virginia, but this fight resulted in the Michigan brigade's highest losses and Custer's greatest personal embarrassment of the war.

After Sheridan's other units had destroyed the railroad station at Trevilian and torn up some track, Custer's men found themselves trapped between Wade Hampton's and Major General Fitzhugh Lee's cavalry. "Custer was everywhere present," Major James Kidd wrote, "giving direction to his subordinate commanders." Kidd added that Custer's behavior made it clear why Custer wore "so singular a uniform. It individualized him. Wherever seen, it was recognized. There was but one Custer, and by his unique appearance and heroic bearing he was readily distinguished from all others."

Custer led his men in one counterattack after another, had three horses shot out from beneath him, and picked up a fallen soldier and carried him off the field. Nevertheless, they were soundly beaten. They lost more than four hundred men, with an additional three hundred captured, before they were able to fight their way back to Union lines. The Confederates also captured Custer's headquarters wagon and all his personal possessions. Libbie joked in a letter home that he lost "everything except his toothbrush. Mother will be glad to hear that he never parts with that. He brushes his teeth after every meal. I always laugh at him for it, also for washing his hands so frequently." But the greatest loss—no laughing matter for Custer—was the bundle of love letters from Libbie, some of which were later published in a Richmond newspaper.

At the end of summer 1864, Grant placed Sheridan in command of a forty-thousand-man army, including Custer at the head of the 3rd Cavalry Division, with a promotion to major general. Custer's orders were to clear out all Confederate forces from the Shenandoah Valley. The men of the 3rd Division welcomed their new commanding general by decking themselves out with red ties, following his example. The unit made a series of saber charges that chased the rebels out, including a West Point classmate of Custer's, Brigadier General Tom Rosser.

Custer approached the battle with Rosser in a knightly fashion, with a proper sense of decorum, theater, and flair. "When his troopers took up their proper stations, [Custer] galloped far out in front of his line, a lone figure in black, stopping where he could be seen by every man on that field. With a swift motion, he raised his right hand to his broad hat and swept it down to his knee in an extravagant salute, bowing gracefully in the saddle. May the best man win!"

Rosser watched the performance. "You see that officer down there?" he asked his staff. "That's General Custer the

Yanks are so proud of, and I intend to give him the best whipping today that he ever got."

Custer chased Rosser and his men some fourteen miles and captured their artillery, supply wagons, ambulances, and even a pet squirrel. It was the most spectacular cavalry victory of the war to date. The *New York Times* wrote that Custer "displayed the judgment of a Napoleon." Custer found Rosser's personal trunk containing his dress uniform and hat. They were far too big for Custer, but he put them on anyway and paraded around camp with the sleeves hanging below his hands. The men thought it was hilarious. He wrote a note to his old friend Rosser and arranged to have it delivered to the Confederate line:

> Dear Friend,
> Thanks for setting me up in so many new things, but would you please direct your tailor to make the coattails of your next uniform a trifle shorter.
> Best regards, G. A. C.

Is it any wonder that reporters wrote so many stories so often about Custer, each one adding to his shining star? Troops cheered whenever he appeared among them. After a skirmish in late October, Custer led thirteen of his men to Washington with thirteen captured Confederate battle flags. At a ceremony at the War Department, each trooper presented his flag to Secretary of War Edwin Stanton.

"General," Stanton said, "a gallant officer always makes gallant soldiers."

One of Custer's men blurted out the sentiments of the entire division.

"The Third Division wouldn't be worth a cent if it wasn't for him!"

The press reported that Custer, with Libbie at his side, looked embarrassed, showing that "his modesty was equal to his courage."

On the morning of October 28, Confederate General Jubal Early attacked Sheridan's army, which was camped along Cedar Creek, 80 miles southwest of Washington. The attack was well planned and caught the Yankees by surprise, sending them running north as fast as they could, some still in their underwear. Although Sheridan was in Washington at the time, he was able to ride to the scene, gathering his retreating army. Custer organized a charge against the left flank of the rebel troops with such force that the enemy line fell apart. Now it was the rebels' turn to run, and they did so for miles to escape Custer's marauding troopers. When it was all over and the Union soldiers returned to camp, Custer, in an even more elated mood than usual, clasped Sheridan with both arms, picked him up, and twirled him about. "By God, Phil!" he shouted. "We've cleaned them out of their guns and got ours back!"

Custer had fought in the first battle at Bull Run over four years before, and now he was fighting the final battles, chasing Lee's army as it fled west from its shattered defenses at Petersburg, Virginia. On April 6, 1865, Custer's 3rd Division, in another of his daring charges, captured a third of the remains of Lee's army at Sayler's Creek, a total of seven generals and nine thousand troops. Two days later, at Appomattox Station, Custer took possession of three Confederate railroad trains loaded with food and ammunition. Those supplies had been Lee's only hope of continuing the war. Without them, he and his cause were truly lost. Custer led his final charge of the war that day, capturing twenty-four cannon.

He and his forces were now positioned directly in Lee's path, with thousands of other Union troops behind and on both flanks of the remnants of the once proud and often victorious Army of Northern Virginia. The next morning, a lone Confederate officer rode to Custer's position, carrying a white towel on a stick. "Fittingly," one historian wrote, "this emblem of war's end came to the young general who, by age twenty-five, had written a record of military exploits that few soldiers exhibit in a lifetime." The long agony was over.

That afternoon, Lee and Grant met in Appomattox Court House in the home of Wilmer McLean, who had once lived near Bull Run. He had left there four years before, following that battle, and moved to Appomattox in order to get as far away from the war as possible. While Grant and Lee discussed surrender terms, Custer greeted old friends—Gimlet Lea, whose wedding he had attended, and Fitzhugh Lee. All were generals, but Custer hugged them and wrestled them to the ground like schoolboys. That night, he invited seven rebel officers to bunk in his tent.

Sheridan paid Wilmer McLean two ten-dollar gold pieces for the little pine table on which the surrender documents had been signed; he intended it as a gift for Libbie Custer. "My dear Madam," he wrote, "I respectfully present to you the small writing table on which the conditions for the surrender of the Confederate Army of Northern Virginia were written by Lieutenant General Grant, and permit me to say, Madam, that there is scarcely an individual in our service who has contributed more to bring this about than your very gallant husband." Custer, clearly pleased, rode off with the table balanced on his head.

Custer had one final moment of glory related to the Civil War, on May 23, 1865, in Washington, DC. The sun was bright, the city festooned with flags, and people by the thousands jammed the streets awaiting the spectacle of the Grand Review, the march down Pennsylvania Avenue of nearly all the Union armies. This was the day for Meade's Army of the Potomac. Sherman's western armies would march the following day. Down the broad avenue they came, an endless blue line of soldiers, bands playing and hundreds of banners waving. The troops marched one last time together, down from the Capitol with its new dome gleaming in the sun, past the huge reviewing stand in front of the White House.

And there was Custer leading the troops of his 3rd Division, each man proudly wearing his distinctive red tie. The crowd easily recognized Custer with his long, golden curls and broad-brimmed hat. He wore the formal coat of a major general's full dress uniform, one of the rare times he abided by the dress regulations.

The crowd went wild when he came into view, screaming his name over and over. A group of three hundred young girls, all dressed in white, was particularly enthusiastic. "We were massed along the sidewalk," one later told Libbie Custer, "waving flags, throwing flowers as we sang. Custer had always been my hero, so as he rode by I tried to throw a wreath of flowers about his horse's neck."

The horse was Don Juan, one of Custer's favorites. He had come under fire many times and had never faltered or changed step. But at that moment, perhaps frightened by the crowds and the wreath hitting him in the head, he bolted and raced ahead, madly out of control of even the greatest cavalryman in the army.

The horse tore past the reviewing stand, past General Grant, President Andrew Johnson, and a host of other dignitaries. All eyes were on Custer. As he flew by, unable to regain control of his horse, he tried to salute Johnson and Grant, as a soldier is required to do. As he raised his saber to give the salute, the tip caught the wide brim of his hat and knocked it off, taking the sword out of his hand.

"Then," as a reporter for the *Detroit Evening News* described the event, "with his long, yellow curly hair floating out behind, he settled himself in the saddle as if he grew there, and by one of the most magnificent exhibitions of horsemanship he reined in the flying charger and returned to meet his troops. An orderly had picked up his hat and sword, and pulling the hat down over his eyes, Custer dashed back past the assembled thousands, and soon reappeared at the head of his division." Custer was the only man to pass the reviewing stand twice, and the only one to receive more press coverage for his performance than most others got in the entire war.

Of course, there were detractors and cynics who insisted that Custer goaded his horse to bolt and run, in a bid for attention. Don Juan had never panicked before, even in the face of cannon fire, and Custer was too good a rider to lose control like that. How could a wreath of flowers spook such a well-trained animal? It was a "show-off trick," one said, his last chance to be the center of acclaim and adulation.

We will never know the truth, but surely Custer did know it was his last opportunity to cling to the fame and glory he had earned in four years of war. When the parade ended, "He had nothing to look forward to, no plans to interest him. The boy who had become a brigadier at twenty-three and a major general at twenty-four, who had received the Confederate surrender flag, and was accustomed to seeing his name continually in the newspapers [would soon] become a forgotten man."

The glory days were over. The man who had trained for war, and who reveled in it, now had no war to fight.

FIVE

WE TOOK
NO
PRISONERS

The end of peace for Black Kettle and his people began on August 17, 1862, in Minnesota, six hundred miles from Colorado Territory. Back East, in a house near Williamsburg, Virginia, behind Confederate lines, George Custer was enjoying the two-week wedding celebration of his friend, Gimlet Lea. In Minnesota on that fateful day, four young men of the Santee Sioux tribe were returning to their reservation when they came across some eggs laid by a hen that had strayed from a local farmer's coop. One of the braves wanted to take the eggs, but another warned him that the farmer would cause trouble for them if he did. The first man told the other that he was being a coward, whereupon the second said he would prove he wasn't a coward by killing the farmer. Before the day was over, the braves had killed the farmer, his wife, and two of their neighbors.

When they got back to the reservation, they bragged about the deed. Their chief, Little Crow, summoned the tribal council to discuss what they should do. He knew the whites would demand retribution. Little Crow, like Black Kettle, had always urged conciliation with the whites because he knew there were far too many of them to fight.

The Santee Sioux were considered to be civilized. The settlers said they were among the "good Indians" because they lived quietly on the lands the government had given them. Some had become farmers, converted to Christianity, wore so-called civilian clothing, and sent their children to white schools. They had remained peaceful even though the government failed to pay their annual annuity that year, even though their crops had failed and the white traders had cheated them again. They had done everything the treaties required of them, and they were still hungry and at the mercy of the whites for their survival. And now this.

The council voted to go on the warpath, despite Chief Little Crow's objections. They might as well go to war, they argued, because the settlers were going to punish them anyway for the killings committed by the four young men. And so the Indians struck the next morning; by the time the sun had set, four hundred whites had been killed, "dispatched with a savagery rarely equaled in the history of Indian uprisings; families burned alive in their cabins, children nailed to doors, girls raped by a dozen braves and then hacked to pieces, babies dismembered, and their limbs flung in their mothers' faces."

The uprising was put down in less than a week, but in all nearly eight hundred whites had been murdered and close to forty thousand forced to flee, leaving behind all their possessions. A month later, a military commission put on trial four hundred captured braves, charging them with rape, murder, and other crimes. Each proceeding lasted fewer than ten minutes; 303 of the men were sentenced to death. However, President Lincoln then studied the trial records and concluded that only 38 actually deserved execution. They were hanged the day after Christmas 1862.

To the people of Denver, the massacre in Minnesota was their worst nightmare realized. They followed every detail of the slaughter with morbid fascination and growing fear. If it could happen there—with Indians who had supposedly been civilized and who went to church every Sunday—then no one was safe; certainly not in Denver with bloodthirsty savages in plain sight on every street. Who knew when the Cheyenne and Arapaho would turn on them?

To add to their fears, residents of Denver thought they had been left defenseless because most of the army had been sent back East to fight the Confederates. Two volunteer Colorado regiments had been formed, but one was in New Mexico keeping the rebels in Texas away from the Colorado gold fields, and the other was in Kansas fighting rebel guerrilla bands. Altogether, almost one thousand eight hundred men in those regiments had gone to war. The locals missed the comfort of seeing men in blue uniforms in their town.

Not that the Cheyenne and Arapaho had actually made any threatening moves. Black Kettle was doing his best to keep his young warriors away from the whites. There had been only one minor altercation. A couple of Cheyenne had gone to a ranch to beg for food. They were given something to eat but asked for more. They quarreled with the rancher and two of his friends over a side of bacon. One of the whites was hit in the head, and then the Indians left. They returned with about sixty others and fired arrows at the house. A few crept inside and tried to drag one of the white men out, but the women in the house clung to him. The Indians left without further incident.

No one was seriously injured and nothing was stolen, but people became jittery nonetheless. Rumors spread that the Great Plains tribes were organizing a conspiracy to murder all the whites living west of the Missouri River. And in truth, other tribes did rise up on hearing of the events in Minnesota. The Ute, Shoshone, Kiowa, Comanche, and others ran rampant, marauding and killing.

Trouble erupted everywhere, it seemed, except in Colorado Territory. The Cheyenne and Arapaho did nothing more threatening than run off a few horses and mules from stagecoach stations, beg for or steal some food, and get drunk and create a small disturbance. Still, how could a settler be sure that the small band of Cheyenne riding up to his isolated ranch only wanted a little food? Look what happened to those poor souls in Minnesota; the Indians there had seemed peaceful too. The suspicions, fears, and uncertainty in Denver were reaching a peak, but the peace Black Kettle worked so hard for might have endured had the situation not been deliberately aggravated for personal gain.

Two men stoked the people's fear and raised it to greater heights, and they did so with cold-blooded calculation. One was a preacher turned soldier, and the other a physician turned politician. Together they started a war.

John Milton Chivington was the quintessential nineteenth-century fire-and-brimstone preacher, a scourge of sinners and backsliders. He looked like a figure out of the Old Testament, with piercing black eyes and coarse, reddish-brown hair, and he had a deep, bellowing voice that rattled the glass in church windows. At six feet four and a half inches and 260 pounds, the self-styled soldier in God's army cut an intimidating figure as he went about his righteous ways. Ordained as a Methodist minister in 1844, Chivington, his wife, and their three children lived a hard life, relocating from one church to another every two years.

Wherever he served, Chivington always left that church more solvent and with more members than when he arrived. He reached out beyond the pulpit into the surrounding communities to build schools and libraries and root out lawless elements. He preached a gospel of social activism and fought against slavery, gambling, drinking, and prostitution. In Illinois, he provided shelter for an escaped slave from

Tennessee, shielding her from a US marshal who showed up at Chivington's front door to take her back. The lawman retreated rather than go up against Chivington.

At a Missouri parish where proslavery sentiment ran strong, he openly preached against it. Told he would be tarred and feathered if he gave another such sermon in that county, he spread the word that he would preach the following Sunday and nobody was going to stop him. A group of men arrived on Sunday with a bucket of hot tar and a feather pillow. Chivington rose up behind the pulpit, gazed out at the parishioners, then reached inside his long black robe and pulled out two revolvers, placing them on either side of the Bible.

"By the grace of God and these two revolvers," he announced, "I am going to preach here today." He delivered his fiery sermon against slavery, and no one threatened him again. That was when he got the nickname "the Fighting Parson."

He arrived in Denver on Saturday, May 4, 1860. The first thing he did was buy enough lumber to build a house for his family. The next morning he held church services in a grove of cottonwood trees; that was the official beginning of the First Methodist Church of Denver. As had happened in other towns, Chivington quickly became a respected and valued member of the community. A year later, at the outset of the Civil War, he was appointed major in the 1st Colorado Regiment of Volunteers. He had been asked to serve as regimental chaplain but insisted that he preferred fighting to praying.

Chivington's chance at glory came in New Mexico Territory on March 28, 1862. The 1st Colorado had been sent south to stop a three-thousand-man force of Confederate troops under the command of Brigadier General Henry Sibley, known as "the Walking Whiskey Keg." The rebels had captured Albuquerque and Santa Fe and were heading for the Colorado gold fields.

While the commander of the 1st Colorado led the majority of the troops forward to meet the Confederates head on, Chivington took a group of 430 men on a challenging trek through the mountains to approach the enemy from the rear. They reached a spot above Glorietta Pass; below them stood the entire Confederate supply train, consisting of more than eighty wagons.

When he heard sounds indicating that the main battle was taking place, Chivington led his men on their dangerous descent. The mountainside was so steep they had to cling to 125-foot leather ropes to keep from falling. They caught the rebels by surprise and in a matter of minutes captured Sibley's supplies. All the Confederates had left was what they wore or carried in their knapsacks. Sibley was forced to retreat to Texas.

Chivington's bold attack most likely saved Colorado from Confederate occupation and was considered so decisive that the battle of Glorietta Pass came to be called the Gettysburg of the West. "The Fighting Parson" led the First Colorado back to Denver in triumph. Crowds lined the streets to cheer the man who saved them from the enemy. He was lauded, toasted, and presented with scrolls, swords, and other expensive gifts, and named commander of the Military District of Colorado. Being the most popular man in the territory was heady stuff for a preacher, and he loved the adulation and acclaim of being a conquering hero. Then the war was over in the West. The rebels did not menace Colorado again, and Chivington found that he missed the glory and fame. But who else was there to fight? The answer would soon become apparent.

In summer 1862, a new governor, John Evans, was appointed for Colorado Territory. Taking stock of the situation, he maliciously set out to exploit the local population's undercurrents of suspicion and fear of the Indians. More than any other individual, he would be responsible for starting a war with the Cheyenne and Arapaho, and he would have a willing ally in Chivington.

Trained as a physician, Evans turned to real estate and made his fortune in Illinois. The city of Evanston, on Chicago's northern border, was named for him, and he helped found Northwestern University and, later, the University of Denver. He was a highly capable organizer and administrator, a generous philanthropist, and an expert whittler. But he was also a cold-blooded opportunist, all too willing to use his office for personal and political gain. He had two overwhelming ambitions in Colorado: to develop the area's natural resources as rapidly as possible, and to become its first US senator.

Every decision he made, every action he took was guided by those goals. He would allow nothing to stand in the way of his political future. He developed close friendships with Chivington and with newspaperman William Byers. All three had the same dream of statehood for Colorado and power for themselves. Evans would be senator, Chivington a congressman, and Byers the power behind both.

As governor, Evans was also ex-officio superintendent of Indian affairs, an unfortunate arrangement since he knew nothing about Indian matters. Nevertheless, he was in a position to exert considerable influence on relations between whites and Indians. He saw the Indians as an obstacle in the path to achieving his goals. He wanted the Cheyenne and Arapaho out of the way, confined to the reservation established by the 1861 Fort Wise Treaty, even though nothing had yet been done to make the land habitable, as had been promised. Evans believed it was his duty to keep the Indians confined to the reservation so that other lands could be developed, farmed, and mined, the way God intended, of course. He needed some way to force the Indians onto the reservation permanently.

If the Indians had been marauding and threatening settlers, then Evans could have raised a militia to deal with them, but the Indians refused to cooperate with his personal plans. They continued, almost obstinately, to live in peace, thwarting Evans's ambition. He tried spreading rumors that the Indians were about to wage war, that Confederate agents were inducing them to fight, and that the Sioux had invited Cheyenne and Arapaho to join a massive uprising to wipe out all the settlers. Evans even threatened the Indians with extermination if they waged war against the whites, or did not stay on their reservation.

In desperation, he announced a council with the Cheyenne and Arapaho chiefs to force the issue, but when he got to the appointed site, no one was there. He then sent Elbridge Gerry, a rancher married to an Indian, to find the chiefs and bring them to the meeting, but they told Gerry they had no interest in meeting with the governor, even though the governor was offering gifts. The reason for their refusal was their dissatisfaction with the Fort Wise Treaty. They told Gerry that they felt cheated because the terms of the treaty had never been fully explained to them.

Cheyenne Chief Bull Bear was especially truculent.

"Does the Great Father want us to live like white men?" he asked.

"The Great Father," Gerry said, "will help you to live comfortably. He will build schools and educate your papooses—."

Bull Bear interrupted.

"Does the Great Father want us to live like white men?"

"Yes, that is what he wants."

"You tell white chief, Indian maybe not so low yet."

Angry that the chiefs refused to meet with him, Governor Evans set out to prove that the Plains Indians were hostile and were preparing for a massive uprising in the spring. Even though men like Charles Bent, who had close ties to the Cheyenne and Arapaho, repeatedly told Evans that Black Kettle and other peace chiefs refused to smoke the war pipe, Evans continued to insist publicly that war was coming.

On December 14, 1862, Evans wrote to Secretary of War Stanton requesting military aid, the authority to form a militia, and permission to station troops along the wagon-train and stagecoach routes. He told Stanton he had done everything he could to keep peace, but that the Indians were only waiting for the grass to grow in the spring to launch their massive attacks.

War did come in the spring, but the Indians did not start it. Some cattle went missing in early April, and the herders responsible for them claimed that Indians had stolen them. The Cheyenne said the cattle had stampeded and that the herders accused the Indians in order to divert blame from themselves for their own carelessness.

John M. Chivington, the "Fighting Parson." (*National Park Service*)

No matter what the truth, the damage was done. The fears and expectations of the whites, reinforced by Evans for months, seemed to be confirmed. Indians were up to no good, and something had to be done.

The governor ordered Chivington to do his duty as commander of the Military District of Colorado. "The Fighting Parson" sent out a detachment of fifty-four men and two howitzers, under the command of Lieutenant George Eayre, to chastise the hostiles. Eayre burned two empty Indian camps and returned to Denver for supplies, commandeering civilians' wagons right off the street. He told Chivington that the Indians had opened fire first. Word had reached town that Indians had run off mules from a ranch, destroyed telegraph lines, and harassed some settlers.

Chivington sent out another detail, commanded by Lieutenant Clark Dunn, who approached a Cheyenne camp and indicated that he wanted to talk. The Indians agreed, but Dunn suddenly signaled for his men to disarm them. Each side claimed the other fired first, and when it was over, four soldiers and three Cheyenne lay dead. On April 15, Chivington received a report that Indians had attacked a ranch, killed two, wounded a third, and run off all the cattle. Dunn led his men to the site and found no bodies or wounded, or any sign that a fight had occurred. Still, the rumors of Indians on the warpath persisted, spreading fear and desire for revenge.

Chivington took a hard line in his orders to his men: "There is but one course for us to pursue, to make them behave or kill them, which latter it now seems we will have to do."

It was Chivington who was on the warpath. The drive for statehood for Colorado was under way, and he was deeply committed to it. His political future, if he was to have one, depended on statehood so he could run for Congress. But other influential and well-connected people also wanted to be the first congressman from Colorado, and some of them were far more popular with voters.

The glory Chivington had earned at Glorietta Pass was now two years in the past, and there had been no further opportunities to keep his name in the public eye. Indeed, his high-handed behavior as commander of the military district had alienated many residents. The praise once lavished on him had turned to criticism, the admiration to indignation. He needed to restore his heroic image; if only he could save the people of Denver from marauding savages, he could be on his way to Congress. The problem was that the Indians were not marauding. The pace of the war he and Evans were trying to foment would have to pick up—and soon.

On April 16, Chivington ordered Major Jacob Downing to take sixty men to investigate a report that drunken Indians had harassed a rancher. The report, like so many others, was not true. Although the settlers Downing interviewed said they feared an uprising, they had seen no signs of any trouble.

Downing did capture one Indian who revealed—after Downing held the man's legs over a fire—the location of a Cheyenne camp. It was a peaceful village occupied by women, children, and old men. The young men were off hunting. Downing attacked anyway and claimed twenty-six warriors killed and thirty wounded. He wrote in his report that there were no women and children among the dead. How they all had managed to escape was a feat he did not explain.

Downing concluded that "though I think we have punished [the Indians] pretty severely in this affair, yet I believe now it is but the commencement of war with this tribe, which must result in exterminating them."

On May 10, Lieutenant Eayre, under orders from Chivington to kill Indians wherever he found them, came across a band of four hundred Cheyenne led by Chief Lean Bear. Eayre claimed the Indians opened fire first and that he killed twenty-eight in a seven-hour battle. The Indians told a different story. Alarmed by the sight of the soldiers and their howitzers, Lean Bear went alone to meet with the whites and tell them the Cheyenne were friendly and meant no harm. He proudly wore a medal around his neck given to him by President Lincoln, assured that it would always protect him. But as he approached within twenty feet of Eayre, the lieutenant gave the command to open fire. Lean Bear fell dead.

The soldiers fired their howitzers on the Cheyenne camp, and as the battle raged, Chief Black Kettle ran to his braves, yelling, "Stop the fighting! Do not make war on the Whites!" Some men obeyed him, but the rest chased the troopers away. Seeking revenge, they ransacked nearby ranches and stage-coach stops within miles, but found no whites to kill. They had all fled.

And so the war began, a merciless war that ultimately cost the US government $30 million and resulted in the deaths of uncounted numbers of settlers and Indians. By May 1864, Black Kettle and other peace chiefs had lost all influence over their young warriors.

The people of Denver and its outlying settlements would not soon forget spring and summer 1864. Every day brought fresh rumors of atrocities and grisly raids all along the Platte River valley. Not that anyone in Denver actually saw victims, or

Indians on the offensive, but everyone knew someone who had heard a story from someone who had heard them from someone else. And everyone remembered the horrors of Minnesota. Every shadow on the horizon, every coyote wail in the night became an Indian, even though there had been no raids near Denver. It was all happening elsewhere in the territory—until June 11, until the Hungates.

Ward Hungate managed a ranch twenty-five miles outside of town, where he lived with his wife and two daughters until the day the Indians came. His body was found some distance from the house, riddled with more than eighty bullets. His wife and the girls, ages three and six, had been stuffed into a well. Their bodies had been mutilated, the children's throats slashed so deeply that their heads had nearly been severed from their bodies.

The ranch owner carted the bloody remains into town and put them on display in a store. It was one thing for folks to hear stories about atrocities; it was something else to see them first-hand. The Hungates became for the whites what Lean Bear was for the Cheyenne: a rallying cry and a symbol. And as symbols often do, these led to greater outrages on both sides.

Several months later it was learned that the Hungates had not been murdered by Cheyenne but by four Arapaho warriors passing through the territory on their way north. But by then the damage had been done. It was obvious to everyone in Denver that the Cheyenne were on the warpath. Terrified families poured into Denver from their isolated ranches. Women and children were sheltered in the two strongest buildings in town. Iron shutters were bolted over the windows, and armed men patrolled outside.

Governor Evans imposed martial law on Denver and sent an impassioned telegram to Secretary of War Stanton claiming that Indian attacks on outlying settlements had commenced and that scalped and mutilated bodies had been brought into town. He pleaded for permission to form a militia unit for one hundred days of service to protect the population.

Denver, Colorado, as it appeared in May 1864. Not only were residents concerned about the threat of Indian attacks in the region, they also suffered a devastating flood, shown here, that spring. (*Library of Congress*)

Receiving no reply from Stanton, Evans then sought assistance from Major General Samuel Curtis at Fort Leavenworth, commanding the Department of Kansas, which included Colorado Territory. He told Curtis that he had reliable information that a full-scale Indian war, led by Cheyenne, was about to begin. Only because of this reliable information, Evans went on, had he been able to avert another Minnesota massacre, although he was vague about how he had accomplished that. Evans concluded that "this Indian war is no myth but a terrible reality." Once again he was exaggerating; there was no war, but there soon would be.

"Dead cattle, full of arrows, are lying in all directions. A general Indian war is anticipated." So wrote William Byers in the *Rocky Mountain News* on July 18, 1864, five weeks after the Hungate family had been killed. The day before Byers wrote that article, war parties of Cheyenne, Arapaho, and Sioux raided stagecoach stations and freight trains along the Platte River trail. They attacked a wagon train, leaving ten men dead.

Chivington shuttled between Denver and the outlying forts, dispatching patrols to find the war parties and providing escorts for the US mail and protection for smaller posts. He had two thousand troops under his command, but only about one thousand five hundred were fit for duty at any one time, and they were scattered over a broad area. It was impossible to protect everyone from the raids, which seemed to increase in frequency and boldness every day.

More ranches were sacked and burned, more men killed, and more women and children kidnapped, carried off into captivity. Many white settlers saved their last bullet for themselves. From August 8 to 18, more than fifty whites were murdered. Chivington notified General Curtis that the Indians had the town surrounded. He asked to raise a company of one-hundred-day men.

Denver was under siege, cut off from the rest of the territory. For nearly six weeks, no stagecoaches could get through, not even the mail. Food grew scarce. The price of flour jumped from nine dollars per one hundred pounds to forty-five dollars. People ran out of coal oil and had to use candles for light. Byers ran out of newsprint and was reduced to publishing smaller and smaller editions of the *Rocky Mountain News*. It appeared on wrapping paper, pink and white tissue paper, even yellow butcher paper.

Governor Evans continued to plead with the War Department in Washington for authority to raise a regiment of one-hundred-day volunteers. He warned that without the extra troops, the white population of Colorado Territory would be slaughtered.

"Extensive Indian depredations, with murder of families occurred yesterday 30 miles south of Denver," he telegraphed Stanton on August 18, after he was told that a man and a boy had been killed south of town. "Our lines of communication are cut. Large bodies of Indians are undoubtedly near to Denver, and we are in danger of destruction both from attack of Indians and starvation. It is impossible to exaggerate our danger."

In late August, General Curtis finally authorized Evans to form the 3rd Colorado Volunteer Cavalry Regiment for one hundred days of duty. Evans and Chivington had no trouble finding volunteers, because someone, never identified, started a convenient rumor that any able-bodied man who did not volunteer would be drafted and sent east to fight the Confederates. It was not true, of course, but the regiment soon enlisted 650 men.

They were a mixed lot who quickly earned a reputation for stealing chickens, going absent without leave, sleeping late, and instigating drunken brawls in Denver's saloons. The officers were as unruly and unreliable as the men. None wanted to drill, do guard duty, or obey orders unless they felt in the right mood. They were a disorderly lot out for some fun, and if they had a chance to kill Indians along the way, so much the better. These were the men Chivington would lead to war.

"The Fighting Parson" was in no hurry to lead his new regiment anywhere just yet. First, he had to win the election on September 11. He waged his war against the Indians in his Sunday sermons and campaign speeches. Wherever he spoke in his fight for Colorado statehood and his own congressional seat, he echoed and incited the public fear of Indians by urging war without mercy. Only one way to deal with savages, he roared—kill them all, even the children, because one day they would grow up to be warriors. Such talk was a good way to get elected, but toward the end of summer, Chivington committed an act so controversial that people began to change their opinion. The incident involved outlaws who had committed a series of robberies. Five of the men had been captured and sent to Denver, where Chivington proposed trying them as guerrillas in a military court because some were renegade Confederates.

He asked General Curtis for permission to execute them if, as seemed inevitable, they were found guilty. Curtis said he was the only person who could pronounce death sentences, and he ordered Chivington to send the prisoners to the nearest army post, Fort Lyon, 240 miles southeast of Denver. Chivington put the prisoners in chains and detailed a one-hundred-man escort to guard them. Ample rations were provided for the troops but none for the prisoners. It turned out they did not need any food, because they were shot to death the second day while allegedly trying to escape. At first, Chivington tried to conceal the event, but then the prisoners' bodies were discovered tied to trees with bullet holes in their skulls.

Now it was Chivington who was in trouble. Many former supporters thought he was assuming too much power, acting as judge, jury, and executioner. The prisoners had at least deserved a fair trial before being hanged. It was bad timing for Chivington, with the election less than two weeks away. In addition, both Chivington and Evans were accused of fomenting the current Indian troubles in an attempt to demonstrate the necessity of direct representation in Washington. Even General Curtis weighed in, charging that Chivington was spending more time on his political career than on his duties as commander of Colorado's military district. He criticized Chivington for staying in Denver electioneering instead of dealing with the Indian troubles throughout the territory.

The bid for statehood lost by a three-to-one ratio, and Chivington's dreams of political glory were as moribund as his faded military glory. He obviously needed a big victory over the Indians to restore his reputation, but Black Kettle was making a peace overture, attempting to bring the war, such as it was, to a premature close, far too soon for Chivington's ambitions.

The move toward peace began at Fort Lyon, formerly known as Fort Wise, site of the 1861 treaty. The fort's commanding officer was twenty-eight-year-old Major Edward W. Wynkoop, known as Ned, a tall, handsome man with wavy black hair and a long drooping mustache. Born to an affluent Pennsylvania family, Wynkoop went west in 1856, seeking adventure and gold. He was involved in the founding of Denver, appointed sheriff in 1860, and married a British woman he met in a traveling theater company in which he sometimes performed. He had also moonlighted as a bartender.

Wynkoop served as a captain under Chivington in the 1st Colorado Regiment at Glorietta Pass, and was promoted to major for his actions in that battle. He and Chivington soon developed a close friendship. When Wynkoop assumed command at Fort Lyon in May 1864, he was in full agreement with Chivington's policy of killing Indians, but his attitude changed after the events of September 4.

Three soldiers from the fort were on their way to Denver, about to be discharged. They came across three Indians carrying a white flag, Cheyenne subchiefs One-Eye and Minimie, and One-Eye's wife. They were quite old, which was probably why the soldiers ignored Wynkoop's standing order to shoot Indians. Instead, the soldiers brought them to Wynkoop, who at first was angry that the men had disobeyed his order. Then he read the two letters from Black Kettle that were pinned to One-Eye's clothing. They had been placed there so they would be found even if the Indians were killed. Black Kettle wrote of his desire to make peace and offered to give up seven white prisoners as a gesture of goodwill.

Wynkoop asked One-Eye how he had the nerve to approach the fort knowing that he might be killed.

"I am young no longer," he said. "I have been a warrior. I was not afraid to die when I was young, so why should I be when I am old? The Great Spirit whispered to me and said, 'You must try and save your people.' I thought I would be killed, but I knew that the paper would be found upon my dead body, that you would see it, and it might give peace to my people once more."

Minimie then added he did not want to see his friend make the journey alone, so he chose to go also, knowing the risk.

Wynkoop was profoundly moved. He wrote, "I was bewildered with an exhibition of such patriotism on the part of two savages, and felt myself in the presence of superior beings; and these were the representatives of a race that I had heretofore looked upon without exception as being cruel and treacherous, and blood-thirsty, without feeling or affection for friend or kindred."

One-Eye told Wynkoop that two thousand Cheyenne and Arapaho were camped at the headwaters of the Smoky Hill River, four days' ride away, and that Black Kettle and the other peace chiefs were awaiting the government's reaction to his offer. One-Eye urged Wynkoop to meet with Black Kettle as soon as possible.

Wynkoop faced a difficult decision. He knew that going to Smoky Hill was in direct violation of Chivington's orders of May 31, which stated, "If any [Indians] are caught in your vicinity kill them, as that is the only way." But with no mail getting through, there was no time to contact Chivington, then 240 miles away in Denver, for permission. Wynkoop had to decide whether to risk himself and his men for the chance of peace and retrieving the seven white prisoners. Over the objections of his officers, who thought it was a trap, he decided to put his trust in the Indians.

On the morning of September 6, he led a column of 127 cavalrymen through the gates of Fort Lyon. He placed the two Indian subchiefs at the head of the column and told them they would be shot instantly if the troopers were attacked. One-Eye said calmly that he was prepared to sacrifice his life if his people had lied to him about their intentions. The Cheyenne always kept their word; if they had failed to do so this time, then he would not wish to live, for life without honor held no meaning.

After four days of riding, Wynkoop and his men saw what they most feared: eight hundred battle-ready warriors drawn up in a line across the plain. Their bows were strung with arrows, and many were armed with rifles and pistols. They outnumbered the troops nearly eight to one, and there was no place to hide. Wynkoop ordered the wagon train to form a circle for defense and led his men slowly toward the Indians. He gave the command to halt two hundred yards from the Indian line and sent One-Eye forward to tell Black Kettle why they had come. The old subchief brought back word that Black Kettle wanted to talk. The warriors fell back, and the troopers

Edward W. "Ned" Wynkoop. (*New Mexico State Libary*)

edged forward to set up camp on the riverbank. Although the Indians kept their distance, they rode circles around the men, whooping and howling.

A few hours later, Black Kettle led a stately procession of Cheyenne and Arapaho chiefs to Wynkoop's camp, and the council began. Wynkoop chose his words carefully. John Smith, a trader and friend of the Cheyenne's, interpreted. Wynkoop told the chiefs he had come in response to Black Kettle's letter, and he offered to escort them to Governor Evans to discuss arrangements for peace.

Some chiefs argued in favor of continuing to fight, saying that the whites had started the present confrontation despite the Indians' efforts to live in peace. Many chiefs gave speeches, but Black Kettle sat cross-legged on the ground listening in silence, a slight smile on his face. Wynkoop later described him as serene and dignified; he appeared to be about sixty years old, well built, with solemn eyes and an intelligent, animated expression. At this meeting, Black Kettle wore leggings, breechcloth, and deerskin shirt, all heavily decorated. A cluster of eagle feathers nestled in his hair, and three silver coins dangled from a leather thong around his neck.

When the other chiefs had finished, Black Kettle took Wynkoop by the hand and led him into the center of the circle of chiefs. "This white man is not here to laugh at us," Black Kettle said, "nor does he regard us as children, but on the contrary unlike the balance of his race, he comes with confidence in the pledges given by the red man. He has been told by one of our bravest warriors, that he should come and go unharmed, he did not close his ears, but with his eyes shut followed on the trail of him whom we had sent as our messenger."

After a night of further discussion among the chiefs at their own camp, Black Kettle returned to Wynkoop's camp and told him that they would accompany him to Denver to speak with Evans. Thus Wynkoop's dangerous gamble paid off. He was given four white prisoners, and Black Kettle promised to get the other three from the Sioux. For the first time since early spring, there was reason to believe the Plains war might soon come to an end.

Evans was furious when he learned what Wynkoop had done and said; he did not want to have anything to do with the chiefs. He refused to talk to the Indians even though they had traveled hundreds of miles to secure peace. Evans insisted that the Indians had started the war, and that there could be no peace until they had been sufficiently punished. If he negotiated with them now, it would acknowledge that they had beaten the US government.

Then Evans revealed his real motivation. He told Wynkoop how hard he had worked to get the authority to raise the 3rd Colorado Regiment of one-hundred-day men. His prestige was on the line. The outfit "had been raised to kill Indians," Evans said, "and they must kill Indians." If he offered the Indians peace, Washington would think he had exaggerated the danger to Denver and the territory, and that there had been no need to bear the expense of raising, equipping, and training them.

So there could be no peace, because it might embarrass Evans. How could he admit that he did not need the regiment, that there was no war for it to fight? But Wynkoop persisted until Evans finally agreed to see Black Kettle, though it was clear to Wynkoop that Evans had no interest in a peace conference. Neither did Chivington. He needed the victories the 3rd Regiment could give him.

Black Kettle and the other chiefs solemnly shook hands with Evans and Chivington on September 28, 1864, at Camp Weld, outside of Denver. They lit the peace pipe and passed it in silence from one man to the next. Evans interrupted the ceremony to ask why the Indians had come. Black Kettle said they had come to talk about a proclamation Evans had issued on June 27, offering places of safety and refuge for all Indians who wanted to live in peace.

Black Kettle said he had accepted the terms of the proclamation when he first saw it, but that it had taken time to gather his people to hold a council on it. To show their good faith, they had returned four white prisoners and were arranging to get three more from the Sioux. The Cheyenne and Arapaho wanted to live in peace. Black Kettle spoke with dignity and eloquence:

> I followed Major Wynkoop to Fort Lyon, and Major Wynkoop proposed that we come to see you. We have come with our eyes shut, following his handful of men, like coming through the fire. All we ask is that we have peace with the whites. We want to hold you by the hand. You are our father. We have been traveling through a cloud. The sky has been dark ever since the war began. These braves who are with me are all willing to do what

I say. We want to take good tidings home to our people
that they may sleep in peace.

Evans responded harshly, accusing Black Kettle of making
an alliance with the Sioux and pursuing war against the
whites. "You have done a good deal of damage, have stolen
stock, and now have possession of it. However much a few
individuals may have tried to keep the peace, as a nation you
have gone to war. While we have been spending thousands of
dollars in opening farms for you, and making preparations to
feed, protect, and make you comfortable, you have joined our
enemies and gone to war."

Evans recounted every raid, real and rumored, of the past
months, demanding to know who was responsible. A few
chiefs admitted that some were committed by their young
men, whom they were trying to bring under control.
Obviously not satisfied, Evans announced that he was not
inclined to make a peace treaty and that his proclamation of
June 27 remained in effect. He said he would be glad to have
them all go to Fort Lyon, a point reiterated in brief remarks by
Chivington.

"I am not a big war chief," Chivington said, "but all the
soldiers in this country are at my command. My rule of fighting white men or Indians is to fight them until they lay down
their arms and submit to military authority. You are nearer to
Major Wynkoop [at Fort Lyon] than anyone else, and you can
go to him when you get ready to do that."

The meeting was over. Black Kettle embraced Evans and
Wynkoop, and everyone shook hands. Photographs were
taken. Black Kettle and the other chiefs came away convinced
that the war was over. They believed Evans and Chivington
had agreed to make peace and that the Cheyenne and Arapaho
who went to Fort Lyon would receive protection.

Two months later, on November 28, 1864, Chivington and more than five hundred troopers arrived at Fort Lyon, preparing to leave for Sand Creek, forty miles away, for a surprise attack at dawn on Black Kettle's village. "The Cheyenne nation," Chivington preached, "has been waging bloody war against the whites all spring, summer, and fall, and Black Kettle is their principal chief. They have been guilty of robbery, arson, murder, and rape, and fiendish torture, not even sparing women and little children. I believe it right and honorable to use any means under God's heaven to kill Indians who kill and torture women and children. Damn any man who is in sympathy with them!"

The morale of his troops was high. The "hundred dazers" were finally going after Indians, which was why most of them had joined up. They did not know which Indians they were going to attack, but most of them didn't care so long as they killed some. They were out for revenge, and one dead Indian was just as good as another.

Two weeks earlier, Chivington had ordered the units of the 3rd Colorado to assemble at the Arkansas River on the way to Fort Lyon. While he headed out from Denver to join his troops, two other actors in the drama were also traveling. Governor Evans left for Washington to appeal for still more troops for a large-scale campaign against the Indians, even though he knew what Chivington intended to do. The Indian war Evans tried to instigate had grown quiet. If it could be stirred up again, a renewed drive for statehood might be successful. A surprise attack on the Indians at Sand Creek, who believed they were under the protection of the American flag, would enrage the Cheyenne nation and other tribes as well. If they took to the warpath in retaliation for Sand Creek, the news would reach Washington while Evans was there and reinforce his argument that he needed more soldiers.

The other person heading east was Major Wynkoop, who departed Fort Lyon on November 26, two days before Chivington arrived. Wynkoop had been relieved of command

and was on his way to Fort Riley, Kansas, to justify his actions for violating the standing order not to allow Indians inside a fort and for leaving his district without authorization to escort the chiefs to Denver. Wynkoop's replacement was Major Scott J. Anthony of the 1st Colorado, who had been a merchant in Leavenworth, Kansas, before going to Colorado to search for gold. When that didn't pan out, he opened a general store in Leadville. A cousin of suffragist Susan B. Anthony's, he fought in Chivington's command at Glorietta Pass. The Indians called him the "Red-Eyed Chief," because his eyes were bloodshot, apparently a result of scurvy.

Anthony's orders from General Curtis were to make no agreement with the Indians or allow them in the vicinity of Fort Lyon. When Black Kettle learned of the change of command, he went to the fort to find out if the terms were the same as under Wynkoop. Were the Cheyenne and the soldiers still at peace? Anthony met Black Kettle a half mile from the fort's gates and said he did not have the authority to make peace, but suggested that Black Kettle establish a camp along the banks of Sand Creek. Major Wynkoop had assured Black Kettle that Anthony would treat him and his people the same way he, Wynkoop, had.

As far as Black Kettle knew, then, the Cheyenne would be safe at Sand Creek, under the protection of Fort Lyon. When Black Kettle left the meeting, several of the fort's officers shook his hand and presented him with gifts of tobacco, which, to the Cheyenne, was a sign of peace. Black Kettle believed all was well.

"Scalps are what we are after," Chivington told a trader at a stagecoach stop where his troops were camped for the night. "I long to be wading in gore," he said to his officers a bit later.

The weather was brutally cold for the trek to Fort Lyon. The men burrowed in their heavy army overcoats and drove their horses through two-foot snowdrifts. They were tired and saddle sore, and they cursed their meager breakfast of moldy hardtack. This was more than they had bargained for when they signed up for one hundred days to kill Indians.

When Chivington reached Fort Lyon, he placed a cordon of his men around the perimeter. No one, not even the fort's own guard, was allowed to enter or leave without his permission. The penalty for disobedience was death by firing squad. Major Anthony welcomed Chivington and told him that hostile Indians were camped forty miles away at Sand Creek. Chivington declared that he would march there that night. Anthony volunteered to accompany him with a battalion of 125, making a total attacking force of over six hundred troops.

Chivington issued marching orders for 8 p.m. The men would have to ride hard and travel light to reach Sand Creek by sunrise. The wagon train with the reserve supplies and baggage would be left at the fort. The troopers could take only what they could jam into their pockets and saddlebags.

Some officers at the fort disagreed with the plan to attack the village of the peace chief, Black Kettle, who could easily have wiped out Wynkoop's men at Smoky Hill. There was also the question of honor. Wynkoop and his officers had guaranteed the safety of Black Kettle and the Indians at Sand Creek; these officers took their protests to Major Anthony. In addition, Lieutenant Joseph Cramer confronted Chivington personally. Cramer later wrote, "I thought it murder to jump them friendly Indians." Chivington refused to listen to the objections and shouted that the protesters, such as Cramer and Captain Silas Soule, should get out of the army.*

Shortly before the command was due to leave, there was one more plea for peace, this one from three junior officers, Indian agent Sam Colley, and several civilians. They argued

---

*Silas Soule and Joseph Cramer are remembered each November at the Annual Sand Creek Massacre Spiritual Healing Run. Runners go from the Sand Creek Massacre National Historic Site to Denver, where honor is paid to both men for their protests to Chivington before the massacre and their later testimony, which would cost them dearly.

that it would be a crime to attack Indians who had been given assurances of refuge in good faith. Chivington glared at them. "Damn any man who is in sympathy with an Indian!"

Colonel Chivington sat on his horse less than a mile from Black Kettle's village of some one hundred lodges as the first light of morning spread across the plains. The Indian dwellings, on the far bank of the dry creek bed, were arrayed in a circle over a half mile in diameter, the distance of three arrow flights from a strong bow. Just west of Black Kettle's village stood ten additional lodges belonging to Arapahos. The creek bed was about two hundred yards wide at that point, and the banks on the Indian side ranged from two to ten feet high. A small herd of ponies and about six hundred horses were on Chivington's side of the creek.

Chivington ordered his men to run off the horses so the Indians would not be able to get to them, and he directed other troopers to approach the village from the east, to prevent anyone from escaping. The bulk of his men would charge the village straight across the creek bed. "Take no prisoners," Chivington shouted. "Remember the Hungates." With the Fighting Parson in front, the troops galloped forward.

The Indians in the village were jolted awake by the thunder of more than six hundred galloping horses. Men, women, and children ran out of their lodges to see the troops rushing toward them. Black Kettle hoisted a large American flag and a smaller white flag over his lodge. The commissioner of Indian affairs, A. B. Greenwood, had given him the flag four years before and told him to show it whenever soldiers approached. The flag would always protect him and his people, the commissioner had said.

Black Kettle cautioned his people not to be frightened. They were in no danger; the camp was under the protection of the American flag. That was when the massacre at Sand Creek began. The troops opened fire, sometimes at Indians, sometimes at each other. All semblance of organization and military control vanished, and Chivington made no attempt to restore it. The tactical genius he had displayed at Glorietta Pass was nowhere in evidence at Sand Creek.

Soldiers fired at random and advanced on the village not as a disciplined army but a lawless band gone berserk. The Indians raced in all directions, not knowing where to hide. Cheyenne Chief White Antelope tied a medal from President Lincoln around his neck. For months he had been assuring his people that the whites were good and that peace would soon be at hand. Now he felt betrayed and no longer wished to live. He ran toward the soldiers waving his hands, shouting for them to stop. Bullets kicked up dust at his feet. Black Kettle called out to him to run away from the soldiers, but White Antelope halted in the center of the creek bed, folded his arms across his chest, and waited to die. He stood impassively, chanting his death song, as bullets tore into his chest: "Nothing lives long / except the earth and the mountain."

Heedless, the troops scalped the body and cut off the nose and ears.

Chief Left Hand of the Arapaho stood outside his lodge, telling his people that he would not fight the whites; they were his friends. He had shaken hands with Governor Evans and Major Wynkoop, who had told them they would be safe at Sand Creek. Moments later he was dead.

Many other Indians also made no effort to fight or escape, either because of confusion, a lingering and sadly misplaced trust, or simple resignation that all was lost. Others approached the soldiers with their hands raised. Joseph Cramer, who had protested against the attack, recalled that many Indians held up their hands as if in supplication, begging the soldiers to spare them. The troopers cut them all down.

Only one detachment did not participate in the attack, the command of Captain Soule. Opposed to killing the Indians to whom Wynkoop had pledged safety, Soule ordered his men not to fire. They rode slowly along the south bank of the creek and witnessed the slaughter.

"I refused to fire," he wrote to Major Wynkoop, "and swore that none but a coward would, for by this time hundreds of women and children were coming toward us and getting on their knees for mercy. [Major] Anthony shouted, 'kill the sons of bitches.' I tell you it was hard to see little children on their knees having their brains beat out by men professing to be civilized. One squaw was wounded and a fellow took a hatchet to finish her, and he cut one arm off, and held the other with one hand and dashed the hatchet through her brain. You would think it was impossible for white men to butcher and mutilate human beings as they did."

About one hundred Indians fled along the creek bed west of the village to a spot where the banks were gouged by steep ravines. Soldiers on foot chased them, and mounted troopers stationed themselves up ahead, cutting off their retreat. Using knives and bare hands, the Indians dug crude trenches so the women and children could hide while the warriors made a stand. Soldiers lined up on both sides of the creek and fired on them at will.

The Indians held off the soldiers for almost four hours until the troopers broke off the fight and returned to the village. Even Major Anthony, no friend of the Cheyenne, admired their courage. He wrote that he "never saw more bravery displayed by any set of people on the face of the earth than by these Indians. They would charge on the whole company singly, determined to kill someone before being killed themselves. We, of course, took no prisoners."

Scattered bands of soldiers chased stray Indians along the sand hills. By midafternoon, most of the men were tired, and they drifted back to their camp. The combat had ended, but the atrocities continued throughout the day, forming a haze of fragmented memories that, according to letters and diaries, scarred many of the men for as long as they lived.

Chivington's men had become a mob, unrestrained and barbaric. They mercilessly avenged the Hungates and the other dead white settlers tenfold, and Chivington did nothing to stop them. The eyewitness descriptions of the actions of the Colorado Volunteers, given as sworn testimony in congressional investigations in the months to come, became part of Chivington's legacy. They brought him not the glory he was desperate to recapture but infamy. When it was over, more than one hundred Indians were dead, though Chivington would later claim that his troops had killed as many as five hundred. About five hundred escaped. Witnesses estimated there were fewer than seventy armed warriors in the village when it was attacked, yet they held off six hundred soldiers while the majority of the Indians got away. Nine of Chivington's men were killed and thirty-eight wounded, some shot by fellow soldiers. As a military exercise, it was a fiasco.

Chivington sent a glowing account of the attack to his friend William Byers, who published a front-page article in the *Rocky Mountain News*. "Among the brilliant feats of arms in Indian warfare, the recent campaign of our Colorado volunteers will stand in history with few rivals. The exploit has few if any parallels. All acquitted themselves well and Colorado soldiers have again covered themselves with glory."

The Indian survivors of Sand Creek made their way northeast toward Smoky Hill. After the soldiers withdrew from the fight among the sandpits on the bank of the creek, the Cheyenne crawled up the creek bed, dragging their wounded. After a few miles, they met up with some warriors who had fled at the onset of the attack to try to save the horses.

An old man made his way back down the creek bed, keeping an eye out for soldiers. He was searching for his wife, who had been shot in the melee at the trenches. He found her alive, with nine bullet wounds. She said that the soldiers kept shooting her as she lay in the sand. The old man hoisted her on his back and carried her away. Then he met an Indian on horse-back who took them both to Smoky Hill. The woman survived; her husband, Black Kettle, had saved her life. He was the only chief from Sand Creek still alive.

The largest body of survivors made camp in a ravine ten miles from the battle site. It was bitterly cold. Few had warm clothing because there had been no time to dress when the attack began. There was no wood, but a few fires were started using grass. The wounded were placed close to the fires and covered with grass to keep them from freezing.

The men sat up all night howling to let other survivors know where they were. In the morning, they traveled on, covering only a short distance before they were met by patrols from the larger camp at Smoky Hill, bringing horses, food, and blankets. As they came within sight of the lodges, the entire village rushed out to meet them. The wailing and mourning would soon become war cries. The betrayal of Black Kettle and the Cheyenne would be avenged.

SIX

DREAMS
OF
GLORY

George Custer appeared haggard and exhausted in the days after the Civil War ended. He had lost his energy and zest for life. The problem, of course, was that he no longer had a war to fight. And without a war to fight, Custer was lost.

Fortunately, there was the possibility of a war, perhaps two. In Texas, a large Confederate army under the command of General Kirby Smith remained intact. Although Smith had not continued the fight after Lee's surrender at Appomattox, officials in Washington were concerned that he might lead a rebellion and try to take Texas out of the Union. His army had to be disbanded and Union troops sent to occupy Texas, just as other areas of the former Confederacy were now under occupation.

There was also the chance of war with the French in Mexico. France had sent several thousand soldiers to Mexico during the American Civil War and had overthrown the Mexican government, establishing Archduke Ferdinand

Maximilian as emperor. This was seen as a way to create a French empire close to the United States, in clear violation of the Monroe Doctrine. Some politicians were ready to invade Mexico to drive the French out. That could be another war for Custer to fight.

General Philip Sheridan was charged with dealing with the Texas situation, and he wanted Custer to command a cavalry division. It was just what Custer needed. In late May 1865, Custer and Libbie and most of his wartime staff packed up and headed south, along with their horses, a dozen dogs, and assorted other pets, including Custer's turtles.

"We were like children let out of school," Libbie wrote about the trip to New Orleans, where Sheridan was headquartered. They took a steamboat down the Ohio River into the broad Mississippi. It was a voyage of leisure and luxury. Custer and Libbie spent enjoyable hours in the comfortable deck chairs watching the scenery pass by. But by the third day Custer had seen enough of the countryside and began exploring the ship in his more typical restless, energetic manner. He took the stairs two at a time and stalked from stem to stern, bottom to top, then back again.

He had become interested in the battle sites he had read about during the war, and he eagerly went ashore to explore when the ship stopped at Vicksburg and Fort Pillow. At one stop, he watched a tall, lean man on crutches make his way up the gangplank. When he overheard someone say it was Confederate general John Bell Hood, Custer raced down to greet him.

"The two veterans sat together and talked cordially about their battles—no bitterness, no regrets. Armstrong sent for Libbie. Hood had trouble rising on his crutches and wooden leg to meet 'the little lady,' but she immediately put him at ease and took care not to interrupt their conversation."

In New Orleans they spent all their money on shopping and eating, staying at the best hotel. They dined in the finest restaurants, had their portraits painted, and Libbie purchased more dresses and hats than any one woman could possibly wear. One evening they joined General Sheridan for dinner at the elegant mansion that served as home and headquarters for the commandant of the Department of the Mississippi. After dinner Sheridan took Custer out onto the verandah to talk about plans for a possible war. They didn't want Libbie to know that Custer might soon be back in combat.

The threat from Kirby Smith and his remaining Confederate soldiers had ended when Smith surrendered on May 26, but the US Army was preparing to invade Mexico to rid the hemisphere of foreign troops. Plans were well along. Custer was studying Spanish in his spare time.

A total of thirty-one thousand troops were being assembled at Brownsville on the Rio Grande River, and at Houston and San Antonio. Pontoon bridges were shipped to Texas, ready to be put into place for troops to cross the river into Mexico. Custer was ordered to Alexandria, Louisiana, to take command of a four-thousand-five-hundred-man cavalry division and march them to Texas. It was an exciting prospect for Custer, who only a month before had not known what to do without a war to fight.

Custer and his staff had to buy their steamship tickets on credit because they had spent most of their money in New Orleans; one aide had only twenty-six cents to his name. The voyage north on the Red River was not as pleasant as the cruise to New Orleans had been. The boat was smaller and more primitive, and the landscape depressing, squalid, and muddy, with moss hanging from dying cypress trees.

When they arrived in Alexandria in late June, Custer found himself facing resentful, almost mutinous troops who were in no mood to keep on soldiering, or to obey the orders of the boy general, no matter how famous he had been. They had had enough of war. Custer now had a different kind of battle, to establish control over his own men.

On the morning of December 1, two days after the massacre at Sand Creek, Colonel Chivington led his men away, heading south toward the Arkansas River to search for Little Raven's band of Arapaho. But they found no more Indians to kill, and by December 5, Chivington had grown discouraged. He called a meeting of his officers, who told him the horses were worn out and the men were grumbling about their limited rations and the constant, fruitless marching.

Chivington agreed that it was pointless to continue chasing after bands of Indians who were never where they were supposed to be. It was time to return to Denver. He rode ahead of his men, wanting to be the first to reap the glory he knew was now his. William Byers, who had been receiving daily reports from Chivington, had trumpeted his victory in the *Rocky Mountain News.*

"Bully for the Colorado Boys!" Byers wrote. He published a glowing editorial informing his readers that the defeat of the Indians at Sand Creek would bring about a quick end to their reign of terror. "Having tasted of the bitter end, the supremacy of our power will be seriously considered, and a surrender or a suing for peace be perhaps very soon proclaimed." Byers had apparently forgotten, or he chose to ignore, that revenge was not practiced only by whites, and that a massacre of peaceful Indians could lead only to terror on a greater scale.

Chivington prepared a lengthy report on Sand Creek for General Curtis. He told Curtis that if he had more soldiers under his command, he could rid the territory of Indians for all time. He said that his men had found a white man's scalp a mere two or three days old, and he criticized Captain Soule for refusing to participate in the attack.

The aptly named "Bloody 3rd" Regiment arrived in Denver on December 22 to a tumultuous welcome and a victory parade through streets lined with cheering crowds. Chivington rode in front, brandishing a live eagle tethered to a pole over his head. After the parade ended, the "hundred dazers" carried on their celebration from one saloon to the next, cadging

drinks, retelling tall tales of valor, and flourishing their trophies of bloody scalps. Curiously, no one displayed the white
man's scalp Chivington claimed to have found. Over the next
weeks, the number of white scalps grew in the telling. Nobody
had actually seen one, but everyone claimed to know someone
who had.

Three young Cheyenne children, two girls and a boy who
had survived the slaughter, were put on display at the Denver
Theatre between vaudeville acts. They stood silently and fearful in front of a rope from which dangled a hundred or more
Indian scalps. The locals agreed it was quite a spectacle and
added excitement to the Christmas celebrations.

Three days after Christmas, the men of the Bloody 3rd were
mustered out of the service. Their one hundred days were up,
and they felt they had reason to be proud. One officer said,
they "won for themselves a name that will be remembered for
ages to come." But a few days later, the people of Denver were
surprised to read a dispatch from Washington about growing
pressure from eastern newspapers for a congressional investigation into what it termed the killing of friendly Indians at
Sand Creek. Byers wrote an indignant editorial about those
supposed friendly Indians.

Denver's saloons echoed with angry talk. Irate residents
cursed the Indian lovers back East who never had to worry
about losing their scalps, or having their wives carried off, or
seeing neighbors murdered. Then they learned on January 10
that the US House of Representatives had ordered the
Committee on the Conduct of the War to hold hearings on the
affair at Sand Creek.

General Curtis requested Chivington's resignation in the
hope of keeping the army from conducting its own inquiry. He
resigned without protest, perhaps hoping even more than
Curtis to avoid an army investigation. But he nonetheless
expressed indignation at the idea that he could be court-martialed for doing his duty and keeping Denver safe.

On December 30, the war pipe was lit at Smoky Hill. Some two thousand warriors had gathered, vowing revenge for the massacre at Sand Creek. Almost all the Cheyenne were there, as well as Sioux and Northern Arapaho. Only Little Raven's Arapaho band refused to fight another war. Black Kettle was in attendance, but he was in disgrace with his people. He had been deposed as chief and replaced by Leg-in-the-Water and Little Robe, whose father had been killed at Sand Creek. The warriors taunted and insulted Black Kettle for placing faith in the whites and betraying his people by leading them to believe they were safe at Sand Creek. They demanded to know why he had not stayed with his people and died an honorable death, like White Antelope.

Jim Beckwourth, a sixty-nine-year-old black trapper, hunter, and guide came to the camp at Smoky Hill to urge the Indians not to go to war. He had lived among the Cheyenne for many years and was so well accepted that they had given him the name Medicine Calf. He told the ruling council that there were too many whites to fight; they were "numerous as the leaves on the trees."

"We know," one chief said, "but what do we want to live for? The white man has taken our country, killed our game; was not satisfied with that, but killed our wives and children. Now no peace. We want to go meet our families in the spirit land. We loved the whites until we found out they lied to us and robbed us of what we had. We have raised the battle-axe until death."

The Indians planned their war of revenge with care, laying in a stock of food for the women, children, and old people so they could have sustenance while the warriors were away. This time there would be no sporadic, independent raids led by small parties, no spontaneous attacks by groups operating on their own. The soldier societies, bands of the most experienced warriors, took charge. They would attack as a combined, united, and organized force.

The warriors moved out, heading northwest for the South Platte River and the tiny settlement of Julesburg, about 190 miles from Denver. No white man saw them pass over the plains.

To Custer, Libbie, and the four thousand five hundred troops he was sent to command, Alexandria, Louisiana, seemed like the end of the civilized world. It was so miserably hot and humid that Custer cut off his golden locks and wore his hair short. Thick clouds of gnats, chiggers, and mosquitoes swarmed, and poisonous snakes were everywhere, indoors and out. The homes and plantations were shabby, run-down, and damaged from the war. Libbie wrote in a letter home, "We found everything a hundred years behind the times."

The Custers moved into one of the better abandoned houses, but he had little time to relax. His new troops gave him trouble from the outset. Westerners from Iowa, Wisconsin, and Illinois, they had an independent spirit and never took well to military discipline. Custer's commands during the war had been mostly of easterners in the Army of the Potomac, who were used to saluting, obeying orders without question, and wearing proper uniforms. While the westerners were outstanding fighters, they didn't like traditional army ways and didn't care who knew it.

They showed their cussedness right away with the boy wonder in the fancy outfit. They went absent without leave, deserting whenever they felt the urge. Custer responded the only way he knew, the way he had been trained at West Point, which had worked for him during the war. And that made him more unpopular.

"These rough Westerners considered him a martinet. At one inspection a regiment turned out in grotesque costumes. Some had on caps, some hats with brims turned up or down. Some wore boots, others shoes covered with ashes. Some wore jackets, some stood in their shirt sleeves. Some had their breeches stuck into their boots. Some carried their cartridge boxes upside down—all very funny to a Western volunteer, but Custer, the practical joker, was not amused."

The troops were angry about still being in the army three months after the end of the war they had signed up for. Most of the other Union troops were already back home. Worse, their rations were awful. Although cattle ranches were all around, their meals consisted of "hog jowls and flour and moldy hardtack. The hog jowls sported tusks, and worms and bugs inhabited the hardtack." Not surprisingly, the men tried to supplement their diet with edible food, and the only way to get any was to steal it from the locals.

A group of citizens called on Custer to complain about the thefts of cattle, chickens, turkeys, and anything else the hungry soldiers could find. General Sheridan had told Custer that one of his responsibilities was to protect the local populace, and another was to maintain discipline among his men, which he proceeded to do by instituting harsh, and illegal, punishments.

Custer ordered that any enlisted man who violated the order against foraging would have his head shaved and receive twenty-five lashes on his back with a leather whip. Congress had prohibited flogging in the army in 1861, but that did not stop Custer. Resentment rose with each crack of the whip; hatred festered with each insect plucked from the rations. But the incidents of stealing from the local citizens did decrease.

The situation became potentially explosive when Custer sentenced two men to death by firing squad. One was a deserter and the other, Sergeant Leonard Lancaster, had been charged with mutiny. He and a number of others had signed a petition demanding the resignation of an officer whose behavior had angered them. Every man who signed the petition was arrested. All but one, Lancaster, apologized and were released. Lancaster was sentenced to death.

The others then sent a petition asking for clemency for the condemned man. Even the officer they tried to get rid of signed it, but Custer refused to rescind the execution order. As the day for the firing squad neared, rumor spread that someone would try to assassinate Custer. Libbie begged him to take precautions, but he refused to carry a revolver, and he would not permit his staff to go armed.

The four thousand five hundred men of the division were formed into a hollow square. Custer and his aides rode slowly around the inside of the square, as if he were daring anyone to take a shot at him. Custer's fabled luck held again. The two men slated to die were brought forward to stand next to their open graves. Blindfolds were wrapped around their eyes.

"The red-faced firing squad and the breathless onlookers made a sight to behold. Except for the reading of the warrant, not a sound could be heard. As the provost marshal prepared to give the fatal command one soldier quietly took the sergeant by the arm and moved him off to one side. With the crash of the carbines the deserter dropped dead and the sergeant fell back in a faint."

When the sergeant revived, he was told that Custer had granted him a reprieve several days before, but had let the deserter believe he was going to be executed, counting off the days and the hours one by one, until there were no more, standing in front of his grave, picturing in his mind the carbines aimed at him. It was an exercise in imperial vindictiveness and cruelty, and a powerful lesson for the others. Thus Custer showed that "his word was law and no man could intimidate him."*

On January 6, 1865, more than one thousand Indian warriors attacked Julesburg, a settlement with a stagecoach stop, a general store, and a warehouse, guarded by the garrison at nearby Fort Rankin. Ten Indians chased a stagecoach and the residents into the fort as part of a plan to lure the soldiers out-

*Sergeant Lancaster was court-martialed and received a dishonorable discharge and a prison sentence for organizing the petition.

side. It worked; forty troopers rode out to chase the Indians, who led them straight into an ambush. Fourteen soldiers died.

The Indian braves rode in circles around the fort, taunting the troops and firing their guns, but they were not about to charge the fort with its two howitzers. Instead, they raided Julesburg and ransacked the store and the warehouse, making off with a huge assortment of food and supplies, including such delicacies as canned oysters.

They also found a strongbox full of cash, which the army paymaster had left in his haste to retreat to the safety of the fort. The warriors chopped up the thick bundles of green paper—useless to them—and tossed them into the wind like so much confetti. The soldiers at the fort fired off their howitzers, but the Indians were too far away to be bothered by the exploding canisters.

Other war parties up to five hundred strong set the torch to every ranch and stagecoach station for eighty miles around. They killed eight people and captured one thousand five hundred head of cattle and two wagon trains of supplies bound for Denver. Most of the white settlers in the territory took the news of the uprising as proof, as if more were needed, that Chivington had been right all along when he said the only way to deal with Indians was to kill them all.

Major Ned Wynkoop returned to Fort Lyon on January 14, a week after the Julesburg attack, with orders from General Curtis to ascertain the truth about Sand Creek. When Wynkoop heard of the massacre at Black Kettle's village, he was horrified. He felt personally responsible because he had told Black Kettle that he and his people would be safe there. Wynkoop compiled an indictment of Chivington, which he immediately dispatched to Curtis.

He described Chivington as a monster, saying that his actions had undone the progress Wynkoop had made toward bringing about peace. "Since this horrible massacre by Colonel

Chivington the country presents a scene of desolation. All this country is ruined; there can be no such thing as peace in the future but by the total annihilation of all the Indians of the plains." Wynkoop's blistering report became the basis for months of congressional investigations that would eventually end the careers of Chivington and Governor Evans—and lead to the deaths of two brave young officers.

A week after the raids in the Julesburg area, the chiefs gathered for a council. The decision was made to leave the land between the Platte and Arkansas rivers and join forces with the Northern Sioux and Northern Cheyenne in Wyoming Territory. But before they departed, they planned to lay waste to the entire South Platte Valley. Black Kettle argued against it and spoke up again for peace, but no one listened. He left the camp saddened by the turn of events and feeling that he had failed. He joined his old friend, Little Raven, and the Southern Arapaho who refused to join in the war. About eighty Cheyenne families went with him.

No whites were safe in a swath stretching some 150 miles in the South Platte Valley. Everything was destroyed or burned, even the telegraph poles. On February 2, a war party numbering one thousand returned to Julesburg on the assumption that the warehouse had been restocked. It had. The Indians stripped the building bare, burned it to the foundation, and held a victory dance well into the night. The soldiers at Fort Rankin could only watch and hope that the Indians did not decide to turn on the little garrison.

"About one o'clock, the orgy seemed to reach its height," Captain Eugene Ware remembered. "The yells were the most bloodcurdling and frantic I ever heard, and although we were a long distance off, perhaps a half mile, we could hear them all upon the midnight air quite plainly. We discussed among ourselves whether or not the bottled liquors would not get them finally worked up to a point that would lead them to besiege us. Suddenly the fire began to grow brighter, and greater, and the Indians circling around it seemed to form a large ring."

The fire had spread to the prairie grass. The circle of flames widened, and by dawn the fort was enveloped by dense smoke; the troopers could see nothing beyond the walls. When the smoke finally cleared, the Indians were gone.

The population of Colorado Territory feared for its survival during the winter of 1864–65. The weather was harsh, and the Indian raids were more devastating than in the past spring and summer. All roads and settlements to the north of Fort Lyon were imperiled; Denver was completely isolated. For more than a month, not a single stagecoach, wagon, letter, or telegram reached the city.

Homes, ranches, and stagecoach stations were set afire. Some fifty whites were killed and many others captured. Six hundred tons of government hay was burned, and untold quantities of food and supplies were stolen. Denver faced famine as stocks of food ran out. Samuel Elbert, acting governor, appealed to the War Department for five thousand troops. The uprising spread from the Missouri River in Kansas to Salt Lake City in Utah, a distance of more than nine hundred miles.

In Denver, Colonel Thomas Moonlight, Chivington's replacement as commander of the military district, had only 450 troops to patrol an area of several thousand square miles. He pleaded with Major General Granville Dodge, who had replaced General Curtis at Fort Leavenworth, for troops to prevent the territory from being totally overrun by the Indians.

The Union could spare no more troops from the war in the East. Colorado was on its own. Elbert and Moonlight tried to raise another regiment of one-hundred-days volunteers, but hardly anyone could be recruited. Judging the situation to be desperate, Moonlight proclaimed martial law in Denver on February 8, and closed down every business until he could find 360 men to draft into the army.

One of Custer's troopers said that nothing he had gone through during the Civil War was as terrible as the two-hundred-mile march in mid-August from Alexandria, Louisiana, to Hempstead, Texas, near Houston. Even though the war had been over for several months, Custer ordered his troops to button their coats regulation-style and carry a carbine, revolver, saber, and seventy rounds of ammunition, a heavy load in the heat and humidity, especially with no enemy to concern them.

"The temperature was about 120 degrees," one of the men wrote twenty years later, "and there wasn't a rebel in the land. When the division reached a narrow bridge that had to be crossed in single file, Custer and his staff stood on either side of the line with sabers drawn and where a soldier overcome with heat had fastened his carbine, revolver or sword to the saddle [to take the weight off of himself] they clipped it off and let it fall into the stream. The arms were charged to the soldier."

The rations were more of the same, hog jowls and hardtack, unfit for human consumption. Some men were so starved that they ate the raw corn used to feed the horses. They remained under orders not to forage for extra food, not even to pull an apple off a tree, but some tried anyway. "Many a poor fellow I have seen with head shaved to the scalp, tied to a wagon wheel and whipped like a dog, for stealing a piece of fresh meat or a peach from an orchard by the wayside."

Although it seemed a nightmare for the men, it was like a "picnic excursion" for Custer and his wife. Libbie Custer wrote home about the abundance of fruits and vegetables they enjoyed. She had little contact with the enlisted men but was perceptive enough to realize that Custer was disliked, even hated. "That is the penalty the commanding officer generally pays," she wrote, "for what still seems to me the questionable privilege of rank and power."

In Hempstead, along the banks of Clear Creek, life for the Custers was pleasant. The local southern aristocracy introduced Custer to a different kind of hunting, using hounds and horns. Each man owned a pack of hounds, and even though there were many dogs and many different horns, each hound responded only to the sound from its owner. Custer was so impressed that he got a horn for himself. The five dogs the locals gave him arranged themselves "in an admiring and sympathetic semicircle," Libbie wrote, "accompanying all his practice by tuning their voices until they reached the same key."

One thing Custer did not do during this pleasant interlude was go to war. The French withdrew their troops from Mexico, so there was no longer any reason to send American soldiers over the border. And since Kirby Smith had surrendered his Confederate army, Custer and his men had only simple occupation duties to fulfill, patrolling the countryside to maintain order. Thus they had become more of a police force than an army. Life may have been pleasant for Custer, but the troops remained resentful, unhappy at still being in the army, and hungry much of the time.

In October 1865, the outfit moved to Austin, Texas. Custer was named chief of cavalry for the Department of Texas. It was an impressive title, but his duties remained the same: patrolling the countryside with little else for the troops to do, adding to their feelings of restlessness and hostility.

In the evenings, Custer's staff and their wives often gathered in his spacious quarters to play the piano and sing, and occasionally Custer and Libbie hosted dances. At one Christmas party, Custer dressed as Santa Claus and distributed presents. There was hunting and daily horse races and all sorts of amusements. "Oh," Libbie wrote, "I am enjoying life so thoroughly."

It could not continue indefinitely. Custer's command grew smaller as more units were finally mustered out of the service. In addition, the army as a whole was being reduced to its prewar size, which meant there were too many generals for too few soldiers. The good life ended on January 31, 1866, when Custer received the news that his commission as a major general of volunteers had expired; he was reduced to his regular rank of captain in the 5th United States Cavalry. Captain—the rank he had held four years earlier as an aide to General McClellan!*

General Sheridan tried to intervene on Custer's behalf to allow him to keep his two-star rank, but even he could not prevent the demotion and the attendant drop in pay and allowances from $8,000 to $2,000 per year. Custer sold most of his horses and dogs and returned to Libbie's home in Monroe for a thirty-day leave. What was he to do now?

On March 13, 1865, Congress began hearings in Washington, DC, conducted by the Committee on the Conduct of the War, to investigate the events at Sand Creek. Among those summoned was Major Scott Anthony, whose testimony was as damaging to him as it was to Chivington. He admitted that he told the Indians they could stay at Sand Creek in safety until instructions were received from General Curtis about making peace.

Anthony criticized Chivington for allowing so many Indians to escape and said that he had protested to Chivington at the time for not pursuing them. No one else recalled Anthony's making such a protest. If he had found fault with Chivington at Sand Creek, he kept his views to himself until he appeared before the committee. Anthony also said he had voiced objections to the attack before the outfit left Fort Lyon. No one else supported that claim either.

Anthony admitted he saw soldiers committing atrocities and mutilations but justified the actions by saying they were no worse than what Indians had done to whites. "The only way to fight Indians," he said, "is to fight them as they fight us; if they scalp and mutilate the bodies we must do the same."

*Like all former brevet generals, Custer was allowed to use the rank and to be addressed as general.

Then he added a curious afterthought: "At the same time, of course, we consider it a barbaric practice."

Anthony disputed Chivington's claim that a freshly taken white person's scalp had been found at Sand Creek. "I did not hear anything about that, until after Colonel Chivington had reached Denver. I was with him for ten days after the fight and never heard a word about a white scalp being found in the camp."*

Governor Evans testified at length but said little. He was evasive about everything, even something as simple as the distance between Denver and Fort Lyon. He tried to give the impression that he knew nothing about anything that might be even remotely connected with Indians. And no, he could not recall the names of the chiefs he had met at Camp Weld.

Of course, he knew even less about the attack at Sand Creek; he was in Washington when it happened. Asked if he thought Chivington had any justification for the attack, Evans refused to commit himself. His reply dissolved into a rambling account of previous attacks by Indians.

The committee finally gave up expecting answers from Evans and dismissed him as a witness. His highly publicized performance was a public relations disaster. He had hoped his testimony would protect him from personal accountability for the attack, but in the end, the disaster at Sand Creek aborted his political career as effectively as if he had lifted a scalp or two himself.

Chivington did not testify in Washington but responded to questions in a lengthy affidavit given in Denver. Some of his statements contradicted his earlier official reports; he increased the size of Black Kettle's village and the number of Indians killed. In the matter of the murder of Cheyenne women and children, Chivington swore there had only been a

---

*Anthony resigned from the army six weeks after Sand Creek and became a wealthy and prominent member of Denver's business community. He was a pallbearer at Chivington's funeral in Denver in 1894.

few. He insisted that he carried out the attack because he believed the Indians at Sand Creek were hostile to whites. He cataloged the atrocities committed by Indians in the previous months and claimed to have found nineteen white scalps in the village.

The congressional Committee on the Conduct of the War concluded that the attack at Sand Creek was an atrocity of the highest order for which there was neither justification nor excuse. They described the killings and mutilations in detail, noting, "It is difficult to believe that beings in the form of men, and disgracing the uniform of United States soldiers and officers, could commit or countenance the commission of such acts of cruelty and barbarity."

Major Anthony was criticized for his role, but greater blame was placed on Governor Evans. The committee concluded that his testimony was characterized "by such prevarication and shuffling as has been shown by no witness in these investigations; and for the evident purpose of avoiding the admission that he was fully aware that the Indians massacred so brutally at Sand Creek were then and had been activated by the most friendly feelings toward the whites, and had done all in their power to restrain those less friendly disposed."

A little over a month later, Secretary of State William Seward sent a terse message to Evans telling him that the president wished him to know that his resignation "would be acceptable." Two weeks later, Evans sent an equally brief note to President Andrew Johnson, tendering his resignation as governor.

In their final report to Congress, the committee members noted, "As to Colonel Chivington, [we] can hardly find fitting terms to describe his conduct. Wearing the uniform of the United States, which should be the emblem of justice and humanity, he deliberately planned and executed a foul and dastardly massacre which would have disgraced the veriest savage among those who were the victims of his cruelty."

Chivington's dreams of glory were finished.

Custer arrived in Washington on March 9, 1866, and spent several days on Capitol Hill testifying before the Joint Committee on Reconstruction about the attitudes of Texans toward the federal government. He told the congressmen that he thought Texas was not yet ready to be free of occupation by US troops.

Libbie had to remain in Monroe because Custer did not have enough money for them both to make the trip. When Custer called on Seward, he found Secretary of War Stanton present. "Custer!" Stanton greeted him. "It does me good to look at you again." He told Custer he would do anything he could to help him. It is not clear if Custer asked anything for himself, but he did request regular army commissions for his brother Tom and for a member of his staff from Monroe. Neither man had been able to find gainful employment in civilian life.

Custer considered the possibility of a diplomatic post, and even thought for a time of serving in the Mexican army, which was offering the staggering sum of $16,000 a year to head its cavalry. He turned down both, however, because he would have had to resign his commission to accept. Even though his rank was now only captain, his army commission was the only secure job he had.

He had a much more exciting time visiting New York City, where he was entertained by wealthy, powerful businessmen who tendered highly lucrative offers to join their firms. He rode in their fine carriages, ate in the best restaurants, and thrived on the fuss and commotion that erupted whenever he walked into a hotel lobby or a restaurant.

He wrote to Libbie every night, describing the events of the day. "After the theater," he wrote one night, "several of us went on an expedition in search of fun. We visited several shooting galleries, pretty-girl-waitress saloons. We also had considerable sport with females we met on the street. 'Nymphs du Pave' they are called. Sport alone was our object. At no time did I forget you."

He attended a masked ball at the Academy of Music dressed as the devil. His picture was published in the April 14 issue of *Harper's Weekly*. "My costume was elegant and rich," he wrote to Libbie. "Cape and coat, black velvet with gold lace. Pants the same, reaching only to the thighs. Red silk tights with not even drawers underneath. Velvet cap with two upright red feathers for horns."

On another night, he was seated beside a baroness at dinner at the elegant home of a financier. Her dress was cut so low that Custer felt compelled to write about it. "I sat beside her on a sofa and 'I have not seen such sights since I was weaned' and yet it did not make my angry passions rise, nor *nuthin* else."

He was living the good life, far beyond his means, and yet it was a life easily within his grasp. All he had to do was to accept one of the many business opportunities dangled before him, but he hesitated. He knew he had no talent for business and that companies wanted him for his name alone. Also, he felt that being a soldier was the only career in which he could ever find fulfillment.

Before he could decide, he heard from Libbie that her father, old Judge Bacon, had died of cholera. He rushed back to Monroe to comfort her, but his future remained uncertain. He had nothing in view that could compare with his glorious past.

On the night of April 23, 1865, at the corner of Lawrence and G streets in Denver, Captain Silas Soule was murdered by a soldier from the 2nd Colorado. Soule and his bride of less than a month were walking home from the theater when he heard gunshots. As provost marshal, it was his job to maintain public order; he immediately ran toward the sound of the gunfire. Charles Squiers, a soldier in the 2nd Colorado, was waiting for him and shot him in the head, killing him instantly; then Squiers escaped.

April 23 was the fifty-third day of the third inquiry into the Sand Creek affair. The second had been held in March by a joint committee of the US Senate and House of Representatives. After hearings in Washington, Fort Lyon, and Denver, the committee concluded that Chivington had perpetrated a massacre of Indians at Sand Creek who had legitimate reason for believing they were under the protection of the American flag.

The third hearing, by a three-man military commission, began in Denver on February 9, 1865, and lasted seventy-six days. It provided a friendly arena for Chivington in which he could confront, attack, and malign his opponents, particularly Captain Soule and Major Wynkoop. Wynkoop felt betrayed by his one-time friend; he blamed Chivington for Soule's murder and never forgave him.

The atmosphere in Denver was tense throughout the lengthy proceedings and tempers were short, not only in the hearing room, but also on the streets. The hearings were held in secret, but word leaked out, and by nightfall most people knew what had transpired. Chivington wrote his own account of the daily proceedings, which William Byers obligingly published in the *Rocky Mountain News*. Most of Denver's residents supported Chivington, and it was considered unwise, not to say dangerous, to speak against "the Fighting Parson."

Angry crowds milled about the saloons and sidewalks when Soule took the stand. Soule, who had protested to Chivington in writing about the attack and ordered his men not to take part, was rigorously cross-examined by Chivington for seven days. Chivington even accused Soule of mutilating the bodies himself after the battle. Soule had volunteered to testify against Chivington despite warnings that his life would be in jeopardy. Threats were made against him and several shots fired, but that only increased his determination to speak out.

On the morning after Soule's death, Lieutenant Colonel Samuel Tappan, second in command of the Colorado troops at Glorietta Pass and now chairman of the commission, glared at Chivington in the hearing room and read a brief statement, not bothering to conceal his anger. He described Soule's death not as a shooting or murder, but as an assassination, with all the malice, premeditation, and revenge that ugly word suggests.

Most people in Denver were shocked by the killing. A few thought Soule had it coming, but the majority, including staunch Chivington supporters, were sobered by the death of the man widely respected for his moral integrity, to the point of reconsidering their opinion about "the Fighting Parson." Some even suggested that Chivington had arranged the murder. No proof of that allegation was ever uncovered, but subsequent events fueled the suspicion.

A huge crowd turned out for Soule's funeral, though only a few had known him personally. Most came to show where their sympathies lay. Denver's leading citizens were there with one exception; in defiance of military custom and common decency, Chivington did not attend, and that cost him more support among the public than all the pages of damaging testimony taken together.

The army hearing ended on May 30. In accordance with their charter, the committee members acted solely in a fact-finding capacity. They issued no conclusions, no judgment of guilt or innocence. Their 228-page record of testimony was not printed until two years later, and then it was filed away in government archives, where it can be found today. With the close of the army inquiry, nearly five months of investigations came to an end, leaving a paper trail of murder, deceit, and treachery, and the name of an obscure creek in Colorado Territory to become a monument to perfidy, at least in the collective memories of the Cheyenne.

Six weeks later, Charles Squiers, who had shot Soule, was arrested in New Mexico. Lieutenant James Cannon, who had protested to Chivington before the Sand Creek attack and who had testified against him, was sent to bring Squiers back to Denver. They arrived on July 12, and Squiers was turned over to the military to be court-martialed. But two days later, Lieutenant Cannon was found dead in his hotel room. He had been in excellent health, and there were no marks of violence on his body. No cause of death was officially determined, though poison was suspected. A few days later, Squiers escaped from the army jail, jumped on a horse conveniently waiting nearby, and rode out of town. No investigation was conducted into the escape, and he was never found again.

Chivington left Denver to try to build a new life but with little success. He moved to Nebraska and started a freight-hauling business that did poorly, in part because of frequent Indian raids on wagon trains, a legacy of the attack at Sand Creek. He tried California, then Ohio, where he had been raised. He bought a newspaper and decided to run for the state legislature. When his opponent raised the issue of Sand Creek, by then twenty years old, Chivington withdrew from contention.

In 1883, he was invited to Denver to speak at the twenty-fifth anniversary celebration of the city's founding. He had not lost his power of oratory; audiences received him with overwhelming enthusiasm, as did Byers of the *Rocky Mountain News*. Chivington was so gratified by this reception that he moved back to Denver and held a succession of minor political offices, including deputy sheriff and county coroner.

There were, however, occasional awkward reminders of his past. When an Indian woman was about to be introduced to Chivington at a social function, she was asked if she knew him. "Know Colonel Chivington?" she said. "I should. He was my father's murderer."

At the same time Chivington left Denver to try to start over, Custer was on a similar path. General Sheridan came through for him again when, in July 1866, Congress authorized an expansion of the army to deal with the Indian uprisings out West. Four new cavalry regiments were formed, and Sheridan pushed for the rank of full colonel and for Custer to command one of the new outfits.

The War Department, however, offered Custer a commission as lieutenant colonel, second in command, of the new 7th Cavalry to be stationed at Fort Riley, Kansas. His commission was dated July 28, 1866.

He was no longer at the major general rank, but still he wasn't a captain, either, and so he and Libbie headed out West, the only place in the country where there might be a war to fight and new dreams of glory to pursue.

SEVEN

WE SHALL HAVE WAR

"My shame is as big as the earth," Black Kettle said.

It was October 14, 1865, some eleven months after the killings at Sand Creek. Black Kettle had aged considerably. He looked worn and beaten as he spoke to a delegation of white officials who had come to offer yet another treaty to the Cheyenne and other Indian tribes. After all he had been through, including being labeled a traitor by many of his own people, Black Kettle was still trying to make peace, a venture he had begun fifteen years before at Fort Wise. He had been a major chief then, but by 1865, only about eighty lodges out of more than two hundred were still with him.

The council was held at Bluff Creek, a tributary of the Little Arkansas River, thirty miles south of Fort Dodge in Kansas Territory. The US government, in an effort to atone for Sand Creek, had sent a number of important officials to parley with the Indians, including the superintendent of Indian affairs and Generals William Harney and John Sanborn.

Friends of the Cheyenne were also present, men Black Kettle trusted. They included the trader and government agent William Bent, and the noted adventurer Kit Carson, who had married into and lived among the Cheyenne and Arapaho tribes. Commanding the military escort was Major Ned Wynkoop, but he was uncertain how Black Kettle and the other Cheyenne would receive him. Wynkoop thought the old chief might blame him for the massacre at Sand Creek.

The last time Wynkoop had seen Black Kettle was when he assured him that he and his people would be safe at Sand Creek. But he needn't have worried. When Wynkoop rode into the camp at Bluff Creek, Black Kettle recognized him immediately.

"I was surrounded and greeted with the utmost kindness," Wynkoop recalled. Nevertheless, some of the older women began to wail, mourning the loss of their loved ones. "After dismounting I was led by Black Kettle to his lodge where surrounded by the other chiefs he stated to me that not for one moment had any of them doubts of my good faith; through their extraordinary natural intelligence they had seemed to comprehend the whole state of affairs."

Black Kettle addressed the delegates to the council. "I once thought that I was the only man that persevered to be the friend of the white man, but since they have come and cleaned out our lodges, horses, and everything else, it is hard for me to believe the white man anymore." He referred to Chivington and his men as a "fool-band" of soldiers who killed women and children. As a result, Black Kettle said, many Indian nations hesitated to meet with whites for fear of being betrayed, as Black Kettle had been at Sand Creek.

For himself, he did not fear whites, but he was afraid of the soldiers. "Your young soldiers, I don't think they listen to you. You bring presents, and when I come to get them I am afraid they will strike me before I get away."

General Sanborn, a friend to the Indians whom the Cheyenne had named "Black Whiskers," spoke first for the government delegation. He conceded that some bands of Indians had been forced to go on the warpath because of Chivington's actions at Sand Creek. But today, Sanborn said, Washington wanted to make restitution to the survivors of Sand Creek for the goods and property they had lost. The government was prepared to offer 160 acres of land to every woman who had lost a husband at Sand Creek, and each child who had lost a parent. Black Kettle accepted the offer for the Cheyenne, as did Little Raven for the Arapahos. Then the terms of the new peace treaty were presented.

Both tribes would have to cede all lands in Colorado Territory that had been given to them in earlier treaties and move to a new reservation south of the Arkansas River. (No doubt these terms pleased former Governor Evans; ridding Colorado of the Cheyenne and Arapaho had been one of his major goals.) Whites would not be permitted on the Indians' new reservation, except for traders and the government's Indian agents. The land would be exclusively theirs where they could live in peace. Each man would receive forty dollars a year for the next forty years. They would be granted hunting rights to the north of the reservation but had to agree to stop raiding white settlements and to stay clear of major travel routes, including the Smoky Hill and Platte River trails.

More promises from the Great Father. More land to give up. Confinement to another barren reservation. It was an old and familiar story. Black Kettle and the other chiefs had heard it all before and seen that promises were not kept. They had witnessed the loss of the great buffalo herds as settlers, railroads, and wagon trains despoiled the vast territories they had once roamed. But Black Kettle knew that unless he agreed to the treaty, the alternative was the annihilation of his people.

On October 18, four days after the beginning of the meeting, Black Kettle made his X on the document—the Treaty of the Little Arkansas—as did Little Raven and five other chiefs.

But after signing, Black Kettle rose and expressed his feelings to the delegation about the new agreement:

> Our Great Father sent you here with his words to us, and we take hold of them. Although the troops have struck us, we throw it all behind and are glad to meet you in peace and friendship. What you have come here for I say yes to. We are different nations, but it seems as if we were but one people. Again I take you by the hand and I feel happy. These people that are with us are glad to think that we have peace once more and can sleep soundly, and that we can live.

Peace remained nothing more than a dream that a piece of paper could not make real and lasting. Black Kettle and Little Raven abided by the terms of the treaty, but other bands of Cheyenne, particularly the so-called Dog Soldiers, did not.

Dog Soldiers were cohesive warrior bands within a tribe, led by their own war chiefs independent of tribal chiefs such as Black Kettle. These highly aggressive, warlike societies had been operating to the north of Black Kettle's village when the new treaty was signed and thus knew nothing about it. Other bands heard about it but continued their raids anyway because their own chiefs had not signed. They did not feel bound by Black Kettle's decision at any time, particularly since many still held him responsible for Sand Creek.

These war parties committed sporadic depredations in areas north of the Little Arkansas River, which previously had been Cheyenne land. Wagon trains, ranches, settlements, and stage-coach stations all came under siege. As whites fell victim to the arrow and the scalping knife, the territory resounded with cries for help and, of course, for revenge.

The attacks continued into January 1866, but then a new Indian agent was appointed for the Cheyenne and Arapaho. It was Ned Wynkoop, whom Black Kettle knew he could trust.

Black Kettle, seated second from the left holding a pipe, with other southern Cheyenne leaders. (*Oklahoma State Historical Society*)

Wynkoop was ordered to contact Cheyenne, Arapaho, and other tribes that had not yet signed the latest treaty, including the Dog Soldier bands.

He arranged for a substantial shipment of food, blankets, and other supplies as an inducement to bring the wandering bands to meet with him. On February 25, at Bluff Creek, he met several chiefs, including two war chiefs of the Dog Soldiers: Medicine Arrows and Porcupine Bears. Despite threats on his life because the Dog Soldiers did not trust Wynkoop the way Black Kettle did, he persuaded them to sign. Although they agreed to the major terms, they actively protested the loss of their favorite hunting grounds around the heavily traveled Smoky Hill Trail.

A month later, Wynkoop met with four hundred Cheyenne, Sioux, and Arapaho warriors and persuaded them to sign the treaty, despite their initial reluctance. Black Kettle came with him to vouch for his trustworthiness. The animosity toward Black Kettle was beginning to lessen, and he had regained a measure of credibility. For several months after that meeting, there were no Indian raids, and it began to appear that a lasting peace was possible—until that summer.

The Dog Soldiers announced that they would not leave the Smoky Hill area, while in Washington, the Senate had not yet ratified the nine-month-old treaty. William Bent traveled to Washington to urge the senators to act. He warned that if they failed to approve the treaty, the result would be the longest, bloodiest war of all time, but still the politicians argued and stalled.

The commissioner of Indian affairs ordered Wynkoop to distribute $1,000 worth of annuity goods to the Cheyenne and Arapaho and to deliver a warning as well. "If the government is obliged to open war upon them, *all* the people will suffer terribly, and such chastisement will be made that there will be nobody left to make war."

On August 14, Wynkoop met Black Kettle and seven other chiefs, including some Dog Soldiers. He persuaded them to give up their last and best hunting ground, the Smoky Hill area. In addition, apparently in response to Wynkoop's warning, the Indians offered to kill any of their own people who attacked whites, if that was the only way to maintain the peace. In return, however, the Indians demanded six hundred ponies and the return of three Cheyenne children captured at Sand Creek. One was in Denver, another on exhibit in a traveling sideshow, and the third had been adopted by Colonel Tappan, who had presided over the army inquiry into Sand Creek.

On October 16, Wynkoop met once more with Black Kettle and other chiefs at Fort Zarah, some ninety miles northeast of Fort Larned on the Arkansas River near the Santa Fe Trail.

The meeting did not go well. The chiefs of the warrior bands wrested power from Black Kettle and the peace chiefs and forced them to renounce the terms of the Treaty of the Little Arkansas. The Dog Soldiers took to the warpath, attacking a stagecoach station on the Smoky Hill Road, stealing its stock, and killing two men. That was the final blow to the peace efforts of Wynkoop and Black Kettle. When news of the killings, the first to occur in several months, reached Major General Winfield Scott Hancock, in command of the Department of the Missouri, he vowed to subdue the Cheyenne for all time. Hancock began to organize the largest army expedition ever mounted in the West. One of the units he called on for this punitive expedition was the recently formed 7th Cavalry.

Custer arrived at Fort Riley in Kansas Territory on October 16, 1866, the day the warrior chiefs seized power from Black Kettle. Custer had traveled with Libbie, four horses, and an unknown number of dogs, including a white bulldog named Tuck.

The 7th Cavalry was commanded by Colonel Andrew Jackson Smith, a rough old soldier—West Point class of 1838, a year before Custer was born. Smith refused to divulge his exact age and took great delight in showing up younger men with his ability to withstand physical hardships. He was considered a good officer with combat experience out West, in Mexico, and in the Civil War, during which, like Custer, he achieved the brevet rank of major general.

Three weeks after Custer reached Fort Riley, he left for Washington to appear before a board of examiners for his new commission as lieutenant colonel, returning a month later. Two months after that, Colonel Smith was reassigned and the 7th Cavalry became Custer's to command, a position he would hold until his death at the Little Big Horn nine years later.

Unlike the men Custer had led during the Civil War, the troopers of the 7th were far less motivated to serve and to fight. Typically, postwar soldiers were less intelligent and less physically fit than those who had served in the Civil War. The official history of the regiment noted, "These recruits represented almost every strata of human society—young adventurers, professional frontiersmen, outcasts from society, fugitives from justice, refugees from the Civil War, both North and South alike, and recently arrived immigrants seeking to enlist in the Army to save enough money to get started in this new land. At least half of this heterogeneous collection were foreign born and many could barely speak English."

George A. Custer, commander of the 7th Cavalry. (*Library of Congress*)

Other descriptions of the men of Custer's 7th Cavalry called them the dregs of society who joined the army because they could not find work elsewhere. They were not openly rebellious like the Texas and Louisiana troops but simply an assortment of mediocrities who, given a choice, would rather have been almost anyplace else. And many did not stay long.

The majority of easterners at that time held a strong negative opinion of the soldiers serving in the territories out West. That was especially true of the abolitionists; with the end of the Civil War, they no longer had slavery to fight against, so they took up the cause of the noble Indian. They lambasted the army as "butchers, rampaging around the West gleefully slaughtering peaceable Indians and taking special delight in shooting down women and children." Custer would soon become a target, to be assailed as no better than a savage himself.

The desertion rate in the 7th Cavalry was more than 50 percent; on average, some fifty troopers left every month. They usually took their weapons, food, supplies, and horses with them. Desertions were highest in the spring. Not only was it easier to travel over the plains then, but jobs on the transcontinental railroad and in the gold mines were more plentiful. In 1867 alone, more than fourteen thousand men deserted from the army as a whole.

It was not surprising that they left in such staggering numbers. Life in the postwar army in the West was grim. Hunger was widespread because of shortages and the terrible quality of the food. Custer wrote about bread and hardtack infested with maggots; the date stamped on some of the boxes was seven years old. "Lunch might be Cincinnati Chicken, otherwise known as bacon, together with salt pork, perhaps eaten raw after being dipped in vinegar, and angel cake, this last being another bakery product guaranteed to chip a tooth. As for coffee, a trooper was issued green beans, and what he brewed was nobody else's concern. Usually he roasted the beans in his mess kit, pounded them with a rock or the butt of his revolver, and emptied the scorched debris into a can of muddy creek water." Custer found a box of stones listed as food, and more stones packed between slabs of bacon. Rocks weighing as much as twenty-five pounds were discovered in packages of food for which the civilian contractor had been paid by the pound.

Because of the poor diet, impure water, and primitive sanitary conditions, cholera, dysentery, and scurvy took an almost daily toll. More men died of disease than were killed by Indians. At one western fort, a soldier wrote, "The spring of 1867 was the time the effects of the spoiled flour and bacon showed up. All of the men got scurvy. Some lost their teeth and some the use of their legs. In the spring when the grass was up there were lots of wild onions and the scurvy gang was ordered out to eat them."

Custer referred to desertion as a popular antidote to the living conditions and the long periods of boredom and inactivity. Most deserters were never caught, but those who were brought back to their forts faced court-martial and imprisonment, suspension in rank and pay, or physical punishments that left some soldiers more dead than alive.

Some deserters were branded on the right hip with the letter *D* for deserter. One was spread-eagled on the ground under a swarm of buffalo gnats that inflicted painful bites. Other common punishments were flogging, confinement in a small steel sweatbox in the blazing sun, dunking in a water barrel to the point of unconsciousness, suspension by thumbs, wrists, or arms so high that the feet could not reach the ground, or marching to the point of exhaustion while carrying a heavy load. Then the soldier was usually drummed out the service. With head shaved, the man was marched around a square formed by his regiment while the band played the "Rogue's March":

> *Poor old soldiers! Poor old soldiers!*
> *Tarred and feathered and sent to hell,*
> *Because they wouldn't soldier well.*

Libbie Custer described the officers of the 7th Cavalry as "a medley of incongruous elements." They were a fractious and quarrelsome lot who generally did not get along well with one another. "Ill feeling arose between volunteers, West Pointers, and appointees direct from civil life; between 'rankers' and officers who felt that shoulder straps did not convert a former enlisted man into a gentleman; and between the commanding officer's 'loyalists' and those who did not like him." And quite a few officers did not like Custer because of how much he had achieved at so young an age. Some felt he had not deserved his rank and the publicity during the war in which they had also fought with considerably less acclaim.

Next in rank to Custer was thirty-five-year-old Major Wickliffe Cooper, from Lexington, Kentucky, who had been a full colonel during the war. Cooper was a competent officer but a heavy drinker, which would shortly be his undoing. Most of the other officers also drank heavily, a constant problem for the teetotaling Custer. Custer's brother Tom would soon join the regiment and was sometimes drunk himself.

Captain Frederick Benteen, a thirty-two-year-old Virginian had risen to the brevet rank of lieutenant colonel; during the war he fought in eighteen major battles. He disliked Custer from the moment he paid the obligatory courtesy call on the commanding officer and his lady at Fort Riley. The evening was not a success. Custer "dominated the conversation and at one point read his farewell address [to his troops at the end of the war], which Benteen dismissed as 'bluster, brag and gush.'" Libbie tried to defuse what she sensed was Benteen's growing hostility. His animosity toward Custer would become a seething and vindictive hatred, which was not helped by his heavy drinking.

Captain Alfred Barnitz, a cheerful, intelligent, thirty-one-year-old veteran of many campaigns, had been a major in Custer's 3rd Division during the last two years of the war. He professed to admire Custer, but that would change.

Captain Myles Keogh, then twenty-four, was from Ireland. He traveled throughout Europe when he was only sixteen and became an officer in the Papal Guards in Rome. Lured by the prospect of action in America's Civil War, he came to the US in 1862, compiled an outstanding war record, and reached the rank of lieutenant colonel. He, too, liked to drink; it was said that he "squandered every paycheck as wantonly as the lowest private."

Captain Louis McClane Hamilton, grandson of Alexander Hamilton, descended from a wealthy, powerful, and influential family. He received a commission in the regular army in 1862 through a family connection and fought with valor and distinction at Fredericksburg, Chancellorsville, Gettysburg, and Petersburg. He remained in the army after the war and joined the 7th Cavalry, at twenty-two the youngest captain in the regular army. He was a highly capable, ambitious troop commander liked by officers and men.

First Lieutenant Myles Moylan, a twenty-eight-year-old soldier from Massachusetts, would not have been an officer were it not for Custer. He joined the regular army four years before the Civil War and was still an enlisted man when the war began. In 1863, he won a commission as a second lieutenant in the 5th Cavalry, where Custer was the first lieutenant of the company. Moylan fought in a number of battles but took an unauthorized leave to visit Washington. Dismissed from the army, he enlisted in another cavalry regiment under an assumed name and worked his way up from private to captain. A year later he reenlisted as a private, using his real name, and was assigned to the 7th Cavalry at Fort Riley. Custer promoted him to sergeant major of the regiment.

Captain Robert West was another officer who immediately disliked Custer. West had joined the regular army five years before the Civil War and by its end was a brevet brigadier general who had led his troops in some of the costliest battles of the war. In the 7th Cavalry, he quickly developed a reputation as one of the regiment's most competent officers, when he was sober. Benteen remembered West as a "distinguished man, but given at time to hellish periodical sprees." Custer noted that West suffered from delirium tremens because of his drinking. Barnitz described a campaign in which West was so drunk he had to be taken in a wagon because he could not sit on his horse.

Major Joel Elliott was described by Custer as having "great courage and enterprise." He became a captain in 1863 but was wounded so severely that he was left on the battlefield for dead. He recovered and went back into action, distinguishing himself in further combat. He tried a career as a schoolteacher in Ohio after the war before deciding to return to the army.

It did not take long for these officers to form competing factions, namely, those who admired and respected their commanding officer and those who despised him, with Cooper,

West, and Benteen in the latter camp. Custer's supporters included his brother, Tom, a captain; Captain George Yates, an old friend from Monroe; as well as Hamilton, Keogh, Elliott, and Moylan. A fractious bunch, but in the wilderness, they had to get along as best they could because they were about to embark on their first campaign against the Indians.

During summer 1866, Major General William Tecumseh Sherman, commander of the Military District of the Missouri, made an inspection tour of the Great Plains of Kansas and Colorado territories. The more he saw, the less he believed there was much danger of an Indian war, not unless elements in the white communities started one.

He observed that ranchers and farmers were exaggerating reported Indian raids so that the army would send more troops. Soldiers and horses had to eat, and the locals were exploiting that fact. The army purchased cattle and grain in large amounts and was willing to pay inflated prices. "All of the people west of the Missouri River look to the army as their legitimate field of profit and support," Sherman wrote, "and the quicker they are undeceived, the better for all."

Sherman found most of the reports of hostile Indian attacks to be questionable. "I find the size of Indian stampedes and stories diminishes as I approach their location. I have met a few straggling parties of Indians who seem pure beggars; poor devils, [they are] more to be pitied than feared."

Despite the lack of evidence of a planned uprising by the Cheyenne, Sherman's deputy, Major General Winfield Scott Hancock, persuaded him that Indians had been responsible for the murders of two stagecoach employees the previous fall. Conceding the point, Sherman allowed Hancock to plan a major campaign against the Cheyenne to commence in the spring.

On December 21, 1866, Captain William J. Fetterman led eighty troops out of Fort Kearny, by the Bighorn Mountains in Wyoming Territory. Fetterman's mission was to rescue a party of woodcutters under siege by the Sioux. As Fetterman rode through the gate, the post commander, Colonel Henry Carrington, shouted orders that he was not to go beyond Lodge Trail Ridge, a little over two miles from the post.

Everyone heard the order; there was no mistaking its intent or purpose. Just two weeks before, troops from the fort had been caught in an ambush beyond the craggy ridge. They had escaped with two dead and five wounded. Carrington was adamant that it not happen again: Fetterman's party was not to cross beyond the ridge.

Before long, Carrington realized that no surgeon had accompanied the outfit, so he ordered one to catch up with them. The doctor reported back that Fetterman had crossed the Lodge Trail Ridge before he could reach them. Mindful of Carrington's orders, the surgeon refused to cross the ridge himself.

Fetterman had seen combat during the Civil War but had been out West only a short time. He was "eager to 'make coups' and had boasted about what he would do against the natives when afforded an opportunity. Shortly before noon he got his chance."

The sound of gunshots lasted twenty-one minutes, Carrington recounted years later. After that, only an eerie silence. Fetterman and all eighty of his troops were dead. Even a dog that had gone along was killed. The Indians systematically mutilated the bodies. Carrington's official report of what came to be called the Fetterman Massacre noted:

> Eyes torn out and laid on rocks; noses cut off; ears cut off; chins hewn off; teeth chopped out; joints of fingers, brains taken out and placed on rocks; entrails taken out and exposed; hands cut off; feet cut off; arms taken out from sockets; private parts severed and indecently placed

on the person; eyes, ear, mouth, and arms penetrated with spear heads, sticks, and arrows; ribs slashed to separation with knives; skulls severed in every form, from chin to crown, muscles of calves, thighs, stomach, breast, back, arms, and cheeks taken out. Punctures upon every sensitive part of the body, even to the soles of the feet and palms of the hand.

The national outrage at the attack quickly turned to a vow of equally brutal revenge. No one seemed to remember that just over two years before, it had been whites, under the command of Colonel Chivington, who had committed atrocities against Indians, including women and children. The army was particularly angered by the Fetterman Massacre and embarrassed as well. It was the worst defeat the army had suffered at the hands of Indians. Soldiers wanted to avenge fallen comrades, and even Sherman now believed that war was inevitable. "We must act with vindictive earnestness against the Sioux," Sherman wrote to Grant, "even to their extermination, men, women, and children." And to one of his brothers, Sherman wrote, "I expect to have two Indian wars on my hands. The Sioux and Cheyennes are now so circumscribed that I suppose they must be exterminated, for they cannot and will not settle down, and our people will force us into it."

But it was winter and the snow was deep, the winds bone-chilling, the prairies empty of grass for the horses. Sherman knew the Indians would stay in their lodges until the grass sprouted in the spring. That gave him several months to plan the campaigns, one in the north against the Sioux and the other in Kansas and Colorado against the Cheyenne.

As Sherman and Hancock prepared for war, Wynkoop tried to defend the Cheyenne, telling Sherman that they had not committed any recent acts of violence. "I have been among them constantly," Wynkoop wrote, "and never knew them to feel better satisfied or exhibit such a pacific feeling." Wynkoop was correct about those who followed Black Kettle, but the Dog Soldiers continued to make raids through the early months of 1867. They ran off stock belonging to a group of buffalo hunters and forced a rancher to give them food, then threatened to kill him when he said he had no sugar to spare for them. They stole horses and mules from a wagon train and took goods from a trader. They held target practice with their new rifles and revolvers, bragging about how much ammunition they now had. Although some whites felt threatened, no one had been hurt.

In March 1867, General Hancock told Wynkoop that the purpose of his expedition was to show the Cheyenne that the government had all the men and resources necessary to punish Indians who caused trouble. He asked Wynkoop to tell the chiefs that if they stopped harassing the settlements they would not be harmed, but if they wanted war they would surely have it. Sherman wrote to Grant, "Our troops must get among them and must kill enough of them to inspire fear, and then must conduct the remainder to places where Indian agents can and will reside among them and be held responsible for their conduct."

The Cheyenne could have war or peace. It was their choice. "We shall have war," Hancock told his men, "if the Indians are not well disposed toward us."

EIGHT

HANCOCK THE SUPERB

"I am sorry to say that the result of the expedition is disastrous." So wrote Major Wynkoop on April 15, 1867, three days after General Hancock met with the Indians. "I am fearful that the result of all this will be a general war."

A month later, on May 13, Thomas Murphy, the district Indian superintendent, echoed Wynkoop's concern in a letter to the commissioner of Indian affairs in Washington. "It would have been for the better, for the interest of all concerned had [Hancock] never entered Indian country with the soldiers. Indians who, at the time he got into their country, were peaceable and well-disposed toward the whites, are now fleeing with their women and children, no one knows where to. What the final results will be is doubtful."

The final results were not in doubt for long. More Indian raids, more killings, more slaughter on the Great Plains, and yet another setback for Black Kettle's efforts to make peace. It came to be called "Hancock's War"; his biographer concluded, "Hancock left an Indian war behind him where there had had been at least a tenuous peace before he came. He failed utterly in his mission of impressing upon the Indians respect for the striking power of the United States Army."

History's judgment on the matter is sharp and clear. Hancock was grievously ill-prepared for the task he set out to accomplish, and a major reason for his failure lay in his attitude toward the Indians. He dealt with them in a condescending and bellicose manner. "He simply did not understand, nor did he try to understand, Indian ways, even when strategically it would have been to his advantage." His 1867 expedition was the worst blunder in an otherwise exemplary record.

During the Civil War, the newspapers had called him "Hancock the Superb." An officer who saw him at Gettysburg described him as "the most magnificent looking General in the whole Army of the Potomac. With a large, well shaped person, always dressed with elegance even upon that field of confusion, he would look as if he was 'monarch of all he surveyed,' and few of his subjects would dare to question his right to command or do ought else but obey."

Winfield Scott Hancock entered the US Military Academy at West Point in 1839, the same class as Pete Longstreet and Ulysses Grant. He was an average student, only a little above mediocre performance in the classroom, but he was quite popular. A classmate wrote, "His handsome face and figure and pleasing manners made him a favorite with his brother cadets and officers of the institution."

Hancock chose the infantry after graduation and served in the territory later called Oklahoma. There were few white residents there in the 1840s, and so relations with the Indians were peaceful. He learned his trade there but apparently learned little about how to relate to the Indians. It would be twenty years and two wars before he found himself out West again.

He led men in combat for the first time in 1847 in Mexico and was awarded a brevet promotion to first lieutenant. After the war he remained in Mexico City as part of the occupation and apparently endeared himself to the young ladies. Humdrum and disappointing times followed the good years in Mexico. Hancock was forced to transfer from the infantry to the quartermaster corps in order to make captain.

During the Civil War, he progressed swiftly through the ranks to major general, fighting bravely in almost every major battle in the East, from Fredericksburg in 1862 to Petersburg in 1865. A colleague recalled, "He was always neatly dressed, and one of the wonders of the Army of the Potomac was the fact that Hancock always wore a clean white shirt, well pressed, even in the midst of a long march or a protracted battle."

He drew admiration and respect from the lowest private to his commanders, and he received favorable and frequent press coverage, largely because he took time to cultivate the news reporters. He played a major role in the victory at Gettysburg; on the final day he repulsed the attack that came to be known as Pickett's Charge.

Hancock sat astride his horse on Cemetery Ridge directing the defense when a rebel bullet tore through the wooden pommel of his saddle and ripped deep into his groin. The bullet carried with it wood splinters and a ten-penny nail from the pommel. Hancock pulled the nail from his wound and was heard to comment that the rebels had to be pretty hard up if they were firing things like that at him.

Aides kept pressure on the wound to try to stop the bleeding as he continued to issue orders. He remained in command until he was certain the Confederate charge had been halted. Only then did he allow himself to be carried to the field hospital.

Following the assassination of President Lincoln, Hancock was appointed military commander of Washington, DC, a post he held during the trials and executions of the Lincoln conspirators. In 1866, Sherman brought Hancock out West to command the Department of the Missouri. In March the following year, they met in Saint Louis to plan Hancock's Indian campaign. Its purpose was to show a force sufficiently large and impressive to persuade the Plains Indians to stop their marauding and harassing of the towns and settlements. Hancock was told to make it clear to the Indians that if they wanted a war, they would have it.

General Winfield Scott Hancock, commander of the Department of the Missouri in 1866. (*Library of Congress*)

Although Hancock still looked impressive enough to be called "superb," the army he now led was definitely not. It was a force designed for traditional warfare such as had been fought against the Confederates, with organized units fighting other organized units in set battles of the kind taught in field manuals, military textbooks, and West Point classrooms.

Hancock had assembled the largest force ever deployed on the plains, consisting of some one thousand four hundred men, but it was of doubtful value for chasing Indians across open lands and for guerrilla-style warfare against quick surprise raids by small bands that refused to stay and fight. About half of Hancock's troops were Custer's cavalry, while the rest consisted of seven companies of infantry, an artillery battery, and a cumbersome pontoon bridge hauled by massive wagons.

Infantry was of no use in going after Indians of the Great Plains who rode some of the swiftest horses available and were skilled in mobile warfare. Hancock's force was limited by how fast and how far men could march in a day, and how slowly a string of pontoon and supply wagons could be pulled by plodding teams of oxen. "The cavalry and infantry were not ready for combat. The men were raw recruits, and the units had only been organized for a few weeks. The cavalrymen scarcely knew how to ride and the infantry had not been hardened for marching. Although they knew the Manual of Arms and had had loading exercises, neither had actually been trained in the use of their weapons. The infantry were still armed with single-shot, muzzle-loading muskets. In experience and ability, the soldiers were far inferior to the Indians."

In addition, Hancock and Custer knew little about fighting Indians, or about their customs and culture. They did not understand how to approach or negotiate with the chiefs in ways they would understand. But the long blue column that left Fort Riley on March 25, 1867, certainly looked impressive. It headed southwest toward Fort Larned, 150 miles away. The expedition also included Delaware Indian scouts, an Indian child, two reporters, and one of the best known white scouts of all time, James Butler "Wild Bill" Hickok.

The Indian boy, then about five years old, had been captured at Sand Creek and was finally being returned to his people. He had been given the name Wilson Graham, after Wilson and Graham's touring circus, in which he had been put on exhibit. "He is a boy of extraordinary intelligence," an observer with the expedition wrote, "and shows the true spirit of the savage by drawing his jackknife on any one who attempts to correct him."

One reporter was Theodore Davis, who wrote for *Harper's New Monthly Magazine*. He had met Custer at West Point while visiting there for a story. The other reporter was listed in the church records of Denbigh, Wales, where he was born in 1842, as "John Rowlands, Bastard." That was not the name by which the world would come to know him.

At age eighteen, in 1859 in New Orleans, Louisiana, John Rowlands became Henry Morton Stanley. Before he startled the world twelve years later by discovering the long-lost missionary, Dr. David Livingstone, at Lake Tanganyika in Africa, he became perhaps the only man to serve in the Union army, the Union navy, and the Confederate army during the Civil War.

Rowlands's father was the village drunkard and his mother an unmarried housemaid who never showed any interest in the boy. He was raised for a time by his maternal grandfather and then placed in a workhouse until age fifteen. He looked for help from other relatives; some kept him for a short period, while others refused to do anything for him. He ended up in Liverpool and signed on as a crewman on an American merchant vessel that took seven weeks to reach New Orleans. A sailor from the ship escorted Rowlands to a brothel where, as he wrote, the girls "proceeded to take liberties with my person." The sailor then took him to a bar for a drink, but Rowlands refused because years before he had signed a pledge not to drink. The sailor offered him a cigar, but the smoke made him sick. And so ended his first night in America.

His situation improved the next day when he landed a job as a junior clerk for a local businessman who took a kindly interest in him. He learned quickly and worked hard. He felt himself becoming more bold and aggressive. As he put it, "within a few weeks of arriving in America, I had become different in temper and spirit."

He then met wealthy cotton broker Henry Morton Stanley, who coached him in etiquette and encouraged him to develop his mind by studying and reading for several hours each day. Although the relationship ended, young Rowlands changed his name and somehow ended up forty miles away in Cypress Bend, Arkansas, clerking in a country store.

As talk of secession from the Union swept the South, the residents of Cypress Bend were caught up in a wave of patriotism for the noble cause. Volunteer regiments were formed, and young men enlisted to teach those Yankees a lesson. Before long, Stanley was the only man of fighting age who had not made the commitment to the rebels.

He probably would not have joined the rebel army had he not received a package from a young woman that contained a chemise and petticoat, which he recognized as symbols of cowardice; he joined up the next day. In hindsight, he admitted,

"Enlisting in the Confederate service because I received a packet of female clothes was certainly a grave blunder."

Stanley fought his first and last battle on April 6, 1862, at Shiloh. He wrote about seeing a small stand of trees "littered by the forms of about a thousand dead and wounded men, and by horses and military equipment. It was the first Field of Glory I had ever seen and the first time that Glory sickened me with all its repulsive aspects and made me suspect that it was all a glittering lie."

He was captured and sent north to Camp Douglas, a prisoner of war camp near Chicago. Scores of rebel soldiers there perished daily from disease, hunger, and despair. After six weeks of these horrendous conditions, Stanley accepted the offer of a way out by joining the Union army. That, too, was short-lived, as he was discharged with a severe bout of dysentery and abandoned, penniless, in West Virginia.

It took a week to walk the nine miles to Hagerstown, Maryland, where a farm family nursed him back to health and bought him a train ticket to Baltimore, where he signed on as a deckhand on a vessel heading for Liverpool. He sailed on other merchant ships for almost a year before returning to the United States in October 1863.

Stanley worked as a clerk in Brooklyn and then decided to try the Union navy. He was appointed the ship's writer for the USS *Minnesota* to record all the activities aboard the ship. He enjoyed the work so much that he started writing stories about life at sea in the wartime navy. Newspapers bought some of the stories to publish as features, and soon Henry Morton Stanley found himself a career as a paid journalist.

He deserted the navy and headed west, intent on a new life. In spring 1867, he was earning $15 a week as a reporter for the *Saint Louis Missouri Democrat*. His assignment was to tell the story of the Hancock expedition to pacify the Indians, whom Stanley would soon characterize as "wronged children of the soil."

One of Stanley's early stories was about the legendary Wild Bill Hickok, who bragged that he had killed more than a hundred men and none without good reason. "He stands six feet one inch in his moccasins," the five-foot five-inch Stanley wrote, "and is as handsome a specimen of a man as could be found. [Hickok] held himself straight and had broad, compact shoulders, was large chested with small waist and well-formed muscular limbs. A fine handsome face free from blemish, a light mustache, a thin pointed nose, bluish-grey eyes with a calm look, a magnificent forehead, hair parted from the centre of the forehead, and hanging down behind the ears in wavy, silken curls, made up the most picturesque figure."

Custer called Wild Bill "a strange character" and a "perfect type of physical manhood." He also wrote that unless Hickok was asked to speak about himself he rarely did, he never used vulgar language, and he was a crack shot with pistol or rifle. Custer envied Hickok's twin pearl-handled revolvers. Others in the expedition talked about Wild Bill's garish outfit: scarlet jacket and black velvet trousers.

Hickok and Stanley got off to a good start. When some soldiers deserted and took a saddle blanket belonging to Stanley, he asked Wild Bill to help chase down the deserters so he could get his blanket back. They found the soldiers twelve miles away, lying drunk in an abandoned house. They were in no shape to put up a fight and were brought back, at Stanley's suggestion, tied together in single file, which won Stanley the hearty approval of Hancock and the other senior officers.

Hancock's expedition reached Fort Larned on April 7, and the men set up their tents outside the fort to await the Indians. Hancock had ordered Wynkoop to tell the chiefs that a meeting would be held there on April 10. On April 9, a fierce spring snowstorm tore over the plains, bringing crippling winds and eight inches of snow, so the meeting was postponed a day. On

April 11, Wynkoop told Hancock that the Indians had been on their way to the fort when they came across a buffalo herd and went after it. That meant another day's delay.

"Hancock was clearly becoming edgy, first a big snowstorm, now a buffalo hunt; what were these people in this strange country really up to? Here he had marched all those soldiers all that way to put it to the Indians—peace or war—and now he could not even find a chief to whom to express his ultimatum." He decided to give them one more day. If they did not appear, he would take his troops to their village, heedless of what had happened the last time soldiers went to a Cheyenne village at Sand Creek. The Indians had not forgotten that.

Finally, on the evening of the twelfth, Chiefs Tall Bull and White Horse and about a dozen men appeared, expecting to be fed and housed for the night. Black Kettle was not present; when the message about the April 10 meeting reached him, he was too far away to get to the fort in time. Hancock was determined to waste no more time. They would meet then and there. He did not know, or perhaps care, that Indians never held councils at night, but only during the day so the sun could bestow its blessing on the deliberations. The chiefs were alarmed by the prospect of a nighttime meeting and felt they were being treated disrespectfully. Thus, each side believed it was being treated unfairly.

The chiefs looked impressive in full regalia, particularly to Hancock, Custer, and others who had never seen Indians before. Stanley was also impressed. He sat by the bonfire and made notes on their appearance:

> The Indians were dressed in various styles, many of them with the orthodox army overcoat, some with gorgeous red blankets, while their faces were painted and their bodies bedizened in all the glory of the Indian toilette. To the hideous slits in their ears were hanging large rings of brass; they wore armlets of silver, wrist-rings of copper,

necklaces of beads of variegated colors, breast ornaments of silver, shields, and [President] Johnson medals, their scalp locks were adorned with a long string of silver discs.

The army officers were also wearing their finest regalia, full dress uniforms with gold epaulettes, tall hats glittering with gold, and gleaming swords. The artillery officers were especially resplendent in their helmets with fiery red horsetail plumes. The officers sat on one side of the bonfire facing the chiefs and Wynkoop on the opposite side. The two reporters, Stanley and Davis, sat off to one side, as did the interpreter, Edmund Guerrier.

Guerrier, whom Hancock called Geary, was a half-breed married to the daughter of trader and Indian agent William Bent. He had risked his life many times carrying messages between whites and Indians. He was still considered a friend by the Indians even though he often carried messages for the soldiers. Perhaps they continued to trust him because they knew he had been at Sand Creek when Chivington attacked and had barely escaped with his life.

The first twenty minutes of the meeting were taken up with the ritual of smoking the peace pipe, a carefully scripted quasi-religious practice of appeasing the gods in the sky by silently exhaling the smoke upward. Everyone present, white and Indian, puffed on the pipe as it was carefully passed from one to another. Then finally, it was time for the impatient and increasingly irritated Hancock to tell the Indians what he had come so far to say.

He rose to his full height, took off his overcoat, and began speaking in a peremptory tone of voice, pausing periodically to allow Guerrier to translate. He said he was disappointed to see so few chiefs attend, and he was angry that he would have to repeat his remarks when the others arrived. He went on to announce that he would lead his soldiers the next day to the Indian camp at Pawnee Fork, about thirty miles away, so he could address the other chiefs. That comment was not received well; the chiefs grunted their disapproval when they heard the translation.

"Now I have a great many soldiers," Hancock said, "more than all the tribes put together. The Great Father has heard that some Indians have taken white men and women captives. He has heard that a great many Indians are trying to get up war to hunt the white men. That is the reason I came down here. I intend not only to visit you here, but my troops will remain among you to see that the peace and safety of the Plains is preserved. I have heard that a great many Indians want to fight. Very well; we are here, and we came prepared for war. If you are for peace, you know the conditions; if you are for war, look out for its consequences."

He told them that the Indian agent Wynkoop was their good friend, but that he would not be able to protect them if they chose war. The soldiers would remain on Indian land to make sure that the new railroad snaking its way across the plains was protected. The "steam car" must be allowed to run, Hancock told the chiefs, and the wagon trains must be allowed to pass along the trails because both carried gifts for the Indians. "You know very well, if you go to war with the white man, you would lose. I will await the end of this council to see whether you want war or peace."

When Hancock sat down, no one said a word. One of the chiefs then lit another pipe, and the Indians passed it among themselves, not offering it to the whites. After the last man had smoked, Tall Bull, a slender, wiry Cheyenne, rose and folded his red and black robe around him. He shook hands with each officer, muttering, "How!" as he did. Then he spoke gravely to Hancock.

"You sent for us; we came here. We have made a treaty with our agent, [Major] Wynkoop. We never did the white man any harm; we don't intend to. We are willing to be friends. The buffalo are diminishing fast. The antelope that were plenty a few years ago are now few. When they will all die away we shall be hungry. We shall want something to eat, and we shall be compelled to come into the fort. Your young men must not fire on us. Whenever they see us they fire, and we fire on them."

Tall Bull warned Hancock not to bring his soldiers to their village the next day, but Hancock interrupted.

"I am going to your camp tomorrow."

The council ended on that acrimonious note.

Edmund Guerrier.
(*National Park Service*)

Tall Bull appealed to Wynkoop to urge the general not to bring troops to the village. He reminded Wynkoop, who surely needed no reminding, that the memory of Sand Creek was still fresh in the minds of his people. If women and children saw soldiers approaching, they would flee in terror.

Later that night, Wynkoop tried to dissuade Hancock from his mission, but he failed. Hancock was determined to see the matter through. His entire command would head toward the village at Pawnee Fork in the morning. And that was his final word.

Custer had never dealt with Indians before; he had never even seen them, and he recorded his impressions about a year after the meeting. They fascinated him, but he thought they possessed a deceitful nature that was displayed during the peace talks. Custer believed they tried to present themselves as simple, peace-loving "sons of nature," living in harmony with their environment, asking nothing more than the right to roam and hunt. He concluded that they were a race of warriors with a deep hatred of other tribes and of whites, and when they adopted the behaviors of whites, it was at the sacrifice of their power as a nation, and their health, strength, and bravery as individuals. "Nature intended him for a savage state," Custer wrote. "Every instinct, every impulse of his soul inclines him to it. Civilization may and should do much for him, but it can never civilize him."

Another observer of the failed council at Fort Larned was Dr. Isaac Coates, a thirty-three-year-old army contract surgeon for the expedition who reflected on how Hancock had treated the Indians. He described the general's speech as arrogant and patronizing. "How galling it must have been to those Indian warriors to be talked to as if they were children. The 'musts' and 'wills' and 'shalls' were more wounding to them than steel-pointed arrows. General Hancock talked to those Indian warriors and orators as a cross schoolmaster would to his scholars."

The historian who edited Coates's journal in 1997 concluded, based on the doctor's observations, that Hancock had "entered a new world" at the Fort Larned meeting. "Suddenly he was negotiating face-to-face with people of a different culture, different traditions and different religious beliefs. His former adversaries, Confederate generals, had often been fellow graduates of West Point. Indian leaders did not follow the same rules. The meeting was the first in a series of events and decisions that would produce intense criticisms of Hancock's leadership, persisting until this day."

The expedition had gotten off to a bad start; it would soon get worse.

NINE

WAR AT
ITS MOST
SAVAGE

It was the most chilling sight the troops of the expedition had ever seen. No more than a half mile ahead of them, stretched in a line a mile wide, stood hundreds of mounted Cheyenne and Sioux warriors. Most of the soldiers, new and inexperienced, gazed in fear, but Custer was fascinated. It was shortly after eleven o'clock on the morning of April 14, the second day of the march from Fort Larned to the Indian village at Pawnee Fork.

Custer described the line of warriors as "one of the finest and most imposing military displays which it has ever been my lot to behold. It was nothing more nor less than an Indian line of battle drawn directly across our line of march; as if to say, 'This far and no further.'"

The Indians were dressed and painted for war with brilliantly colored bonnets, crimson pennants strung on their lances, and arrows ready to fire. In addition to bows, arrows, and tomahawks, each man carried a revolver or a modern breech-loading rifle. Many had both, thanks to what Custer sarcastically described as "the wise foresight and strong love of fair play which prevails in the Indian Department, which, seeing that its wards are determined to fight, is equally determined that there shall be no advantage taken, but that the two sides shall be armed alike."

Small groups of Indians dotted the landscape leading to the village beyond. Estimates of the number ranged as high as five hundred. Although they were outnumbered by three or four to one, the warriors held their ground as the troops advanced, prepared to die where they stood rather than allow the whites to reach their women and children.

Hancock ordered his men to form a battle line with the infantry arrayed in a solid front and the artillery behind it. Custer's cavalry, sabers drawn, galloped to the front, prepared to charge. The troops halted, waiting while the Indians advanced slowly. "Everything now looked like war," Dr. Isaac Coates wrote, "an engagement was momentarily expected."

The Indians stopped a few hundred yards from the soldiers. For what seemed like an eternity to the troops, no one moved or spoke, as if the two armies had been painted on a canvas, colorful lines of blue on one side and a rainbow of shades on the other. Custer described the scene in grand terms, a clash of civilizations on the empty prairie: "Here in battle array, facing each other, were the representatives of civilized and barbarous warfare. The one with but few modifications, stood clothed in the same rude style of dress, bearing the same patterned shield and weapon that his ancestors had borne centuries before; the other confronted him in a dress supplied with the implements of war which the most advanced stage of civilization had pronounced the most perfect."

To Custer, it was a glorious tableau, a sight to be celebrated in flowery prose. To others, it was a barren plain that could become their grave.

The Cheyenne chiefs and elders had been trying to dissuade Hancock from going to their village ever since he led his men out of Fort Larned. On April 13, the first day of the march, small groups of Indians were spotted. Some came close enough to the soldiers to say "How!" and then ride away, leaving the troops to wonder about their motive.

Several times during the first day, Indians set fire to the prairie grass, leaving red scars of flame and columns of black smoke. They hoped the fires would destroy enough grass so that the army's horses would go hungry and the soldiers would return to the fort, but the expedition's wagons carried its own supply of hay and corn for the horses—and the blue-clad line of troopers kept moving closer to the village.

When the fires did not stop the soldiers, the Indians sent delegations to talk to Hancock. In the early afternoon, Pawnee Killer (a Sioux chief), White Horse (a Cheyenne chief), and a few Sioux and Cheyenne braves rode along with Hancock for a while, pleading with him to stay away from their village. Hancock invited them to spend the night when the troops set up camp if they would agree to bring all the chiefs to camp the following morning, Sunday, April 14.

Pawnee Killer left Hancock's camp early in the morning to bring the chiefs back by nine o'clock, a time he indicated by pointing to a spot in the sky midway between the horizon and the sun's highest point. Hancock waited. The designated hour came and went, but no chiefs approached. A half-hour later, Bull Bear of the Cheyenne rode into the camp and said the other chiefs were on their way, but by then, Hancock was visibly agitated.

He was "a punctual West Pointer," his biographer wrote, "and he found it hard to understand how these fellows could treat dates and appointments so casually." Coates wrote in his journal, "This want of punctuality on the part of the savages, the General treated with as much rigor as if the Indians had been white soldiers."

Hancock told Bull Bear he would not wait. He planned to march to Pawnee Fork and set up camp beside the village. Bull Bear rode away to spread the word that their attempts to stop the soldiers had failed. There was only one course of action open to them: the Indians must arm themselves and block the soldiers' path. And that was why Hancock's men found themselves facing a line of warriors after they had covered only a few miles that morning.

As the two armies continued to face each other in silence, Wynkoop asked Hancock's permission to talk to the chiefs. It seemed a dangerous gamble, but most of the Indians were glad to see Wynkoop and welcomed the prospect of a peaceful outcome to the standoff. They agreed to talk with Hancock.

Twelve chiefs, led by the Cheyenne Roman Nose, rode out from the line of warriors, led by Wynkoop carrying a white flag. Hancock, Custer, and several other officers went forward to meet them at a point midway between the armies. Roman Nose was the fiercest chief in appearance.

"He is one of the finest specimens, physically, of his race," Coates wrote in his journal. "He is quite six feet in height, finely formed with a large body and muscular limbs. His appearance is decidedly military; on this occasion he wore the full uniform of a General in the Army. A seven-shooting Spencer carbine hung at the side of his saddle, four large Navy revolvers stuck in his belt, and a bow, already strung, with a dozen or more arrows were grasped in his left hand. Thus armed, and mounted on a fine horse, he was a good representative of the God of War; and his manner showed plainly that he did not care much whether we talked or fought."

Reporter Theodore Davis had a similar impression: "From his manner it was quite evident that he was indifferent whether he talked or fought." Actually, Roman Nose planned to do more than fight. As he approached the white soldiers, he told Chief Bull Bear that he intended to kill General Hancock.

Bull Bear begged him not to do it. He said that if Roman Nose murdered Hancock, the soldiers would slaughter the women and children in the village. Roman Nose grudgingly agreed. He stopped his horse beside Hancock and glared at him. Both men were angry. Hancock demanded to know if the Indians wanted peace or war.

"We don't want war," Roman Nose said. "If we did, we would not come so close to your big guns."

Hancock introduced Custer and the other officers and then asked why Roman Nose had not come to the Fort Larned council.

"My horses are poor," the chief said, "and every man who comes to me tells me a different tale about your intentions."

Hancock abruptly dismissed the chiefs, saying it was too windy to continue to hold a council there. He would establish camp near their village, and the chiefs should all come to his tent that afternoon. Roman Nose turned and rode away, without another word. Bull Bear stayed behind to remind Wynkoop that the women and children would be frightened if the soldiers came close to the village. Wynkoop understood Bull Bear's fears about the memory of Sand Creek. "This I communicated to General Hancock," Wynkoop wrote later, "but he did not agree with that view of it."

The troops marched on to within a half mile of the village by two o'clock that afternoon. The Indian settlement consisted of some 250 lodges. Hancock established his camp, posted guards, placed the troops and artillery in defensive positions, and waited once again for the chiefs to come to him.

As he looked out over the beautiful landscape of the Indian village, Hancock made a surprisingly sympathetic observation in a report to General Sherman: "I am not surprised that the Indians do not wish to give up this country." But ultimately, that was what his mission was all about.

He waited throughout the afternoon for the chiefs to arrive, all the while growing increasingly irritable. Four men finally rode out to the army camp at dusk and told Hancock that the women and children had fled, fearing for their lives. Hancock was furious.

"You must get them back," he demanded, "and I expect you to do so."

He offered the chiefs fresh horses so they could overtake the women and children, and settled back to wait again. At 9:30 that night, interpreter Edmund Guerrier brought word that the men of the village also planned to leave.

"Poor Hancock," his biographer wrote. "One of the great leaders of the Union army, he had marched across Kansas to coerce these Cheyennes into peace, with infantry, artillery, cavalry, and pontoons, and he could not even get them to stay around and talk."

Hancock ordered Custer to take his cavalry and surround the village to keep the chiefs and warriors there. "Easily said," Custer wrote later, "but not so easily done." His men were assembled under cover of darkness; he ordered that there be no talking and that sabers be left behind. The slightest noise could betray the outfit's presence. They encircled the village, stationing men every few yards to form a cordon. If the Indians tried to escape, they would find their way blocked by the mounted troopers.

"No sooner was our line completely formed," Custer wrote, "than the moon, as if deeming darkness no longer essential to our success, appeared from behind her screen and lighted up the entire scene. And a beautiful scene it was. The great circle of troops, each individual of which sat on his steed silent as a statue, the beautiful and in some places dense foliage of the cotton trees sheltering and shading the bleached, skin-clad [Indian] lodges. . . . [A]ll combined to produce an artistic effect, as beautiful as it was interesting."

It was also potentially deadly. The hundreds of warriors Custer and his men had seen on the prairie that morning could be anywhere—concealed along the banks of the stream, behind the trees, burrowing in the undergrowth, or waiting inside the lodges. If they broke out, the 7th Cavalry would face the worst conditions imaginable, fighting hand-to-hand in the darkness with a determined enemy who knew the terrain, were better trained fighters, and might have Custer's force surrounded.

Custer slid his revolver out of its holster and summoned Guerrier, Lieutenant Myles Moylan, and Coates. The four of them would enter the village alone to see if the warriors were still there. This was Custer's way from his earliest days in the Civil War; when in doubt, forge ahead.

Why he selected Coates, who had no military experience, to accompany him is not clear. According to the historian who edited Coates's journal, it is likely that "he enjoyed Isaac's company and wanted him to share in the excitement. Custer, whose own courage, if not judgment, was beyond question, knew a brave man when he saw one."

The four men crawled on their hands and knees. Custer said later that he believed the Indians were asleep. His plan was to get close enough to the lodges for Guerrier to call out in the Cheyenne language that they came in peace. But the only responses to Guerrier's shouts came from a pack of dogs barking fiercely. The presence of so many dogs persuaded Guerrier that the Indians were hiding in the shadows.

Custer and his men continued to venture into the village. "Each one grasped his revolver," Custer wrote, "resolved to do his best, whether it was running or fighting. I think most of us would have preferred to take our own chances at running." They crawled to within a few yards of the first lodge, stopping to listen for the slightest noise, but again heard nothing but the barking dogs.

The Indians were gone. Only the dogs were left, plus a warrior too sick to travel and an eight-year-old Indian girl who had been raped, perhaps by soldiers who had sneaked into the camp before Custer arrived; Wynkoop insisted that Indians never raped their own. The Indians had abandoned the settlement in such haste that they left a fortune in possessions.

Henry Morton Stanley walked through the deserted camp the next morning. "The Indian village consists of about three hundred hide lodges," he wrote. "They show unmistakable traces of the haste of their owners to get away—dogs half eaten up, untanned buffalo robes, axes, pots, kettles, and pans, beads and gaudy finery, lately killed buffalo, stews already cooked in the kettles." The Indians had taken little more than the clothes on their backs, and their horses and weapons.

Hancock was angry when he heard the news. How could he deal with Indians if they would not stay where they were supposed to? "This looks like the commencement of war," he said. He vowed to destroy the encampment in order to punish the Indians for fleeing.

Wynkoop pleaded with him to spare the camp. Destroying the village, he argued, would make the Cheyenne chiefs even more reluctant to talk and also make it harder to arrange councils in the future with other tribes. One of Hancock's senior officers supported Wynkoop, but the general would not commit himself either way. He might burn the village or he might not. It would depend on what the Indians chose to do, he said.

Hancock placed guards around the deserted camp, but they could not keep out the determined souvenir hunters among the soldiers. "[I]n spite of the strict guard kept," Stanley wrote, "the 'boys in blue' are continuously carrying away mementoes of their bloodless victory, such as stiff buffalo robes, dog skins, calumets [ceremonial pipes], tomahawks, war clubs, beadwork, moccasins. Arrows and knives are picked up by the dozen, and also little dolls, which had been the gratification of the papooses. The soldiers rummage and pick up things in the most senseless manner, and after carrying them a few yards throw them away, when they are soon picked up by somebody else, and thrown away again."

Hancock then ordered Custer to take eight companies of his cavalry and make a forced march to go after the Indians. His mission was to find them and escort them back. If they refused to return with him or threatened to do battle, he was to attack.

Custer told his men to travel light. "Blankets were carefully rolled so as to occupy as little space as possible," he wrote.
"Every useless pound of luggage was discarded, for in making
a rapid pursuit against Indians, much of the success depends
upon the lightness of the order of march."

Some of the Delaware scouts went with them, along with
Hickok, reporter Davis, and interpreter Guerrier. Custer led
his men out of Hancock's camp at dawn on April 15. "Oh!"
Coates wrote in his journal, "it was a glorious sight to behold
our army splendidly organized and equipped with every comfort and martial invention of modern civilization, like blood-
hounds on the trail in hot pursuit. A martial spirit had taken
possession of every soul in the command."

Davis's observations were quite different. He had no confidence in the troops. One historian wrote that to Davis, "The
men in this army he found to be mostly bums or broken-down
adventurers, some of them ex-Confederate soldiers seeking
free transportation to the Colorado mines. They showed no
interest in the service or in Indian fighting and would certainly desert at the earliest opportunity."

Custer never realized that the person he most depended on,
Guerrier, undermined the mission from the outset. As they left
camp, Custer ordered Guerrier to ride ahead and alert any
Indians he saw that the soldiers only wanted to talk and that
he would not attack if they stopped running from him.

Guerrier was about three miles ahead of the column when
he saw a Cheyenne warrior looking for horses that had
escaped when the people fled the village. The man was some
distance away and in a ravine, but he spotted Guerrier, who
communicated through sign language that soldiers were coming so he should get away.

Then Guerrier headed off in another direction, and when
Custer caught up with him, Guerrier said the Indians had scattered in all directions. When he asked Custer which trail he
should follow next, Custer chose one heading north toward
the Smoky Hill Trail.

The Indians had a twelve-hour start, Custer wrote, but because they were "encumbered by their families, we hoped to overhaul them before many days." But the soldiers encountered an obstacle early on the first day, at Walnut Creek, where the banks were too steep to climb. The column had to detour three miles upstream to find a spot where it could cross.

Reaching the opposite bank, they saw that the Cheyenne had crossed at the same place. Fires the Indians had used for cooking breakfast were still burning. Coates believed the Indians had been warned about the soldiers because they departed in such haste that they abandoned a mule and some ponies with packs still on their back. The Delaware scouts examined the packs and found the ornaments Roman Nose had worn to his meeting with Hancock. One of the scouts attached Roman Nose's crimson feather to his own headdress.

The soldiers pushed north and by the afternoon came across lodge poles and other objects the Indians were discarding in their flight. By three that afternoon, Custer was certain he would accomplish his mission that day. "No obstacle seemed to stand in our way," he wrote later. "The trail was broad and plain, and apparently as fresh as our own. A half hour, or an hour at furthest, seemed only necessary to enable us to dash in upon our wily enemy." But, he added, "Alas for human calculation!"

The Indians were too clever for Custer and his scouts. Instead of remaining together as a band, leaving one broad trail to follow, they separated into smaller groups, each one marking its own trail. Now there were scores, then hundreds of paths fanning out in many directions. Custer decided that because the Cheyenne had originally headed north toward the Smoky Hill Trail, he would continue that way.

By five o'clock that afternoon, the one remaining trail north had become so narrow and indistinct that it was impossible to follow. The exhausted troopers had been on the march for twelve hours, stopping only to water their horses. They had covered thirty-five miles; it was time to set up camp for the night.

Custer roused the men at two in the morning, and they were in the saddle two hours later. By daylight, still moving north, Custer chose to head out on his own to have some fun. Astride his thoroughbred horse Custis Lee, and with five hunting dogs racing behind, he rode alone through Indian country even though he knew it was foolhardy. But Custer believed in his own luck. It had gotten him through a war and had never failed him yet. Besides, it was a glorious day for hunting.

He was several miles ahead of his men and had just decided to turn back when he saw a magnificent buffalo as big as his horse. He immediately gave chase. After three miles of hard riding, he caught up with the animal and rode alongside. He pulled out his revolver and took aim. The buffalo swung toward him, causing his horse to shy. At that instant Custer squeezed the trigger, the gun roared, and Custis Lee fell dead with a bullet in its head.

Custer pulled his feet out of the stirrups and tumbled off the horse. His only thought as he rolled to the ground was about what the buffalo would do. For a moment, Custer was too stunned by the fall to move. He and the buffalo eyed one another, then the huge beast shook its head and lumbered away. Custer rose, brushed off his clothing, and considered his situation. It was not good.

"Here I was, alone in the heart of the Indian country, with warlike Indians known to be in the vicinity. How far had I traveled, or in what direction from the column, I was at a loss to know. In the excitement of the chase I had lost all reckoning."

Even the dogs seemed uneasy, as if sensing danger. They "whined piteously," Custer wrote, and seemed eager to leave the dead horse. Custer decided to follow the dogs, which had all turned to look in one direction. With a revolver in each hand, he set out with them, expecting Indians to appear at any moment.

No Indians appeared; such was Custer's fabled luck. After walking several miles, he spied a column of dust in the distance. Something was on the move. It could have been Indians, soldiers, or buffalo, so he herded the dogs into a ravine and scanned the dust cloud with his binoculars as it got closer until he made out a cavalry guidon from his own outfit.

Custer was lucky in not finding Indians, but he also could not find water. That afternoon, his men had to retrace nine miles of their march because the scouts reported there was no water in any other direction. They reached the same stream they had left hours earlier and set up camp again.

Theodore Davis observed that the usually ebullient Custer was growing moody. A biographer noted that he had reason to be unhappy. "This was his first independent command since coming to the West, and it promised to be a failure." Nevertheless, Custer reasoned that if the Indians were still heading north, then they would have to cross the heavily traveled Smoky Hill Trail. This was a major road west to Denver. and they would surely be spotted by a wagon driver or someone from a stagecoach station. Eventually Custer would be able to track them down.

He ordered his men to saddle up at seven that evening for a night march, after only five hours of rest. By daylight, they reached the Smoky Hill Trail, where employees at Downer's Station, on the stagecoach route, said they had seen groups of Indians moving north throughout the last twenty-four hours. They also warned Custer that the Indians had committed raids on other stations.

Custer led his column east and found that all the stations, which were located at ten-to-fifteen-mile intervals, were deserted. Periodically, he came across groups of employees from the abandoned stations who had banded together at one site to better defend themselves. They told him about atrocities they had seen at Lookout Station, the next stop down the line. Custer saw the smoke coming from that direction and led his troops toward the station.

Nothing was left of the station's buildings but smoldering ashes and the charred, mutilated bodies of its three employees. Custer wrote that the bodies were "so mangled and burned as to be scarcely recognizable as human beings. The Indians had evidently tortured them before putting an end to their suffering. They were scalped and horribly disfigured."

The men were horrified by the sight. "This was the first deadly work of the savage Indians that we had seen," Coates wrote in his journal, "and it sent a chill of horror through the whole command. Men whose nerves had been unshaken by the spectacle of a battlefield strewn with dead, shuddered at these victims of Indian wrath who had been brutally murdered, scalped, and burnt. We ourselves had sown the wind and this was the first harvest of the whirl-wind. Our Christian, civilized soldiers swore vengeance; and every man was big with brutal and murderous projects to revenge on the morrow, the deaths of their brothers that they had mourned today."

Custer's Delaware scouts searched the wreckage for clues as to which tribe had passed through but found nothing to indicate the guilty parties. There was no way for Custer to know whether it was Cheyenne, Sioux, or some other Indian nation, but it was clear in his own mind that the killings had been committed by the Indians he was pursuing.

That night, April 17, he sent couriers back to General Hancock's camp on the Pawnee Fork, some seventy miles away, to tell him about the killings at Lookout Station, saying that he was sure they had been committed by the Indians who had been at Pawnee Fork. Two days later, however, Custer learned from other stagecoach employees that the raid had occurred only a day after the Cheyenne and Sioux had left Pawnee Fork, too soon for them to have reached Lookout Station.

Custer amended his report to Hancock: "Lookout Station was burned and the men massacred on Monday, the 15th, which clears those Indians who were at Pawnee Fork the day of our arrival from the charge of being present at the murder."

But his latest message was too late. Hancock had already burned the Indian village in retribution.

The soldiers set the torch to all 251 lodges at Pawnee Fork. Prior to the burning, Hancock ordered an inventory of the Indians' possessions so he could report to Washington on the extent of damage done to the enemy. Stanley cataloged the items for his readers:

> The following is a true list of the miscellanea which were consigned to the flames this morning: 251 lodges, 942 buffalo robes, 436 horn saddles, 435 travesties, 282 bead mats, 181 axes, 190 kettles, 77 frying-pans, 350 tin cups, 30 whetstones, 212 sacks of paint, 98 water kegs, 7 ovens, 41 grubbing horns, 28 coffee mills, 144 lariat ropes, 129 chairs, 303 parflecks [a rawhide suitcase the Indians used to carry personal belongings], 15 curry combs, 67 coffee pots, 46 hoes, 81 flicking irons, 17 hammers, 4 scythes, 8 files, 19 bridles, 8 pitchforks, 1 sword, 1 bayonet, 1 US mail bag, 74 stone mallets, 1 lance, 33 wooden spoons, 251 doormats, 48 raw hide ropes, and 22 meat stones.

Stanley added that it would take three thousand buffalo to replace the skins on the destroyed lodges. It was the entire wealth of the tribe, worth a fortune to them, accumulated over the years. The contents of the typical lodge were valued at approximately one hundred dollars, a staggering sum to an Indian family.

The soldiers tore down the lodges and tossed everything onto a half dozen mounds, all of which were set afire at the same moment, making a colorful, sad, even dangerous display. "The dry poles of the wigwams caught fire like tinder," Stanley wrote, "and so many burning hides made the sky black with smoke. Flakes of fire were borne on the breeze to the prairie, setting the grass on fire. With lightning speed the fire rolled on and consumed an immense area of grass, while the black smoke slowly sailed skyward. Every green thing, and every dead thing that reared its head above the earth, was consumed, while the buffalo, the antelope, and the wolf fled in dismay."

The odors settled into the soldiers' wool uniforms and filled their lungs, and the sight of the six towering columns of smoke blending into one could be seen for miles around. It was an omen, a herald of the fire and smoke and darkness that would stain the sky and the lives of hundreds of people, Indian and white, for years to come.

The news of the burning village spread over the prairie almost as fast as the fire itself. Roman Nose and other warrior chiefs vowed a bloody revenge. Hancock had "stirred up a hornet's nest. Revenge was mandatory. War had come to the central plains."

Black Kettle, despite these events, still believed that peace was the only way to preserve his Indian nation. Not long after the burning of the village at Pawnee Fork, he offered to hold a council with Hancock at Fort Larned, but Hancock could not get there in time. Instead of a meeting to discuss peace, Hancock offered food and protection for Black Kettle and his followers at any army post Black Kettle chose. Although he was willing to take advantage of that offer, many of his people were not. The promise of protection by the army sounded too much like the promises made by the government before Sand Creek.

In the meantime, Hancock's War was fully under way. Unlike the killings at Lookout Station, there was no question of who was responsible for destroying the Indian village at Pawnee Fork. Cheyenne and Sioux were now out for revenge for the destruction of their community. For their raids, they focused particularly on what Hancock called the steam car, the Union Pacific Railroad Line across Indian territory north of the Smoky Hill Trail. From late May to late June, Indian forays almost brought construction on the railroad to a halt.

As one Cheyenne war party walked across a set of railroad tracks, a man named Porcupine was heard to have said, "Now white people have taken all we had and made us poor, but in these big wagons that go on this metal road, there must be things that are valuable. If we throw these wagons off the iron they run on and break them open, we could take whatever might be useful to us."

First they attempted to wreck the trains running to the construction site, but soldiers were guarding much of the finished line. Also, the Indians underestimated the strength of the steam cars. One warrior tried to lasso a locomotive. "Apparently the diminutive 4-4-0 wood burner seemed tame to [him] at the time, but it jerked him off his horse and dragged him over the prairie for some distance before he let go."

Other attacks were more successful and more deadly. One war party tied a log to the track and waited for the next train, but instead a handcar pumped by two railroad employees came along. It jumped the tracks when it struck the log. The men were thrown off and tried to scramble away but were quickly overtaken and killed.

Another war party pulled the spikes out of a rail bed and bent the rails. Before long, two freight trains came down the track. The first one hit the bent rails, sending the locomotive flying into the air; the cars behind it rammed one into another. Only one crew member survived the wreck, and the Indians finished him off. The second train stopped in time and slowly backed away. An observer noted that the war parties "plundered and burned the wrecked train and scattered the contents all over the prairie. They tied bolts of calico to their horses' tails, galloped about, and had much amusement."

Isolated stagecoach stations were also targets, with attacks recorded over a distance of 170 miles along the Smoky Hill Trail. From June to August, every station was raided at least four times. Coaches and freight wagons were kept off the road out of fear of fresh attacks. For several weeks, the only movement was of the parties of Cheyenne and Sioux warriors.

Cheyenne warriors attacking a working party of the Union Pacific Railroad, August 1867. (*Library of Congress*)

The plan for hitting the stagecoach stations was the same. "The [Indians] would ride up to a station about 2 o'clock in the morning, set fire to the haystack, and also to the station if it was made of combustible material. While some of the Indians rode whooping in a circle around the station, firing into it, a few others would steal the stock. As soon as the station attendants and soldier guards could return the fire, the Indians would ride away."

They typically attacked in bands of ten to twenty warriors and took care to avoid getting shot. If one of them was hit and toppled off his horse, two others would gallop up at top speed and snatch him up without dismounting. It was an amazing feat, developed through years of practice; rarely was a wounded man left behind. As a result, it was difficult for the government to calculate the extent of the Indian casualties.

Newspapers from Denver to Boston published lurid stories about bloody Indian raids. Stanley wrote, "Between Bishop's Ranch and Junction Cut Off, 80 miles from Denver, there are no less than 93 graves, 27 of which contain the bodies of settlers killed within the last 6 weeks. Dead bodies have been floating down the Platte River. The Indians, indistinguishable from the earth they lie on, continue to watch patiently from behind the hills or from the sagebrush that screens them from view. As soon as they perceive a chance to get scalps or plunder they dart down, and the deed is done."

Soldiers were not immune. They seldom ventured far from
the forts that summer of 1867, and those who did were often
attacked within sight of the post. One lieutenant and ten
troopers were ambushed by a band of Cheyenne and Sioux
who murdered them and then hacked and disfigured the bodies. Victims were often dismembered, leaving only indistinguishable pieces to be buried by the roadside.

On June 26, near the Pond Creek stagecoach station, a
detachment of the 7th Cavalry that had remained with
Hancock while Custer led the rest of the regiment in pursuit of
Indians came under attack. Captain Alfred Barnitz was in
command, and his outfit was forced to retreat, leaving several
wounded men behind. "Bugler Charles Clark fell, pierced by
five arrows. A brawny Indian leaned far over the side of his
horse and picked up the boy, much like an eagle would snatch
a rabbit. He stripped the bugler, smashed his head with a
hatchet, and flung him back to the ground under the pound-
ing hoofs," all in a matter of a minute or two while riding at
top speed.

Barnitz had his men retreat, leaving Sergeant Frederick
Wyllyams and four men on their own. One by one they fell.
Barnitz ordered his troops to dismount and form a semicircle,
with three out of every four men kneeling and firing their
repeating carbines as fast as they could; the fourth man held
the horses.

After repeated assaults, the Indians finally left, and
Wyllyams, an Englishman and a graduate of Eton, earned a
kind of posthumous fame as the subject of what may be the
only photograph of a white man's body mutilated by Indians.
The snapshot was taken by Dr. William Bell, an English physician traveling through the West. Bell wrote:

> I have seen in days gone by sights horrible and gory . . .
> but never did I feel the sickening sensation, the giddy,
> fainting feeling that came over me when I saw our dead,
> dying, and wounded of this Indian fight. Sergeant

Wyllyams lay dead beside his horse; as the fearful picture met my gaze, I was horror-stricken. Horse and rider were stripped bare of trappings and clothes, while around them the trampled, bloodstained ground showed the desperation of the struggle. A portion of the sergeant's scalp lay near him, but the greater part was gone.

General William T. Sherman, on learning of the extent of the carnage that summer, declared that the Indians should be removed completely from the land between the Platte and the Arkansas rivers, despite the Treaty of the Little Arkansas, which had ceded them the rights to that territory. He toured the area and informed Secretary of War Stanton that "if fifty Indians are allowed to remain between the Arkansas and Platte we will have to guard every stage station, every train, and all railroad working parties. Rather get them out as soon as possible and it makes little difference whether they be coaxed out by concessions or killed."

Writing to General Grant, however, Sherman sounded a bit more sympathetic, though no less convinced that there was only one solution to the problem. "The Indians are poor and proud. They are tempted beyond the power of resistance to steal of the herds and flocks they see grazing so peacefully in the valley. To steal they sometimes kill. We in turn cannot discriminate. All look alike and to get the rascals, we are forced to include all."

Sherman wanted to add substantially to his forces and go on the offensive with an army of sufficient size to sweep away everything before it. But before he was able to bring more troops to the West, Congress established yet another Indian peace commission, scheduled to reach the plains that fall. Until that time, the army was restricted to defensive operations, patrolling the roads and maintaining the garrisons.

Sherman held out little hope for this latest in a string of attempts to make peace. He was certain that this peace commission, like all the previous ones of equally good intention, would be unable to mollify the younger warriors who were out for revenge. The commission members would most likely only be able to talk with the older peace chiefs, led by Black Kettle, who no longer had the influence they once had. "And to talk with the old ones," Sherman told Grant, "is the same old senseless twaddle."

Hancock did what he could, but he, too, lacked enough soldiers to cover so large an area. As the deadly summer of 1867 came to an end, so did Hancock's command. On August 26, he was transferred to the 5th Military District, which included Louisiana and Texas. His controversial tour of duty in the Great Plains was over. But the war he started would continue.

TEN

THE TIME HAS COME THAT I MUST GO

Custer missed most of Hancock's war. After finding the bodies at Lookout Station on April 18, and failing to find the Cheyenne and Sioux who had fled Pawnee Fork, Custer took his men to Fort Hays. Hancock had promised to arrange for a shipment of forage to be sent there for the horses, along with food for the men, but nothing had arrived. The only food and supplies they had was what they carried with them or found at the fort, and that was not sufficient for Custer's force. He was trapped, unable to continue the hunt for the Indians, which left him unhappy and embarrassed.

Fort Hays was a dismal place. "Miserable log shanties with stone chimneys stood in a square around what passed for a parade ground. In the best cabins canvas had been tacked under the pole ceiling to catch sand drifting down from the dirt roofs. Occasionally a rattlesnake dropped into the billowing ceiling and remained trapped for weeks, startling the people below with its threatening whir."

Custer set up camp a half mile from the fort, but the conditions there were little better. The horses were weak from eating prairie grass, all they had since leaving Pawnee Fork. Soon they were dying of malnutrition at the rate of four or five each day.

The troopers were also ill, most commonly with scurvy. Officers ate no better than the men. They were all reduced to a diet of hard bread, bacon, and beans, and not enough of that to ease the gnawing hunger. To add to the misery, a cold rain fell daily and turned the camp into a deep sea of sticky mud. These miserable, soon desperate conditions prompted many to desert.

In one night alone, ten men left, taking their weapons and ammunition. Soon a dozen more deserted. By the end of May, at least ninety had run off. Captain Barnitz wrote to his wife, Jennie, on May 18, describing how fourteen more had "gone off armed and mounted! [They] broke through the guards and departed. So they go. If General Custer remains long in command, I fear that recruiting will have to go on rapidly to keep the regiment replenished."

Custer grew more irritable and moody, according to reporter Theodore Davis. His manner was tyrannical and overbearing, and he was much like the martinet he had been in Texas and Louisiana. Barnitz and others recorded their increasing frustration:

"General Custer has become bilious. He appears to be mad about something, and is very much on his dignity."

"Things are becoming very unpleasant. [He] is injudicious in his administration and spares no effort to render himself obnoxious. I have lost all the confidence I ever had in his ability as an officer and all admiration for his character as a man. I am thoroughly disgusted with him. He is the most complete example of a petty tyrant I have ever seen."

In his frustration and anger, Custer turned once again to severe punishments for minor infractions. On May 17, he ordered that six enlisted men have one side of their heads shaved clean, while the other half was left untouched. They were paraded through the camp in disgrace. Their crime? They had gone to the sutler's shop at the fort to buy canned fruit. They were away from camp less than forty-five minutes and did not miss role call or duty assignments, but they had not obtained a pass to leave the area. At the time, there were seventy-five active cases of scurvy, and they were in desperate need of fruits and vegetables. Many officers and men felt the punishment was extreme, far more severe than warranted for a minor offense.

Another soldier forgot to water his horse at the prescribed time. "A halter was placed around the man's neck and he was led to the creek where the horses were watered. This was done quite a number of times, and thereafter the man never failed to regularly give his horse water."

To boost his sagging spirits, Custer urged Libbie to come to Fort Hays so they could be together, even though it was dangerous for anyone to travel over the plains. "You remember how eager I was to have you for my little wife?" Custer wrote to her. "I was not as impatient then as I am now." In an eerily prophetic statement he added, "I almost feel tempted to desert and fly to you." Space was limited in the army wagons bringing supplies to isolated outposts such as Fort Hays, but that did not deter Custer.

He told Libbie to bring one hundred pounds of butter for the officers along with lard, potatoes, and onions. She would need calico dresses as well as white ones. He also wanted a croquet set but said she should leave her clothes press at Fort Riley. And she must bring Eliza and the cookstove, as well as a woman friend who was looking for a young officer for adventure and romance.

When Libbie arrived, she was not surprised to see that Custer had turned his otherwise bleak headquarters into a zoo, with "wolves, coyotes, prairie dogs, jackrabbits, raccoons, porcupines, wildcats, badgers, rattlesnakes, owls, eagles, hawks, young antelope, deer and buffalo calves, and a slew of hounds and horses." He also had a pet beaver that followed him around, cuddled in his arms, and slept and cried like a human baby.

Custer's spirits lifted dramatically when Libbie arrived, along with the end of the rains and the pleasant spring weather. Hancock also came in May and noted the deplorable condition of Custer's men and horses. He expedited the shipment of hay and oats for the horses and food for the troops. And then, finally, General Sherman offered Custer a chance to go back to war. Sherman alerted the friendly Indians, including Black Kettle and his people, to go to the forts along the Platte River or to stay north of it, out of the army's way.

He ordered Custer to ride into the country south of the Platte and clear out Cheyenne and Sioux between the Smoky Hill and the Platte. On the morning of June 1, 350 troopers of the 7th Cavalry, along with twenty wagons, left Fort Hays to begin their search for Indians. In the lead rode Major Wickliffe Cooper, in temporary command for the day. Custer was not yet ready to be parted from Libbie, so he let his men begin the mission without him. He stayed with her until midnight and then rode hard through the night with an escort of seven soldiers, reaching his command at reveille. It would be many weeks before he would see her again.

Reporter Davis accompanied the expedition, along with a new scout, William Comstock, who preferred the name of Medicine Bill. Born in Michigan, the twenty-five-year-old Comstock had lived with Indians for two years and knew the terrain in detail. Custer enjoyed his company and invited him to meals so he could learn more.

He was amused when Comstock revealed that he had named his dog Cuss, after Custer. "Perfect in horsemanship," Custer wrote, "fearless in manner, a splendid hunter, and a gentleman by instinct, as modest and unassuming as he was brave, [Comstock] was an interesting as well as valuable companion on a march such as was then before us."

Comstock was called Medicine Bill because, like the Indians, he had a medicine or cure for anything that might happen. He "referred to every object or event in his life as either 'good medicine' or 'bad medicine.' If he had bad luck, he had to do something to change his 'medicine.' His two greatest wishes had been to meet Custer and to see a railroad engine." Not long after he started the trip with Custer he saw a locomotive, which he declared to be good medicine.

The troopers saw no Indians and had no problems for the first week, but on the night of June 8, tragedy struck. Davis was dining with Custer at the officers' mess. Custer mentioned the absence of Major Cooper and said that someone should see if he was all right. He suggested that Davis go, but before the reporter could leave the table, they heard a pistol shot.

Cooper was found in his tent, shot through the head. He had recently been depressed and was drinking more heavily than usual until he ran out of liquor. Custer wrote to Libbie, describing how they had found Cooper "lying on knees and face, right hand grasping his revolver, ground near him covered with blood, [the] body still warm, pulse beating, the act having been committed but three or four minutes before. Another of rum's victims. But for intemperance, Cooper would have been a useful and accomplished officer. He leaves a young wife, shortly to become a mother."

Custer and his men reached Fort McPherson on June 10. He took on fresh supplies, telegraphed Sherman of his arrival, and set up camp ten miles away from the fort to avoid the commanding officer, Colonel Carrington, who had been transferred there after the Fetterman Massacre. Custer even declined a dinner invitation from Carrington, a highly disrespectful act, because he did not want it to be perceived officially that his outfit was located at Fort McPherson, where he then might have to take orders from the more senior Carrington.

A delegation of Sioux chiefs, led by Pawnee Killer, soon visited Custer's camp. Custer smoked a pipe with them, gave them gifts of sugar and coffee, and tried to persuade them to bring their people closer to the fort, where they could live in peace. He warned, however, that he was prepared to kill any Indians he found between the Arkansas and Platte rivers. Pawnee Killer, who had taken a liking to Custer's pet antelope and had begun to gently stroke the tame animal, assured Custer that he wanted to live in peace. He agreed to relocate his people to the protection of the fort, but he kept pressing Custer to reveal details of the plans for his future movements and overall campaign against hostile Indians. Custer refused.

General Sherman arrived the next day. When Custer told him about the meeting with Pawnee Killer, Sherman was annoyed. He said that Custer should not trust the word of any Indian, nor should he meddle in politics by trying to negotiate with them. Sherman, now shouting at Custer, said he should have taken the chiefs hostage to force their people to come to the fort. He ordered Custer to pursue Pawnee Killer's band and any other Indians he could find, and shoot them on the spot. His job was to fight, not parley.

A few days later, Custer led his men west, then turned south toward the Republican River. Sherman had ordered him to scour the countryside of northwestern Kansas and eastern Colorado in his search for Indians. He would then head north to Fort Sedgwick on the South Platte River, to be resupplied and await further orders.

Custer deliberately chose to disobey Sherman's directive because of growing concern about Libbie's safety. He had written for her to meet him at Fort Wallace, 150 miles south of Fort Sedgwick. He was now midway between the two forts; if he went to Sedgwick, he would be following orders but getting more distant from where she was supposed to be. If he went to Fort Wallace, he would be disobeying orders but would be reunited with her.

Custer tried to have it both ways. He sent a wagon train to Fort Wallace to get supplies, and, if Libbie had indeed gone there, it could bring her back. If she were still at Fort Hays, the wagon train could send word for her to come to Fort Wallace and join it for its return journey. Custer also sent a detail of eleven men, under the command of Major Joel Elliott, to Fort Sedgwick to bring back any orders Sherman may have left for Custer there.

Both were bad decisions, perilous not only to the two groups of soldiers traveling alone through Indian territory but to Libbie as well. He was deliberately exposing his men and his wife to great danger just so they could be together while he was in the middle of a military campaign against Indians. One historian wrote that "Custer's mistakes were overwhelming, even if understandable. His desire to have Libbie join him clouded his judgment. He was supposed to be scouting for ene-mies, [yet] one third of his fighting men escorted his wife safe-ly to his side and another group ran an errand to Fort Sedgwick for him. He was in the middle of the Great Plains, the territory swarming with hostile Indians, and he had divid-ed his relatively small force into three parts."

It was the beginning of a series of bad decisions, actions that would cloud Custer's record of glorious service in the Civil War. "His every major decision for the rest of the opera-tion had more to do with Libbie than with Sherman, Indians, his mission, or the welfare of his command." It was reason enough for a career to end in disgrace, but for Custer it was only a temporary setback on the road to everlasting glory.

On the morning of June 24, the day after both detachments left, Custer's camp was attacked by Indians. Custer raced from his tent clad in a red flannel robe, brandishing his Spencer car-bine, with no shoes, and his long hair uncombed. The troop-ers quickly drove off the attackers, but the Indians regrouped within sight of the camp. Custer sent Edmund Guerrier to arrange for a meeting. The Indians agreed.

Custer and six officers, with revolvers stuck in their belts— and the rest of the soldiers on alert, ready to move at a moment's notice—met the Indian delegation on the riverbank. It was Pawnee Killer and six other chiefs who once again spoke of friendship and peace with the whites. Through the interpreter, Pawnee Killer and Custer questioned each other about their intentions, but neither provided any useful information. Custer refused Pawnee Killer's request for coffee and sugar as well as ammunition. When the Indians left, Custer ordered a detail to follow, but it could not keep up with the faster Indian ponies.

Major Elliott's detail arrived safely back from Fort Sedgwick with orders from Sherman for Custer to continue the hunt for hostile Indians. On June 29, the wagon train returned from Fort Wallace; it had been attacked by some five hundred Cheyenne and Sioux warriors. The siege lasted more than three hours, but there were no fatalities.

Custer rushed to meet the wagons, but Libbie was not with the soldiers. She had not been at Fort Wallace and was no longer at Fort Hays. Heavy rains had led to severe flooding at Fort Hays, forcing Libbie to change her plans. It was known that she was traveling to the east, perhaps to Fort Riley, but Custer did not know where she was. "I was never so anxious in my life," he wrote. He set out immediately, exhibiting "the willfulness and lack of judgment which seemed to increase with his advancing age." He pushed his men in a series of forced marches in blazing heat without sufficient water, driven by his worry about his wife.

The troops began deserting on the first day, but Custer drove them on relentlessly. On July 15, he reached a railroad stop and telegraphed Fort Sedgwick. He was ordered to report to Fort Wallace and was told that a duplicate set of those orders had been sent to him with a detail of ten soldiers, led by twenty-five-year-old Second Lieutenant Lyman Kidder, who had no experience in Indian warfare.

Now Custer had a greater motivation—not only to find Libbie but also to locate Kidder's outfit before Pawnee Killer or some other Indian band got them. If that small detail of soldiers was wiped out, Custer would be blamed. If he had been where he was supposed to be, Kidder's party would not be out on the plains trying to find him.

Custer covered a grueling sixty miles that day, and thirty men deserted that night, nearly 10 percent of the regiment. He could not take the time to chase them down, so he pushed on the next morning. At noon, after marching fifteen miles, Custer halted the column for coffee and a brief rest. And then, in full view of the entire regiment, thirteen men headed across the prairie back the way they had come. It was the most blatant and astonishing example of desertion anyone had ever seen. If Custer let the men get away, as he had the thirty who deserted the night before, there would be no stopping anyone else who wanted to leave. He would likely arrive at Fort Wallace bearing the shame of having lost most of his regiment. He would be the laughingstock of the army. He had to make sure no one else deserted.

"Stop those men," he shouted. "Shoot them where you find them. Don't bring in any alive."

Tom Custer, Major Elliott, and Lieutenant William Cooke, the only officers whose horses were still saddled, rode off after the deserters. Less than thirty minutes later, shots were heard. Three were brought back wounded, but the rest got away. When Dr. Coates moved to tend to the wounded soldiers, Custer ordered him away. The men were placed in a wagon, the march resumed, and Custer later claimed that desertion was never a problem again.

About two hours later, making certain no troopers could hear him, Custer told Coates to treat the wounded. One man later died, apparently from the failure to treat his wounds in time.

They found Lieutenant Kidder and his men four days later. The first sign was an army-issue horse shot to death. Two miles farther on, they discovered another dead horse, with the saddle and equipment missing. Custer spotted buzzards circling in the air up ahead. He knew what that meant. Medicine Bill Comstock and the Delaware scouts raced ahead to explore and signaled the regiment to move forward.

As Custer described it, "A sight met our gaze which even at this remote day makes my very blood curdle. Lying in irregular order, and within a very limited circle, were the mangled bodies of poor Kidder and his party, yet so brutally hacked and disfigured as to be beyond recognition save as human beings. "The sinews of the arms and legs had been cut away, the noses of every man hacked off, and the features otherwise defaced so that it would have been scarcely possible for even a relative to recognize the unfortunate victims. We could not even distinguish the officer from his men. Each body was pierced by from twenty to fifty arrows, and the arrows were found as the savage demons had left them, bristling in the bodies."

They buried the dead in a trench and pushed on to reach Fort Wallace on July 13, but Libbie was not there. She had headed for Fort Riley, three hundred miles east. Cholera had broken out at Fort Leavenworth in Kansas and was reported to be spreading toward Fort Riley. Now frantic, Custer was determined to reach her, regardless of the condition of his men and horses, or his orders from General Sherman.

He abandoned his search for Indians, claiming that his horses were too tired to continue and that there were insufficient supplies at Fort Wallace. Both claims were true, but that did not prevent Custer from departing two evenings later, accompanied by one hundred men astride those horses judged to be in the best condition. They were escorting empty wagons for bringing back supplies from Fort Hays, a 150-mile journey. If he couldn't resupply the outfit there, he said, he planned to go seventy miles on to Fort Harker, which had a telegraph line.

They rode through the night, and the following day and night, stopping no more than an hour occasionally to feed the horses and brew coffee. The troopers fell asleep in the saddle and some lagged behind, their horses too exhausted to keep up. Indians, most likely from Pawnee Killer's band, ambushed a group of six men Custer had sent back to pick up his mare.

They were attacked while Custer was taking a rest at a stagecoach station. The station's officer recalled, "While at dinner, [Custer's] rear guard was attacked about three miles west of here, and those who came in reported two killed. Custer remained unconcerned, finished his dinner, and moved on without saying a word to me about the bodies, or thinking of hunting the Indians. Custer's lack of concern caused angry threats of mutiny among the men with him."

Elizabeth "Libbie" Custer. (*Library of Congress*)

In an incredible feat of endurance and stamina, they reached Fort Hays at three in the morning on July 18, having covered 150 miles in sixty hours with no more than six hours of rest. But Custer was not satisfied. He departed almost immediately for Fort Harker, accompanied by only two officers and two enlisted men. He believed they were far enough east to be safe from Indian raids. He ordered the remaining men and wagons to proceed to Fort Harker to pick up supplies.

Custer reached the post at two the following morning, after twelve hours in the saddle. He learned that a train was leaving for Fort Riley in one hour. He roused old Colonel Smith, who had previously been in command of the 7th Cavalry, and insisted that he had to get on that train. He had not seen his wife in six weeks, he explained, and promised to be back by the time his wagons reached Fort Harker. Smith, still half-asleep, agreed.

Libbie Custer described their reunion. She awoke to hear "the clank of a saber and with it the quick, springing steps of feet, unlike the quiet infantry around us. The door opened and with a flood of sunshine that poured in came a vision far brighter than even the brilliant Kansas sun. There before me, blithe and buoyant, stood my husband!"

Later that morning, a now wide awake Colonel Smith decided he had been wrong to grant Custer permission to go to Fort Riley when he was supposed to be fighting Indians. Custer had gone off for personal reasons and left his command. Smith telegraphed Fort Riley, ordering Custer to return on the next train. When he arrived, Smith had him arrested for desertion and held for court-martial.

The trial lasted a month, the verdict handed down October 11, 1867. George Armstrong Custer was found guilty on all counts: being absent from his command without authority, ordering deserters shot in the absence of a hearing, failing to attempt to find and bury the bodies of the troopers killed near Downer's Station, and excessive forced marching that was damaging to the horses.

Yet the sentence was surprisingly lenient: suspension from active service and forfeiture of pay for one year. He had jeopardized the lives of his men and had failed to carry out orders, all because he hadn't seen his wife in six weeks. He risked everything to be with her in a romantic, foolhardy, even juvenile gesture, one Custer never publicly regretted and that Libbie never forgot.

Years later, long after he had died, she would write, "There was in that summer of 1867 one long, perfect day. It was mine, and—blessed be our memory, which preserves to us the joys as well as the sadness of life!—it is still mine, for time and for eternity."

While the court-martial proceedings were under way in early autumn 1867, Black Kettle was attending yet another peace treaty council. Congress had established a new commission on July 20. Its charter was ambitious, as they all had been: to put in place a permanent peace with the hostile tribes of the Great Plains and to remove all of them, without exception, from proximity to roads and railroads. They were to be confined to reservations and learn to live like the whites, in wooden houses, tilling the soil and abandoning the ways of their ancestors and their culture. They would be taught how to be civilized.

Messengers were sent out at the end of summer to those bands of Cheyenne, Arapaho, and Kiowa-Apache known to be friendly, requesting their presence at Fort Larned. Little Raven and his small band of Arapaho arrived first, on September 2. They were poorly dressed and hungry but said they felt no need to make peace because they had not been at war. It was the Cheyenne, they insisted, who had been on the warpath all summer.

Black Kettle came the following day, with seven other Cheyenne. They appeared well dressed and well fed, and rode strong, healthy ponies, but were not overly friendly. Even Black Kettle was uncharacteristically sullen and morose. He shook hands reluctantly with the post commander but spoke very little.

Perhaps he had lost hope that a permanent peace could ever be achieved, having seen so many previous attempts fail. Treaties on which he had made his mark in trust had not improved the lot of his people. Indeed, it continued to worsen as more settlers, roads, and railroad cars scarred the land that was once Cheyenne.

Or perhaps it was because he had lost standing among his people, increasingly the target of blame for the failure to achieve peace. Black Kettle had little influence beyond his own small band. Many younger warriors ridiculed and shamed him for still having faith in the government's promises. Worse, the Dog Soldier chiefs taunted him and called him a coward; some even threatened his life if he persisted in dealing with the whites.

Neither Black Kettle nor the few remaining peace chiefs had been able to persuade the Cheyenne warriors to stop their raids. Despite his lack of success and the threats against him, Black Kettle still chose to meet this latest in a string of peace commissions from Washington. In addition to the lengthy sessions held over the coming weeks, he talked with the government representatives at night, albeit surreptitiously.

"When the other Cheyennes arrived, [Black Kettle] dropped into the background, though it was clear to the reporters that he was still insisting on negotiations. The newsmen agreed that Black Kettle placed himself in grave personal danger by speaking out so consistently for a treaty."

Fort Larned, as with other army posts, was no longer considered an appropriate place to hold a council. The Indians distrusted the soldiers too much. Too many times, troops had fired on Indians for approaching a fort, and so there was the danger that even a small incident could spark a major clash. If these latest meetings were to have any chance of success, they would have to occur on neutral territory where the Indians would feel less threatened.

Little Raven suggested that the talks be held at Medicine Lodge Creek, where the Indians often camped, sixty miles south of Fort Larned. Superintendent of Indian Affairs Murphy agreed. On September 17, he and Wynkoop left the fort with wagons full of supplies. They had an Indian escort of forty Arapaho, Kiowa-Apache, and Cheyenne braves to protect them from roving hostile bands. When they arrived three days later they found one thousand five hundred Arapaho camped at Medicine Lodge Creek, with a large village of Kiowa and Comanche twenty miles away. Murphy and Wynkoop were informed that a band of hostile Cheyenne led by Roman Nose, Tall Bull, and other war chiefs were three days' ride away. Edmund Guerrier was sent out with a letter from Murphy inviting the war chiefs to the council. He returned with them a week later.

Using the language of the time, Murphy told the Indians he wanted to take them by the hand and make a good road to peace and happiness. Some chiefs remained skeptical because they had heard the same words before, but all were encouraged by the fact that Murphy had come to them without bringing soldiers. The Cheyenne chief Grey Beard, one of the skeptics, said that the only reason they had gone to war was that General Hancock's soldiers had burned their village. "We are only revenging that one thing," Grey Beard said.

Murphy replied that Hancock had burned the Indian village without the approval of the Great Father in Washington and that he had been sent far away from Indian country. Apparently satisfied, Grey Beard and Roman Nose agreed to return to their camp and bring other war chiefs to the council.

Murphy went back to Fort Larned to escort the peace commissioners to Medicine Lodge Creek. On October 13, a train of sixty-five wagons left the fort with the seven commissioners, including Colonel Tappan, who had presided over Chivington's army hearing in Denver. The governor, lieutenant governor, and senator from Kansas came along, together with eleven reporters (including Stanley), and a photographer. Major Elliott led five hundred men of the 7th Cavalry, well armed and supplied, carrying forty-four thousand rounds for their carbines and ten thousand rounds for a battery of Gatling guns, an early type of machine gun.

When the delegation arrived at Medicine Lodge Creek, more than five thousand Indians had assembled, waiting to hear what the promises would be this time. But first, an appropriate setting had to be constructed for the meetings. The men of the 7th Cavalry set to work. Stanley described the scene for his readers:

"A vast amphitheater had been cleared in the center of a grove of elms. Logs had been arranged so as to seat the principal chiefs of the southern nations. Tables were erected for the

accommodation of the various correspondents. Before these
tables were the seats arranged in a semicircle for the commissioners. Facing the commissioners were a few of the select
chiefs of the different tribes."

The council proceeded, a lively affair on both sides, characterized by bizarre costumes and colorful behavior. Reporters
were drawn to the only woman present at the meetings,
Margaret Adams, an interpreter for the Arapaho. She was in
her early thirties, had been married three times, and was
accompanied by her thirteen-year-old daughter. Margaret's
father had been a French-Canadian trader and her mother an
Arapaho. She had spent most of her life with the tribe.

Stanley was quite taken with her; he described her as
"dressed in a crimson petticoat, black cloth coat, and a small
coquettish velvet hat, decorated with a white ostrich feather."
At the opening meeting, she created a sensation by appearing
in a red satin dress. Another reporter wrote that she seemed to
be drunk.

Among the commissioners and other officials were the
memorable Major General John Sanborn—"Black Whiskers"
to the Indians—who looked "resplendent in a purple suit."
General William "White Whiskers" Harney, "physically huge
and ceremoniously erect, would have made a show by himself.
With a great masculine head topped by an epicene little cap of
the sort college sophomores used to wear, he could be mistak-
en for a gingerbread general." General Alfred Terry was
described by one writer as "calmly dumb," by another as
"intrepid."

Tappan sat through the sessions amusing himself by whit-
tling sticks. Sanborn picked his teeth and laughed a great deal,
while Harney glared from one Indian face to another. Terry
doodled, printing the letters of the alphabet in sequence over
and over as though preparing for a schoolroom test. Colonel
Jesse Leavenworth, then Indian agent for the Kiowas and
Comanches, watched his children play nearby; one sat beneath
the commissioners' table.

The chiefs were arrayed in their most elaborate finery, with faces painted in red ocher and multicolored designs. After US Senator John Henderson of Missouri completed his obligatory, and probably dreaded, embraces with the chiefs, reporters noted that the Indians' face paint tended to rub off. Henderson's "nose was yellow, one cheek retained a red streak, and the other cheek had several green tattoos. No color photos exist, but a black-and-white picture reveals a middle-aged man with a grizzled beard, plenty of forehead, and frazzled hair. The pupils' of his eyes are distinctly enlarged, giving him a dazed look, as though he could not believe it."

In deference to the importance of the occasion, some chiefs had taken the colorful blankets they draped around their bodies and spread them over anthills. The ants swarmed over the blankets and picked them clean of lice. A vigorous shake of the blanket then got rid of the ants, an effective cleaning method.

Black Kettle was dressed in a long blue robe and a dragoon's hat. The Kiowa chief Santanta had a brass bugle hanging around his neck, which he played from time to time. His face was smeared with red paint. For battle, he painted his entire body, but for the peace council he had donned a blue US Army officer's uniform with epaulets, and tiny brass bells attached to the leggings.

Other chiefs wore shiny brass medallions and silver crosses, feathered bonnets, moccasins decorated with beads, and pieces of army uniforms, which, they boasted, were taken from the bodies of dead soldiers but more likely had been gifts from the president in Washington.

As the meetings began, the Indians' attention was deliberately diverted to the wagons piled high with some $150,000 worth of goods. The gifts were displayed in three huge piles: one for Kiowa and Comanche, one for Arapaho, and the third for Cheyenne. The array was dazzling: bushel baskets of glass beads, boxes of knives and trinkets of every color and shape, and of the most questionable taste. Even frilly dresses had been included, which Wynkoop had complained about to no avail.

"Nothing had changed," he wrote. "Many of the gifts would prove useless. The [Indians] might delight in touching them, but they would never use them." The chiefs were allowed to look over the mound of goods, but they could not touch them or claim them until they signed the treaty.

Surplus items from the Civil War were also in the stacks: 2,000 army blankets, uniforms complete from hat to boots, and, by actual count, 3,423 brass bugles, which would often be heard in battles to come. There were guns, too, and kegs of black powder, percussion caps, and lead and paper cartridges.

Once the warriors got their hands on the guns, they tried to fire them right away. Quite a few were disappointed and injured when the revolvers exploded in their hands. These were cheap, shoddy weapons made by a war profiteer, but among the rubbish were also fifty-four fine repeating rifles and one hundred Colt revolvers. The Indians knew that Colts always worked, and they, too, would be heard in future battles.

Some civilian commissioners were concerned about giving away guns and powder, but the generals assured them that the Indians needed weapons and ammunition for hunting. One reporter argued that the Indians were low on ammunition because they had used so much of it to kill white settlers and remarked sarcastically that it was quite sporting of the government to give them more.

Among the presents were heaps of groceries, more food than most Indians saw in a year, and more than they could load onto their ponies to carry away. The government's system of purchasing, accounting, and inventory had no provision for returning anything from where the prescribed form said it should be delivered, so nothing could be brought back. Much of this food would be left to rot in the field.

The chiefs all delivered brief speeches about wanting peace and being pleased to be receiving the gifts. But sounding a different note, Black Kettle petulantly blamed other tribes for the current troubles. Stanley recorded his words: "We were once friends with the whites, but you [other tribes] nudged us out of the way by your intrigues, and now when we are in council you keep nudging each other. Why don't you talk and go straight, and let all be well?" Little Raven agreed and urged the other chiefs to behave.

The commissioners spoke about friendship and good will. They wanted to protect, feed, and house the Indians, but of course the tribes would have to give up their old way of life. Senator Henderson told them bluntly what they would have to change:

> What we say to you may at first be unpleasant, but if you follow our advice it will bring you good, and you will soon be happy. You say you do not like the medicine houses of the whites but you prefer the buffalo and the chase, and express a wish to do as your fathers did. We say to you that the buffalo will not last forever. When that day comes, the Indian must change the road his father trod or suffer and probably die. We tell you that to change will make you better. We wish for you to live, and we offer you the way.
>
> The whites are settling all the good lands. They have come to the Arkansas River. When they come, they drive out the buffalo. If you oppose them, war must come. They are many and you are few. You may kill some of them, but others will take their place. And finally [you] will have no homes. We are your best friends, and now, before all the good lands are taken by whites, we wish to set aside a part of them for your exclusive home. We will build you a house to hold the goods we send and when you become hungry and naked, you can go there and be fed and clothed. We will send a physician to live with you and heal your wounds and take care of you when you are sick. We will send a blacksmith to shoe your ponies so that they will not get lame. We will send a farmer to show your people how to grow corn and wheat, and we will send a mill to make your meal and flour.

We propose to make that home on the Red River and around the Wichita Mountains, and we have prepared papers for that purpose. Tomorrow morning at nine o'clock we want your chiefs and head men to meet us at our camp and sign the papers.

A long, sullen silence settled over the council like a dank fog. No one spoke until Henderson asked if anyone had questions about the terms of the treaty. Santanta rose to his feet and, with a visible effort to hold his fury in check, spoke briefly. His words were terse, clipped, and cold:

"I ask the Commission to tell the Great Father what I have to say. When the buffalo leave the country, we will let him know. By that time we will be ready to live in houses."

The following morning was cold and windy; the sky was gray and menacing. The ground was damp, and water filled the deep ruts made by the wagons so overloaded with presents. So much bounty the Indians' for the taking; just sign the treaty, giving up all the desirable land they had been awarded by the terms of the last treaty, land they had been told was theirs forever. They would also have to pledge not to interfere with the railroad, settlements, or wagon trains, and not to kill and scalp any whites.

But first, the Indians had more remarks to deliver. Stanley listened to them all, but the one he found most moving was by Satank, the aging chief of the Kiowa. He held up the silver medal he wore around his neck. It showed the profile of James Buchanan, fifteenth president of the United States. "Look at the medal I wear," he said. "By wearing this, I have been made poor. Before, I was rich in horses and lodges. Today I am the poorest of all. When you gave me this silver medal on my neck, you made me poor. Do for us what is best. Teach us the road to travel. We know you will not forsake us; and tell your people also to act as you have done. And now the time has

Cheyenne leaders shaking hands with the American commissioners after the negotiations at Medicine Lodge Creek in 1867. (*Library of Congress*)

come that I must go. You may never see me more, but remember Satank as the white man's friend."

The old chief walked silently down the line of commissioners, solemnly shaking each one's hand. He said no more.

Black Kettle did not speak again before the commission. A few days before the signing ceremony, he was called away by the Dog Soldiers, who had threatened to kill his horses if he signed the treaty. He managed to dissuade them, and they permitted him to return to the council. There he made his mark on the Medicine Lodge Creek Treaty of 1867.

Other chiefs also signed, but some war chiefs, including Roman Nose, did not. Several agreed to make their mark "only after Senator Henderson took [them] aside and promised them, contrary to the terms of the document, that they would still be able to roam and hunt the buffalo prairies of Western Kansas." Stanley and Major Elliott, among others, believed that the Indians did not understand the terms of the document they were signing, how much of their land and way of life they were giving away. Stanley reported that not a single word of the treaty was ever read aloud at the conference.

Captain Barnitz of the 7th Cavalry wrote that the Cheyenne were "superstitious in regard to touching the pen, or perhaps they supposed that by doing so they would be signing away their rights, which is doubtless the true state of affairs, as they have no idea what they are giving up, or that they have given up the country they claim as their own. The treaty amounts to nothing, and we will certainly have another war sooner than later with the Cheyenne, at least, and probably with the other Indians, in consequence of misunderstanding of the terms of the present and previous treaties."

No matter. It was done. After the signing, the Indians accepted the presents from the commissioners. They heaped as much of the loot as they could onto their ponies and filed slowly away across the empty plains to their winter camps. Shortly after, the commissioners and the soldiers rode away from Medicine Lodge Creek, leaving stocks of rotting food behind them. Vultures and coyotes stood ready to devour the decaying feast.

ELEVEN

WAR IS
SURELY
UPON US

B lack Kettle's Cheyenne lived in peace with the whites through the winter of 1867–68, even though they stayed on the land between the Platte and the Arkansas rivers. They fought their traditional enemies, the Kaw and Osage tribes, and continued roaming the territories freely to hunt buffalo, as their ancestors had done for generations.

They still traded buffalo robes for food, gaudy trinkets, and whiskey. It was illegal to sell whiskey to Indians, but the chances of being caught were low and the profits enormous, so the practice flourished unabated, sometimes within sight of army posts. Cheyenne men tended to become truculent with a bellyful of liquor, and they harassed any white settlers whose paths they crossed. But no one died and no scalps were taken.

In February 1868, Black Kettle, Little Raven, and several war chiefs brought their people to Major Wynkoop at Fort Larned for the distribution of food for the winter, as promised by the Medicine Lodge Creek Treaty. Wynkoop gave out eighty tons of beef, sixty tons of flour, twenty tons of bacon, five tons of coffee, ten tons of sugar, and four and a half tons of salt. He informed Superintendent of Indian Affairs Thomas Murphy that the food provided should keep the Cheyenne content and help to civilize them by persuading them to give up hunting.

Wynkoop was wrong. The supplies were not sufficient to see the Indians through the winter, nor did the quantity meet the terms of the Medicine Lodge Creek Treaty. The problem was that Congress had not yet ratified the treaty, though four months had passed since the chiefs had made their marks. As a result, Wynkoop did not have the money to purchase more food to distribute.

Wynkoop pleaded with Black Kettle to be patient and to keep his young men from going to war while they waited for Congress to approve the treaty. Black Kettle was disappointed. He knew that if the Indians did not receive what had been promised, the warriors would blame him yet again for signing a treaty with the government.

"Our white brothers are pulling away from us the hand they gave us at Medicine Lodge," Black Kettle told Wynkoop, "but we will try to hold on to it. We hope the Great Father will take pity on us and let us have the guns and ammunition he promised us so we can hunt buffalo and keep our families from going hungry."

Wynkoop also hoped to obtain the weapons due the Cheyenne, but there were other difficulties as well, eroding the chances of success for the Medicine Lodge Creek Treaty. Black Kettle's Cheyenne and Little Raven's Arapaho were becoming increasingly discontent. Both chiefs told George Bent that, despite having signed the new treaty, they were not willing to be confined to a reservation along the Red River.

They wanted to move west and go into the Rocky Mountains, where they believed they could live on their own and avoid all contact with the whites. They did not yet realize, or accept, that virtually all the territory was rapidly filling up with settlers. The Cheyenne were running out of land, and time.

Peace lasted until summer. In May, after losing a battle with the Kaw, Cheyenne braves stole some cattle and scared a few settlers away from their ranches around Council Grove in east-central Kansas. When word of those incidents reached Superintendent Murphy, he ordered Wynkoop to withhold the guns and ammunition from the distribution the Cheyenne were due to receive in July.

When some fifteen thousand Indians arrived at Fort Larned on July 20 for their goods, Wynkoop had prepared everything the Medicine Lodge Creek Treaty promised, except for the guns and ammunition. These were being held back, he told the chiefs, because of the raids on cattle ranches. The chiefs conferred and said they would not accept any supplies until they got the weapons. They needed to be able to hunt during the summer and fall in order to store up enough meat for their people in winter. Otherwise the tribes would starve.

After several weeks, Wynkoop was finally given permission to distribute the arms, as long as he was confident they were necessary to keep the peace and that Black Kettle understood they were not to be used against whites. On August 9, the Indians were given 160 revolvers, 12 kegs of powder, 1 1/2 kegs of lead, and 15,000 percussion caps. They were admonished to use these only for hunting. The following day, Wynkoop wrote to the Bureau of Indian Affairs in Washington:

"I have the honor to inform you that I yesterday made the whole issue of annuity goods, arms, and ammunition to the Cheyenne chiefs and people of their nation. They were delighted at receiving the goods, particularly the arms and ammunition, and expressed themselves as being so well contented, previous to this issue. I made them a long speech. They have now left for their hunting grounds, and I am perfectly satisfied that there will be no trouble with them this season and consequently with no Indians of my Agency."

Wrong again. On the day Wynkoop wrote that letter, August 10, a band of Cheyenne went on a rampage north of Fort Larned, beating a white settler and repeatedly raping his wife and her sister. That was only the beginning. Within a week, two hundred Cheyenne, along with some Sioux and Arapaho, had killed more than a dozen settlers, kidnapped several children, set homes and barns afire, stolen cattle, and forced hundreds to flee for their lives.

On Sunday, August 16, a band of Cheyenne killed Medicine Bill Comstock, Custer's favorite scout, who had previously been welcome in the camps of the Cheyenne and other tribes. They shot him down on the prairie under the pretext of escorting him and a companion to safety. His friend, wounded, managed to flee.

There was no question that Cheyenne were involved in these depredations during August. Each tribe and each band within a tribe made its own arrows, which provided identification as unique and distinctive as a fingerprint. The arrows found on the dead settlers in western Kansas came from the camps of Medicine Arrows, Bull Bear, and Black Kettle.

In a harsh judgment on the peace chiefs in this instance, one historian wrote:

> Black Kettle and the other chiefs were, without doubt, in their villages when the criers were calling among the tipis for warriors to assemble for the preliminary war dance and smoker at which plans for the raid would be discussed. Indian raids were always carefully planned, and the medicine man was called upon to determine whether the omens were favorable. The chief of each village must have been aware that a foray was in the making.

Perhaps the so-called friendly chiefs tried to prevent the raid. More likely they did not. In any event, they continued to profess friendship to the whites and to receive government bounty, even after the war party had started on its way. And they did nothing to warn their white 'friends' that some of their people were about to be murdered by Indians who had recently promised to give up such practices.

Attitudes were hardening on both sides. Murphy felt betrayed when he learned about the rampage. "I can no longer have confidence in what they say or promise," he wrote. "War is surely upon us."

Indeed, it was all-out war. Savage attacks continued into September. Raiding parties even attacked small detachments of soldiers. Wynkoop tried to defend the Indians as best he could. He did not deny that some Cheyenne participated in the killings—the evidence was too damning to deny—but he argued that they had become violent because of food shortages. If only Congress had appropriated more money for supplies, Wynkoop believed, there would have been no outbreaks of violence.

Murphy disagreed with Wynkoop and demanded that the Cheyenne and Arapaho be held accountable. He insisted that the US government had fulfilled its part of the Medicine Lodge Creek Treaty obligations and had given the Indians all the goods to which they were entitled. The Indians had broken their pledge not to attack whites, and as a result the army should fight them until they sued for peace.

Wynkoop felt betrayed by the peace chiefs who could not (or did not) restrain their warriors, but he disagreed with Murphy's conclusion that only the army could deal with the Indians. On October 17, he resigned as Indian agent, having served the Cheyenne and Arapaho for four years. His resignation was an admission of failure. This well-intentioned soldier-turned-Indian agent disappeared from the history of the West, leaving the Cheyenne with no more influential friends in high places.

Now it was up to the army to deal with the Indians. The last time it attempted to do so, General Hancock destroyed a Cheyenne village at Pawnee Creek, setting off a new round of violence. And before that, Chivington destroyed a Cheyenne village at Sand Creek, spawning a war.

The raids and murders continued throughout the fall. Lieutenant Francis Gibson of the 7th Cavalry compiled a report for the period August to November 1868: "murdered 117, wounded 16, scalped 32, women outraged 14, women captured 4, children captured 2, horses and mules stolen 619, stock cattle stolen 938." There was also an unverified report of fourteen white children being found frozen to death in what had been an Indian encampment.

Wagon trains, ranches, stagecoach stations, and army detachments were targets. Men were cut down by bullet, arrow, and lance; women carried off into a long night of captivity that few survived. War parties two hundred strong laid siege to army units for hours or days before reinforcements raised a trail of dust in the distance, a most welcome sight when a soldier was down to his last bite of hardtack, his canteen was empty, and the few bullets he had left could be held in one clenched fist.

Colonel George Forsyth commanded a group of fifty scouts and frontiersmen, a special unit designed to travel light and fast enough to catch Indians. They were ambushed by Cheyenne led by Pawnee Killer on September 17 while camped on the bank of the Arikaree Fork of the Republican River. The scouts took up defensive positions on an island, thereafter to be known as Beecher's Island, named for Lieutenant Frederick Beecher, a nephew of Henry Ward Beecher's, the prominent social reformer and abolitionist. Lieutenant Beecher had fought valiantly in the Civil War but did not survive the eight-day siege by Indians. Men suffered horrible wounds that could not be treated. The heat was awful, the food supply gave out, and there was the constant fear of being overrun. On the fourth day one man wrote, "It was very hot, our meat had become putrid, and the stench from the dead horses lying close around us was almost intolerable."

"Still looking anxiously for relief," wrote another on the seventh night. "Starvation is staring us in the face, nothing but horse meat."

The charge of Roman Nose against Colonel George Forsyth's command. (*Library of Congress*)

And on the last day: "All fresh meat gone. Made some soup tonight from putrid horse meat. My God! Have you deserted us?"

The warrior chief Roman Nose was killed on the first day. He knew he was going to die but led the charge anyway. A medicine man had warned that if he ever ate food that had been touched by iron, he would die. "At the Sioux camp the other day something was done that I was told must not be done," he said. "The bread I ate was taken out of the frying pan with something made of iron. I have been told not to eat anything so treated. If I go into this fight, I shall certainly be killed."

On the ninth day of the siege, with nearly half of Forsyth's command dead or wounded, a column of riders appeared, a troop of Buffalo Soldiers from the 10th Cavalry. The racial origin of the rescuers was noted in the language of the day in the memoirs of one survivor: "[They] were Negroes, but boy, were we glad to see them!"

A larger military force was going after the Cheyenne to the south and east. Composed of nine companies of the 7th Cavalry and a company of infantry, the outfit was commanded by Brigadier General Alfred Sully, son of Thomas Sully, the well-known portrait painter. Sully had extensive combat experience in the Mexican War, the Civil War, and against Indians in the Dakotas. He led his men out of Fort Dodge on the Arkansas River on the afternoon of September 17. His orders were to do battle with the Cheyenne and Arapaho. It was a huge display of US military might, but it was ungainly and slow, limited to the speed of the heavily laden wagons and the marching cadence of the infantry.

Even this massive force was not safe from Indians. Three days later, Cheyenne warriors ambushed it and fought the troopers to a standstill. After three days of continuous attacks, Sully retreated to the fort to await reinforcements. Cheyenne warriors followed the troops all the way back, thumbing their noses at the soldiers and slapping their buttocks, traditional gestures of scorn. Sully noted that he was impressed by the precision with which the war chiefs controlled the movements of their men, signaling their commands with bugle calls. (Sully did not say if he knew the Indians had gotten the bugles from the government as part of their annual bounty.)

Sully's show of force had failed to resolve the Indian problem, and so had Forsyth's smaller, more mobile group. Both failures reinforced the Indians' confidence that they could defeat any soldiers sent after them. Consequently, they became even more daring in planning raids.

General Sherman refused to acknowledge defeat and remained determined to punish the Indians severely for their assaults on white settlements and railroads. "All the Cheyenne and Arapaho are now at war," he wrote to the secretary of war. "Admitting that some of them have not done acts of murder, rape, et cetera, still they have not restrained those who have, nor have they on demand given up the criminals, as they agreed to do."

The Indians' only choices as far as Sherman was concerned were war or peace, extermination or survival. They could move to their assigned reservations or be hunted down like the buffalo. He requested that food supplies be made available at Fort Cobb, south of the Arkansas River, for whatever Indians survived the army's next campaign, but he also made it clear that he did not think there would be many survivors.

Nor did he want there to be. On September 23, while Forsyth's men remained under siege and shortly after Sully retreated, Sherman wrote to his brother, "The more we can kill this year, the less will have to be killed in the next war, for the more I see of these Indians, the more convinced I am that they will all have to be killed or be maintained as a species of paupers. Their attempts at civilization are simply ridiculous."

Sherman told Colonel Tappan that he had approved of the peacemaking policies of the Bureau of Indian Affairs in the past, but now it was too late to talk of peace. "They laugh at our credulity," he said, "rape our women, burn whole trains with their drivers to cinders, and send word that they never intended to keep their treaties. We must submit, or we must fight them."

The new campaign against the Cheyenne would be mounted by General Sheridan, whom Sherman had appointed to command the Department of the Missouri. The obstinate Sheridan made his attitude toward the Indians clear from the start; he remarked that the only good Indians he ever saw were dead. That sentiment swept the national consciousness, rephrased as, "The only good Indian is a dead Indian." Sherman knew what he was getting when he selected Sheridan to carry out the nation's policies.

"The Indian is a lazy, idle vagabond," Sheridan wrote in an official report in 1869. "He never labors and has no profession except that of arms, to which he is raised from a child; a scalp is constantly dangled before his eyes, and the highest honor he can aspire to is to possess one taken by himself."

Sheridan's beliefs were supported by his observations on a tour of the territory four months after the signing of the Medicine Lodge Creek Treaty, and by his meeting with a Cheyenne chief at Fort Larned. Chief Stone Calf said, "Let your soldiers grow long hair, so that we can have some honor in killing them."

Sheridan's war was to be without mercy, without pity. On October 15, Sherman sent a message to Sheridan that sanctioned any action whatsoever, as long as it led to victory. Sherman wrote that as soldiers they had to

> accept the war begun by our enemies, and hereby resolve to make its end final. If it results in the utter annihilation of these Indians, it is but the result of what they have been warned again and again, and for which they seem fully prepared. I will say nothing and do nothing to restrain our troops from doing what they deem proper on the spot, and will allow no mere vague general charges of cruelty and inhumanity to tie their hands, but will use all the powers confided to me to the end that these Indians, the enemies of our race and of our civilizations, shall not again be able to begin to carry on their barbarous warfare. You may now go ahead in your own way and I will back you with my whole authority, and stand between you and any efforts that may be attempted in your rear to restrain your purpose or check your troops.

Sherman was granting him license to do whatever was required to end the Indian problem. No matter what Sheridan and his troops did in the field, Sherman would support and protect him. It was, essentially, a more genteel and polished version of what Chivington had told his men before he set them loose at Sand Creek.

Sheridan had his orders, as well as assurances of no recrimination. Now he needed a new and daring approach to the battle, and a new and daring commander to carry it out. He decided to launch a winter campaign— when the snow and cold would keep the Indians in their camps, when their ponies were weak from lack of prairie grass, and when they would not be expecting an attack, for they believed that white troops could not hunt Indians in the freezing winds and snows on the Great Plains.

General Philip Sheridan after the Civil War. (*National Archives*)

So that was Sheridan's plan; now he needed someone capable of leading such a bold, unorthodox attack.

TWELVE

THE STAR
OF THE
WASHITA

Headquarters, Department of the Missouri,
In the field, Fort Hays, Kansas,
September 24, 1868
To General G. A. Custer, Monroe, Michigan
Generals Sherman, Sully, and myself, and nearly all the officers of
your regiment, have asked for you, and I hope the application will
be successful. Can you come at once? Eleven companies of your reg-
iment will move about the 1st of October against the hostile Indians.
(signed) P. H. Sheridan
Major General Commanding

Custer received this telegram while he and Libbie were having
dinner at a friend's house. He wired Sheridan immediately that
he was coming, and took the train west the following day. He
had served ten months of the twelve-month suspension from
duty the court-martial had imposed on him, and he was eager
to get back.

What a glorious sense of vindication and satisfaction he felt, knowing that the army wanted him—needed him—to fight the Indians. He had followed the news closely during his suspension and knew about every campaign, every foray and raid, and, more important, every failure the army had suffered at the hands of the Indians. Even though Custer, too, had failed because he had not been able to find any Indians, he was convinced that he could do a better job than any other army commander. All he needed was a chance, and now he had it.

But why, considering Custer's record against the Indians, did Sheridan select Custer to lead the new offensive? And why did Sherman approve of this choice? One historian suggested that "Sheridan had seen Custer in action in the Civil War and knew that the boy general would fight if he had the opportunity, while Sherman may have reasoned that Custer would be so determined to salvage his reputation that he would either get the job done or die in the attempt." Whatever the reason, Custer's exile from active service was over.

But Sherman was wrong about Custer's wanting to salvage his reputation; Custer did not believe it needed restoring. He insisted that his name was still prominent and felt no shame or embarrassment about the court-martial. He thought he had been made a scapegoat for Hancock's failure and brought to trial to divert public attention from Hancock's disastrous campaign, not because he had done anything improper himself. Even Sheridan had stated publicly that he thought Custer had been wronged.

The result was that Custer had enjoyed a pleasant, ten-month holiday. He and Libbie had spent the winter and spring with friends at Fort Leavenworth, residing in Sheridan's quarters on the post. They attended all the dinners, dances, and other social activities that marked the winter season. As one historian observed, "It could hardly be said that Custer did penance for his misdeed in leaving Fort Wallace, for he had quite an agreeable time with his comrades at Fort Leavenworth."

In the spring they returned to Monroe, to the house of Libbie's late father. Custer spent his days hunting and fishing, and working on his memoirs, published as *My Life on the Plains*. He was so circumspect about his court-martial that he never mentioned it directly. He wrote that he was "living in involuntary but unregretful retirement from active service." He also wrote about "official examination of certain events and transactions to determine if each and every one of my acts had been performed with due regard to the customs of war in like cases. To enter into a review of the proceedings which followed, would be to introduce into these pages matters of too personal a character to interest the general reader. It will suffice to say that I was placed in temporary retirement from active duty." Custer always referred to that period as a forced and temporary retirement. The term *court-martial* was never used, and once he received that telegram from Sheridan recalling him to active duty, there was no need to ever refer to it again.

"Now I can smoke a cigar in peace," Sheridan said when Custer reported for duty at Fort Hays on October 4. Custer was also welcomed warmly by most of the men of the 7th Cavalry when he rejoined the regiment a week later at their camp forty miles south of Fort Dodge. One trooper wrote, "We are all glad to see him again, as he was the only man capable of taking charge of the regiment." An officer described how the outfit had deteriorated in Custer's absence, "but with his coming, action, purpose, energy and general strengthening of the loose joints was the order of the day."

Those in the anti-Custer clique, however—some of whom had testified against him at his court-martial—were not so pleased. It was to Custer's credit that he never sought revenge against those he believed had wronged him. While he was less than cordial, even refusing to shake hands with one of them, he never took action that might have harmed their careers.

"My official actions shall not be tarnished by a single unjust or partial act," he wrote to Libbie.

About two hours after Custer returned to his outfit, just as he was sitting down to dinner, Indians attacked the camp, riding in circles around the perimeter. He grabbed his carbine and joined his men. "I wish you could have been with us," he wrote to a friend. "You would never ask to go to a circus after seeing Indians ride and perform in a fight. It was like shooting swallows on the wing, so rapid were they in their movements."

The Indians stayed out of rifle range but near enough to be seen making defiant gestures to the troopers. Custer was told the Indians attacked almost every day now and that the regiment was effectively under siege, with orders to stay within the camp's perimeter. Custer immediately set out with a contingent of men to strike back at the Indians, but they disappeared.

He began an ambitious program of reorganization and training to prepare the men for a strenuous winter war. He started with target practice, holding daily drills for firing at targets set at one hundred to three hundred yards away. They had an incentive to shoot well: Custer told them that the best forty would be labeled sharpshooters and form an elite unit led by Lieutenant William Cooke. They would march separately from the main column and be excused from guard duty, which meant they could count on sleeping through the night.

Next, he ordered all officers and men to turn in their horses, a practice known in the cavalry as coloring the horses. The horses were arranged so that each company rode horses similar in color—gray, black, sorrel, chestnut, and brown—to bring about uniformity in the appearance of the regiment. It looked nice, of course, but it meant that the men had to give up the horses they had cared for and bonded with over time. Captain Barnitz noted that he was "indignant and provoked in consequence of Custer's orders with regard to the new horses. All my old horses were well trained, and very carefully trained, and the men were much attached to them, and now, just as we are to march on the campaign, everything is to be turned topsy-turvy!"

Custer then turned his attention to the regimental scouts, whites and Indians. His Indian scouts were twelve Osage led by Chief Little Beaver. "They are painted and dressed for the war-path," Custer wrote to a friend, "and well armed with Springfield breech-loading guns. All are superb horsemen. We mounted them on good horses, and to show us how they can ride and shoot, they took a stick of ordinary cordwood, threw it on the ground, and then, mounted on their untried horses, they rode at full speed and fired at the stick of wood as they flew by, and every shot struck the target."

Custer's favorite white scout was Moses Embree Milner, known as "California Joe," even though he was from Kentucky. He was a big, shaggy, unkempt man, perhaps in his forties, and he preferred to ride a mule instead of a horse, claiming that was fast enough for him. He wore an old sombrero, buckskin trousers, and a flannel shirt. An observer described his "ponderous mat of flaming red whiskers. Both his hair and whiskers were well powdered with a series of layers of dust intermingled with stray blades of dry grass, leaves, and chips, reminding the beholder forcibly of the previous night's slumber on the bosom of mother earth."

"California Joe" had spent thirty years out West, and there was not a trail he could not track or an Indian he could not find, but he had one problem. He kept his canteen full of whiskey and seemed to be always thirsty. He got drunk the night Custer appointed him chief scout, so Custer reluctantly demoted him, but kept him with the regiment for the coming expedition. Custer chose the more sober and serious twenty-six-year-old Civil War veteran Ben Clark, who had spent years leading freight trains out West, to be his chief scout.

On November 12, 1868, Custer led the 7th Cavalry north. Behind the long line of troopers, four hundred wagons guarded by five companies of infantry stretched across the open prairie. Six days later they reached their destination, two hundred miles south of Fort Dodge: an empty stretch of ground a mile from the confluence of two creeks joining the North Canadian River.

There they built a fort with walls ten feet high, constructing two block-houses at opposite corners. Named Camp Supply, this was where the goods carried by the four hundred wagons would be stored for Custer's winter expedition. The five infantry companies would stay behind to guard the fort.

Moses Embree "California Joe" Milner. (*National Archives*)

Custer's plan was designed to catch the Indians by surprise while they were holed up in their winter camps. Despite Chivington's success four years earlier in attacking an Indian village in the snow and extreme cold, the Indians remained convinced that regular army troops would never be able to follow the example of those Colorado volunteers. "We are going into the heart of the Indian country," Custer wrote to Libbie, "where white troop have never been before. The Indians have grown up in the belief that soldiers cannot and dare not follow them there." Custer was out to prove them wrong.

General Sheridan arrived at Camp Supply on November 21 to see the expedition off and to bring gifts of buffalo overshoes and a fur hat with earmuffs for Custer. That evening, Custer ordered his regimental band to serenade Sheridan while he and his officers paid a courtesy call. Captain Barnitz wrote to his wife, "We all went up and called on General Sheridan. He received us in his good, genial way, shaking hands with all, and seemed well pleased to see us. He received us in the open air, around a big campfire."

Sheridan gave Custer his orders. He was to head south toward the Washita River, find the winter settlements of the hostile Indians, and burn the camps to the ground. Kill all the warriors, destroy all the horses, and take the women and children prisoners. This would be Custer's first chance to reclaim the glory he had known during the Civil War.

Barnitz wrote in his journal, "Considerable snow fell last night, and sleet, alternating with snow and rain today. The Seventh Cavalry is to march southward tomorrow at 6 AM with a month's supplies, in search of Indian villages. Reveille is to be at 4 AM, two hours before daylight."

A foot of snow covered the ground. As the troopers prepared to leave, Custer stopped at Sheridan's tent. When Sheridan asked if he was concerned about the snow, which was still falling heavily, Custer said it was just what he wanted. The worse the storm, the less watchful the Indians would be.

Second Lieutenant Frank Gibson of A Troop recalled the morning of their departure in a somewhat romanticized manner:

> Everybody was in prime condition as regards health and spirits, and the whole outfit was in for it, whether it turned out to be a fight, a fluke or a frolic. We dispatched a very hasty and early breakfast that morning, so early that it was like taking it the night before, and for all the good it did it might as well have been left for the crows. At the proper intervals the different signals for breaking camp and packing up were sounded, and finally everything being in readiness, the men mounted, the sharp notes of the advance cracked through the crisp air and the column moved forward to that old tune whose inspiring strains have cheered the heart of many a weary soldier, 'The Girl I Left Behind Me.' If each one had a girl, there were upward of eight hundred of them left behind on that occasion.

Sergeant John Ryan of M Troop had a more sober recollec-
tion: "To this day I have not forgotten that morning's march.
We had the capes of our overcoats drawn up tightly around
our heads and while marching in fours we could hardly see the
next set ahead of us because the blinding snow was so bad that
we had to turn our faces from it."

The snowstorm raged, fierce winds blew, and the horses
had to struggle with every step to break through the foot of
crust-covered snow. Everyone was blinded by the white,
swirling blur, and the troopers were warned to keep watch as
best they could on the man in front, for if someone accidental-
ly wandered off to one side, he would disappear. The regiment
managed to cover only fifteen miles that day before making
camp on Wolf Creek. Men and horses were exhausted, chilled
to the bone. "This has been a very disagreeable day," twenty-
five-year-old Lieutenant Edward Godfrey wrote in his journal.

Reveille sounded at four the next morning, and the men set
off again. By the third monotonous day of traveling, the snow
finally stopped, leaving a foot and a half covering the ground.
The scouts reported back; they had seen no Indians or any
Indian trails. When the troopers reached the banks of the
Canadian River, they found it wider than expected and partial-
ly iced over, making the crossing difficult, tedious, and time-
consuming.

The men had been ordered to carry no more clothing than
they could wear. But when one of the wagons got stuck trying
to cross the river, Custer ordered that it be unloaded. The men
found a trunk belonging to Lieutenant Owen Hale. "The
trunk was burst open and the contents, consisting of long
topped boots, corduroy pants, velvet pants, etc., dumped out,
and the men were given orders to help themselves, which they
promptly did. The owner of the clothing could do nothing, as
he had disobeyed orders."

Custer dispatched Major Elliott to press on ahead with
three troops of cavalry to keep up the search for Indians while
the main body of troops and wagons continued to cross the

river. When they were ready to resume the march, one of the scouts with Elliott returned with the news that they had found a trail left by a war party of about one hundred Indian warriors. It was roughly ten miles up the river, and less than a day old.

Custer sent the scout back on a fresh horse with orders for Elliott to follow the trail as quickly as he could through the snow. He also told the scout to inform Elliott that the rest of the expedition would try to catch up by nightfall. To do that, however, Custer would have to pare down to essentials. When the troopers moved out again, they left the wagon train to follow at its own pace, with an escort of eighty men. Each man carried only one hundred rounds of ammunition, a small amount of coffee and hard bread, and forage for the horses. Even tents and extra blankets were left with the wagons.

Custer led them on a hard ride all afternoon. The sun came out and began to melt the snow, so they were able to catch up with Elliott's group by nine that night. They found them in a small valley close by the Washita River. Custer permitted men and horses one hour's rest. He was determined to push on, even after dark, regardless of the possibility of an ambush. All that mattered to Custer was that Indians might be camped somewhere up ahead.

The Osage scouts wanted to wait for the morning to move on; they believed it was bad medicine to fight at night, but Custer refused. "Custer's rule, all through the Civil War, had always been to attack first and, if outnumbered, cut his way back afterwards. He had done this repeatedly at Beverly Ford, at Gettysburg. No superstitious Indians could bluff him."

By ten o'clock they were on their way, with the Osage three hundred to four hundred yards out in front, carefully tracking the Indians' trail. Lieutenant Gibson of A Troop remembered the concern about not alerting the Indians to their presence. He wrote that "no talking [was] permitted except in suppressed whispers; even the tramp of the horses as they broke through the top crust that had formed on the snow since sundown, made a noise that caused dismay in the command lest the hostiles be aroused by it."

Around midnight, the two scouts halted in the darkness, waiting for Custer to catch up.

"What is the matter?" Custer asked.

"We don't know," one of the scouts said, according to Custer's account, "but me smell fire."

Neither Custer nor any of his officers smelled anything unusual. They decided the scouts were wrong, and Custer ordered them to press on. The scouts stopped again after no more than a half mile.

"I told you so," one said.

This time they all smelled smoke, and they soon spotted the embers of a dying fire about one hundred yards distant. The scouts examined the area around the fire and reported that it had not been made by the war party they were tracking but by boys from a village who had been tending the ponies. That meant that an Indian camp was nearby.

Custer followed the two scouts as they slowly moved forward. As they approached each hill, they would crawl to the crest and peer over the top to see what lay ahead. They moved silently from ridge to ridge until one came back to tell Custer that he had spotted many Indians beyond the next hill.

Custer crept to the top of the ridge, peered into the valley, and saw a large number of animals a half mile away. Thinking it might be a herd of buffalo, he asked the scout why he thought Indians were there. The man said he had heard a dog bark. Custer listened, and soon he heard the ringing of a small bell and the cry of a baby. He had found his quarry, a village of nearly fifty lodges.

It was after midnight. Custer summoned his officers and told them to go quietly to the top of the ridge and see for themselves. Then he issued orders for the attack, to be made at the first light of dawn. He divided the command into four detachments. One would remain with Custer while the other three made their way right and left until they surrounded the village.

"General," one officer asked when the orders were given, "suppose we find more Indians than we can handle?"

"Huh," Custer answered, dismissing the question. "All I am afraid of is we won't find half enough. There are not Indians enough in the country to whip the Seventh Cavalry."

Had Custer sent scouts farther down the Washita Valley beyond the camp he was preparing to attack, he would have discovered a string of villages stretching ten miles and housing some six thousand Indians, many of them warriors. But, as was his habit in the Civil War, as he would do later at the Little Big Horn, Custer failed to reconnoiter the territory before attacking. He was unaware of the size and disposition of the enemy's forces.

Something else Custer did not know, and it would have made no difference if he had, was that the village ahead of him was the camp of Chief Black Kettle. And ironically, it was two days shy of the fourth anniversary of Chivington's attack on Black Kettle's village at Sand Creek.

Once Custer's troops were in place, there was nothing left to do but wait for morning. The men could not light fires to keep warm or boil coffee, for Custer had ordered them to be still. They were not to walk around or stamp their feet to keep warm, lest the sound of the snow crunching underfoot give them away. So concerned was Custer with maintaining silence that he and his brother Tom strangled Custer's greyhound with a lariat. Other dogs that had followed the detachments were also garroted or had their throats slit to keep them from barking.

Sergeant Ryan of M. Troop wrote, "One dog in my company, of whom the men were very fond, was a little black dog called Bob, harmless as a kitten. We had to part with him and one of the men drove a [spike] into Bob's head and he was left for dead." Ryan also recalled, "We were obliged to sit in our saddles, as we were under orders not to dismount. We were pretty cold, especially our feet, and we tried two ways of keeping them warm: first, to take the feet from the stirrups and let them hang down, thus allowing the blood to circulate; then to kick the feet against the stirrups and keep the blood stirring. The officers dismounted and with the capes of their overcoats drawn over their heads, sat down in the snow. We could occasionally hear the Indian dogs barking, and the outcry of some infant, although we could not see the camp."

"Daylight never seemed so long in coming," Lieutenant Gibson wrote, "and the cold never so penetrating. It was an infraction of orders to talk or move about, so there was nothing left to do but remain perfectly quiet and immovable, thus maintaining a death-like silence, while spending the night in moody meditation, broken occasionally by spasmodic shivers and involuntary shakes. At break of day, the band, which was with the main column, was to strike up 'Garry Owen,' the signal for each command to charge into the village. At last the first faint signs of dawn appeared while the morning star still shone in majestic splendor like a beacon light, as if to warn the silent village of approaching danger."

Custer saw the morning star and called it the "Star of the Washita." He believed it was a fortunate omen, a sign that a great victory was his for the taking.

THIRTEEN

HERE GOES
FOR A BREVET
OR A COFFIN

Black Kettle returned to his camp on the Washita the same night Custer's scouts located it. The precise time is not known, only that it was sometime after dark and before the troops encircled the village. If Black Kettle had arrived after that, they would have seen him—or, more likely, he would have spotted them first.

Black Kettle and several other chiefs had been to Fort Cobb, eighty miles southeast. He still clung to the hope of making peace for the Indian nations, but the army officer he met at the fort, Colonel William Hazen, was unable to help, even though he was sympathetic to Black Kettle's situation. (It was Hazen, as a captain at West Point, who had arrested the newly graduated Custer for failing to stop a fight between two cadets. Hazen had testified for Custer in that first court-martial, but Custer never forgave him.)

General Sheridan also disliked Hazen because of an incident at the Civil War battle of Missionary Ridge. They had argued over whose troops reached the ridge first. Grant sided with Sheridan, and Sheridan held a grudge against Hazen for contesting the matter.

Hazen did have an important patron in General Sherman, who outranked Sheridan. Hazen had served under Sherman in the Atlanta campaign, and they had formed a strong personal bond that continued after the war. Hazen's job at Fort Cobb as Sherman's personal representative was to establish an Indian agency where friendly Indians could gather in peace.

That put Hazen in a difficult position. Sheridan was in command of the area and in charge of all military matters. Hazen's primary task in running the Indian agency put him in charge of issuing goods and supplies to the Indians in the territory. He was caught in the middle as an army officer under Sheridan who was expected to act as a quasi-Indian agent under Sherman. Not an enviable position for a career man.

On November 20, while Custer was still at Camp Supply, Black Kettle and the chiefs met with Hazen to try to convince him that they still wanted to live in peace with the whites, a position Black Kettle had maintained since 1861, when he signed the first peace treaty. "I do not feel afraid to go among the white men," he told Hazen, "because I feel them to be my friends. I have done my best to keep my young men quiet but some will not listen, and since the fighting began I have not been able to keep them all at home. But we all want peace, and I would be glad to move my people down this way; I could then keep them quietly near camp."

Big Mouth, an Arapaho chief, also made an appeal for peace. He told Hazen, "I look upon you as the representative of the Great Father at Washington, and I came to you because I wish to do right. Had I wished to do wrong, I never would have come near you. I do not want war and my people do not, but although we have come back south of the Arkansas, the soldiers follow us and continue fighting. We want you to stop

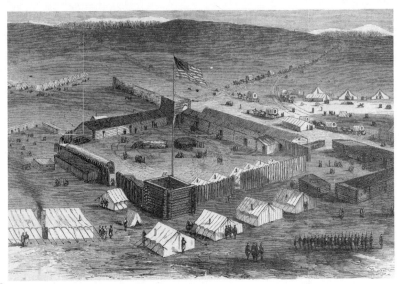

Camp Supply, Indian Territory. For its location, see the reference map on page 270. (*Library of Congress*)

those soldiers from coming against us. We want no more of it."

Hazen wanted to help Black Kettle and Big Mouth because he believed they were sincere about peace. But Sheridan had formally declared the Cheyenne and the Arapaho to be hostile tribes and therefore legitimate targets of the soldiers and of the new expedition about to get under way. Hazen was concerned that if he invited Black Kettle and Big Mouth to bring their people close to Fort Cobb, Custer's troops might attack them there, even though the Indians would believe they were under the protection of the American flag. It would be a repeat of Sand Creek. Hazen could not take that risk.

"I am sent here to this territory as a peace chief," Hazen said, "but north of the Arkansas is General Sheridan, the great war chief, and I do not control him. He has all the soldiers who are fighting the Arapahoe and Cheyenne. You must go back to your country, and if the soldiers come to fight, you must remember that they are not from me but from the great war chief. [It is] with him you must make peace. I am glad to hear that you want peace and not war. I cannot stop the war, but I will send your message to Washington and if they send me orders to treat you like the friendly Indians, then I will send for you to come in.

"I am satisfied that you want peace, that it has not been you but your bad men who have made the war, and I will do all I can for you to bring peace. I hope you understand how and why it is that I cannot make peace with you."

Although Black Kettle said he understood, he knew that his efforts had failed again. Hazen then told the chiefs that he was not allowed to give them food. Sheridan had forbidden him to distribute goods to tribes identified as hostile. Before they left the fort, however, a friendly trader supplied them with sugar, coffee, tobacco, and hard crackers. It was a welcome, but meager, substitute for what they had expected.

It took Black Kettle and the chiefs six days to return to their village because of fierce winds and heavy snow. While they were traveling, another band of Indians was converging on the Washita, but these were coming from the north. It was a war party 150 strong, including some men from Black Kettle's tribe. They were returning from raids in the Smoky Hill area; this was the group Custer's men were tracking. The war party broke up into separate bands as they neared the Washita, each one taking a different route to Black Kettle's village.

Crow Neck was with the war party, but his pony was so tired from tramping through deep snow that he left it tied to a bush about fifteen miles from the camp, intending to return for it the next day. After resting for the night, he went back for his pony, but before he reached it he thought he detected some movement in the distant hills. He was not sure if it was animals or people, and he did not wait to find out. He abandoned his pony and rushed back to the Indian camp. He told Bad Man that he thought he had seen soldiers coming and that they had better move away quickly, but Bad Man refused to believe him. Crow Neck told no else for fear of being laughed at. Also, he was afraid Black Kettle would be angry if he learned that Crow Neck had been out with a war party killing whites.

That same day a Kiowa war party found a large fresh trail that could only have been made by soldiers heading toward the Washita. The Kiowa stopped at Black Kettle's village on the way to their own camp to report what they had seen, but people laughed at them and sent them away. Sheridan and Custer had been correct; the Indians would never think that US soldiers would conduct a winter campaign against them.

When Black Kettle got back to his village, he invited Big Man and his son, fourteen-year-old Magpie, to his lodge to describe the meeting with Colonel Hazen. He told them that a large force of soldiers was searching for the Cheyenne and Arapaho to punish them for the actions—as Black Kettle put it—of a few wayward braves who had attacked whites even though Black Kettle had told them not to. Now, Black Kettle insisted, the tribes faced the risk of punishment, even extinction, for the actions of a few.

Black Kettle decided to summon a council to inform the tribe's leaders of Hazen's judgment and to discuss the courses of action open to them. Black Kettle and Big Man agreed, however, that even if soldiers were looking for them, they could not travel far with the snow so deep and the wind so strong. The leaders went to Black Kettle's lodge later that evening. His wife, Medicine Woman Later, gave them the hard crackers and coffee sweetened with sugar Black Kettle had brought back from Fort Cobb. After they ate, they lit the pipe and passed it around. Then Black Kettle told them of Hazen's words: the Indians would not be allowed to camp near the fort for safety, and soldiers were heading south toward the Washita.

The discussion, and much smoking of the pipe, went on well into the night, at the same time Custer's men were already quietly surrounding the village. The chiefs reached a decision:

Custer leading the 7th Cavalry toward Black Kettle's camp along the Washita River. (*Library of Congress*)

at sunrise they would move down the river, closer to the other camps and the protection of greater numbers. They also agreed to send out peace emissaries to find the soldiers and ask them to hold a council. They wanted the war chief, Sheridan, to know that those Indians living south of the Arkansas River had deliberately moved there because they did not want war with the whites.

By the time the meeting ended, the moon was high and the snow glittered in the light. They returned to their lodges, sure of their belief that soldiers would never be out on such a bitterly cold night. And yet, there was a lingering sense of uneasiness, even dread.

Medicine Woman Later was especially apprehensive. And she was angry. She stood outside their lodge in the moonlight speaking to herself. "I don't like this delay. We should have moved long ago. It seems that we are crazy and deaf, and cannot hear."

The night wore on in cold, forbidding silence, as if death already lay over the land. "Toward morning the moon disappeared, leaving the valley wrapped in dense fog. Then suddenly, mysteriously, Voohehe, the Morning Star, rose high in the sky, glowing in the darkness like a great signal fire lighted above, to warn the people below that enemies were near."

Many of the Cheyenne who survived the coming battle later claimed they had forebodings that night and that they awoke earlier than usual. One couple near Black Kettle's lodge packed their belongings well before dawn. They intended to leave the village right away, concerned that the stories they had heard about the soldiers coming were true. The wife walked down to the herd to collect their pony and saw the horsemen heading toward the village. She ran back through the snow, apparently unseen by the troopers, and screamed at her husband. A fourteen-year-old girl, Moving Behind, heard her cries: "Wake up! White Men! White men are here! The soldiers are approaching our camp."

Black Kettle heard her warning. He grabbed his rifle and told the woman to run through the camp to warn everybody she could find. He fired a shot into the air to wake people up. It was the first shot of the battle.

Custer was approaching the village from the far side. As he slowly led his line of troopers forward, he saw thin columns of smoke floating out of the open tops of some of the lodges, but he saw and heard no movement. "We had approached so near the village that from the dead silence that reigned I feared the lodges were deserted, the Indians having fled before we advanced."

The band was directly behind him, and he was about to give the signal to play when Black Kettle's rifle shot rang out. Custer turned in his saddle and gave the order to play "Garry Owen," but only a few notes sounded. It was so cold that the trumpeters' saliva froze and clogged the instruments, but they made enough noise for the troopers surrounding the village to hear. Cheers rang out, the men charged, and volley after volley of rifle fire split the early morning stillness.

The battle was on, and Custer and his scout, Ben Clark, rode hard for the village. "I rode right beside Custer just ahead of his command," Clark wrote. "He would allow no one to get ahead of him. His horse cleared the stream at one jump and up the bank we went and into the village."

"We became frightened," Moving Behind wrote, "and did not know what to do. We arose at once. At that instant, the soldiers let out terrible yells, and there was a burst of gunfire from them."

Captain Louis Hamilton tried to keep up with Custer and was almost at his side when he was hit, the first soldier to die. He was not supposed to be part of the charge. Custer had assigned him to command the wagon train, but the eager Hamilton pleaded so earnestly that Custer relented, if he could get another officer to take his place with the wagons. He did, and now he was dead, shot in the chest by a Lancaster rifle.

As Custer rode into the village, a Cheyenne warrior leaped in front of him, raised his rifle, and took aim. Custer yanked on the reins, brought his horse to a stop, and shot the Indian in the head. Another brave lunged at him. Custer dug in his spurs, urged his horse forward, and rode the man down. He continued on to a hill on the south side of the village. It was a good vantage point, and Custer and Clark stayed there to observe the battle.

Black Kettle had no time to reload after firing the warning shot. Medicine Woman Later, who still bore the scars of the nine bullets she had taken at Sand Creek, brought up Black Kettle's pony. He jumped on, pulled her up behind him, and headed toward the river. If they could cross, they might have a chance of reaching safety in the next village. But now mounted soldiers confronted them:

> One of their bullets caught [Black Kettle] in the pit of the stomach. In spite of the pain he stayed on his horse, swerving the pony to the right, but still heading for the river. Just as the horse splashed into the water, another soldier-bullet caught him between the shoulder blades. Black Kettle slumped, sliding from the horse's back, dead before he ever hit the water. The frightened pony splashed

on, Medicine Woman Later holding fast to his back. Then soldier-bullets caught her too, leaving her dead in the shallow river. The horse scrambled to the top of the opposite bank. Then he fell too. The troopers raced on, without stopping, riding right over Black Kettle and his wife, splashing mud all over their bodies.

The battle deteriorated. There was no front line, no orderly flanking movements, no longer even a charge. Warriors grabbed their weapons and shot at soldiers from behind logs and trees, and kneeling along the riverbank. Screaming women and children ran one way, then another, but the troopers were everywhere. Some Indians hid in their lodges even as bullets sliced through the buffalo hide roofs. "We did not show much mercy," recalled Sergeant S. F. Statler forty years later, "for they had not shown much mercy."

Moving Behind was staying at the lodge of a friend. Over the cacophony of shots and screams she heard her aunt, Corn Stalk Woman, wailing for her. She left the lodge, shaking with terror. Her aunt grabbed her hand and pulled her along behind her. "Hold my hand tightly," her aunt said. "Don't turn it loose whatever happens. We will go somewhere and hide."

"The air was full of smoke from gunfire," Moving Behind remembered, "and it was almost impossible to flee because bullets were flying everywhere. Somehow we ran, we could see the red fire of the shots. We got near a hill and there we saw a steep path where an old road used to be. There was red grass along the path, and although the ponies had eaten some of it, it was still high enough for us to hide." They hugged the ground and hoped their trembling would not cause the grass to sway and give them away. All around them, Cheyenne were dying.

Big Man, whose lodge was next to Black Kettle's, had just come outside when Black Kettle fired his rifle. His son,

The 7th Cavalry charging into Black Kettle's camp on the morning of November 27, 1868. (*Library of Congress*)

Magpie, grabbed a pistol and a knife and joined him. Together they ran toward some thick chinaberry bushes, but before they reached the protection of the brush, troopers raced toward them. Big Man and Magpie changed direction, but a bullet tore through Magpie's calf. It missed the bone, and he picked himself up and started running again, but Big Man was nowhere to be seen. As Magpie approached a ridge, a soldier bore down on him, wielding a saber. Magpie was exhausted from running. His leg cramped and he realized he would never reach the ridge. He turned to face the trooper, dodged the slashing saber, and jumped up beside the horse. He shoved his pistol against the man's stomach and fired. He and another Indian pulled the wounded soldier out of the saddle, mounted the horse and fled.

The officer Magpie shot was Captain Alfred Barnitz, who lived to tell the story. Magpie, Barnitz wrote, "stood so near me that the blaze from his gun burnt my overcoat. His ball appears to have struck the lower edge of a rib, and then glancing downward, as I was leaning forward at the time, cut the next rib in two, a piece out of the next rib below, where it was deflected, and passed through my body and out through the muscles near the spine, passing again through my overcoat and cape. You see he was loaded to kill."

Barnitz, in his written account of the battle, claimed he killed the Indian who shot him, then lay down "in the expectation that I would very speedily die." When he was taken to the regimental surgeons, they pronounced his case hopeless, and said they would try to make him comfortable for the short time they expected him to live. Word was sent out that he had been killed; his obituary was printed in the Cincinnati newspapers. He died forty-four years later, in 1912, at age seventy-seven. During the autopsy, a piece of his overcoat from the battle at the Washita was found in his body, driven there by the force of the bullet.

Captain Frederick Benteen came upon a Cheyenne boy on a pony. He was Blue Horse, Black Kettle's twenty-one-year-old nephew, though he looked much younger. Blue Horse charged Benteen and fired two shots; both missed. Instead of returning fire, the captain made peace signs, indicating that he did not wish to fight. He was under the impression that Blue Horse was a child. The Indian fired again and closed on Benteen. The bullet struck Benteen's horse in the neck. When Blue Horse raised his pistol for another shot, Benteen took aim, squeezed off a single shot, and killed him.

Some two dozen women and children plunged into the icy Washita River and tried to scramble up the opposite side, but Custer's sharpshooters, concealed by a stand of timber, shot the first ones to reach the riverbank. The rest turned away, to wade downstream from the camp, breaking the ice as they went. They had little warm clothing. Awakened by Black Kettle's rifle shot, they had not taken the time to dress. Some did not even have moccasins or any other foot covering, but they had no way to escape beyond the river. The choices were either freeze to death or be shot.

The water rose to chest height. Women with babies clutching them close for warmth had to hold them high enough to keep them out of the river. As more and more soldiers spotted the group, more shots rang out. Behind the main group, a girl named Tahnea plunged into the icy river and was shot in the leg by a sharpshooter. She had been an infant at Sand Creek. Tahnea forced herself to keep going down the river and managed to survive Washita as well.

Young Bird, a fourteen-year-old girl, was also with the women in the river. In 1937, at age 83, she recalled:

> We could hear the women singing; they sang some war songs and some death songs, because all the men were now trying their best to defend us and themselves and many were lying on the ground dead and very many wounded. I cannot tell the horror that was experienced that awful cold morning when the soldiers started shooting and we jumped out of our sleep and ran for safety and very many of our people were shot down like rabbits. No mercy was shown to either the babies or children of any age and no mercy was shown to the women. As I think back to those times how terrible those days were, it makes tears roll off my eyes to think of our loved ones as they were suddenly taken away from us.

The group of women and children reached a sharp bend in the river where the ice was thicker. Chief Little Rock and two warriors had joined them as a rear guard to hold off the soldiers. They were poorly armed, with only an outmoded muzzle-loader and bows and arrows. Nevertheless, Little Rock shot a cavalryman's horse, but he was killed when a bullet entered his forehead. One warrior fired an arrow that missed one soldier but got close enough to stab his horse with another arrow, gripping it like a knife. They kept the soldiers back long enough for the women and children to round the bend and reach the Arapaho village two miles downstream.

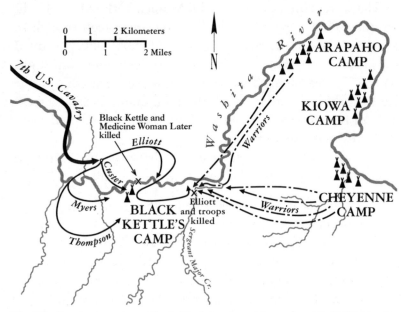

The 7th Cavalry attack on Black Kettle's camp, November 27, 1868. For its location, see the reference map on page 270.

Many others were not so fortunate, particularly those caught by the Osage scouts. The Osage had been uneasy in the hours before the attack. If the soldiers were beaten back, the Osage knew that the Cheyenne, their long-time enemies, would be merciless in taking revenge. When the assault began, they remained behind with Custer at the edge of the camp until they were certain that all Cheyenne warriors had been killed or driven away. Only then did they enter the Cheyenne village. One historian wrote: "Not in years had [the Osage] enjoyed such a glorious opportunity to vent their blood-lust on their hereditary enemies. Scalping knives were soon dripping. Nor were their wielders satisfied with the mere lifting of scalps. Breasts of their women victims were slashed. Arms and legs were severed and bodies otherwise mutilated."

The Osage chief Little Beaver was particularly intent on revenge. As he rode into Black Kettle's village, he fired almost at random, at every Cheyenne he saw, but then he spotted the body of a man lying in the snow; it was the warrior who had killed Little Beaver's wife several months before. Little Beaver jumped from his horse with his scalping knife at the ready, only to discover that someone else had already taken the scalp. Mad with fury, he "fell upon the body with the ferocity of a beast of prey, and severed the throat from ear to ear. Again he stood erect, his whole frame quivering with rage. Once more he fell upon the lifeless form. Completely severing the head from the trunk, he took his knife between his teeth, clutched the gory object in both hands, and raising it high above him, dashed it upon the ground at his feet."

Another Indian named Little Beaver was a twelve-year-old Cheyenne boy. He had run from the lodge with his father, while his mother stayed behind. When the boy and his father had almost reached the safety of the timberline, he remembered that he had left his most prized possession, a revolver that his father had given him, back in the lodge. Disregarding the bullets and the blue-clad troopers bearing down on them, Little Beaver retrieved his gun and went to rejoin his father, but the man was gone. Not knowing where else to turn, he joined the women wading down the river. As long as they stayed in the water, they were partly hidden by the high banks, but at one point the water was too deep, and they had to haul themselves up on land. At that moment, Major Elliott and his band of troopers rode up, guns drawn. They held their fire and took the group prisoner.

Elliott ordered Sergeant Major Walter Kennedy to escort them back to the village, and then Elliott took his men off in pursuit of other Indians. Kennedy motioned for the Cheyenne women to head back in the direction of the camp. Little Beaver was with them. Kennedy followed behind. Kennedy had not searched the prisoners so did not know that the boy was armed with a pistol in a holster under his arm. Little Beaver asked a few of the women to distract Kennedy's attention so he could draw the gun and shoot him. They refused. They already feared for their lives. If Kennedy saw the gun, or if Little Beaver fired and missed, he might shoot them all. Little Beaver was not certain the gun was loaded. He tried to conceal his actions as he carefully took the gun out of the holster to check, but Kennedy saw him and told the boy to give him the gun.*

As the prisoners neared the Indian village, White Buffalo Woman spotted a warrior on horseback on the far side of the river. Then she saw two more and thought they must be Arapaho from the next village who had heard the shooting. Surely more would be coming as word spread of the attack. If she could somehow delay the group that Kennedy was escorting, that would allow time for more rescuers to appear.

She had an idea. The two youngest children with them were not wearing shoes. Their feet were bleeding, leaving red streaks in the snow. White Buffalo Woman gestured to the children's feet, making sure that Kennedy saw her. She stopped, tore the sleeves from her dress, and began to bandage their feet. She worked as slowly as she dared, looking up periodically at Kennedy for permission to continue. It was a humane gesture on Kennedy's part, and the last he would ever make.

Four Arapaho on horseback charged. Kennedy got off two shots but missed. As he tried to reload, the carbine jammed. One Arapaho warrior, Little Chief, struck Kennedy with a hatchet. The others pulled him off his horse and killed him.

---

*In 1930, Little Beaver and Magpie, the Cheyenne boy who had shot Captain Barnitz, returned to the Washita for the sixty-second anniversary of the battle. As part of the ceremonies, Magpie, then a Cheyenne chief, said that "he forgave General Custer for the part he had in the Battle of the Washita, and that he prayed that God would forgive Custer."

An old, gray-haired Indian woman stood alone wielding an army saber, swinging it at any trooper who came near, as if daring them to attack her. Instead of shooting her, some soldiers persuaded her to give up the weapon and join the group of captives.

Custer's chief scout, Ben Clark, stopped one band of troopers who were about to shoot some women who were fleeing. They probably would all have been killed, but Clark let them escape. But even he could not save the life of a Mexican man named Pilan who worked for William Bent. The man carried his little girl in his arms and begged the soldiers to save her. One of them gently lifted the girl from Pilan's arms and told him to run. Then he shot the man in the back.

An old man hid among a group of women being rounded up by some troopers. When the soldiers were not looking, the old warrior whipped out his bow and arrow from under his blanket, fired, and shot the bugler boy in the head. The arrow grazed the skin but did not penetrate the boy's skull. He pulled the arrow out, shot the old man and scalped him, holding up his bloody trophy with a grin of triumph.

One woman was determined that the soldiers would not take her and her baby. She had heard the stories, told and retold around many campfires, about the fate of the women and children at Sand Creek. As one writer described it, "Now, with the others dead around her, she rose from behind a pile of dirt. In one hand she held the baby, extended at arm's length in front of her, while in the other hand she grasped a long knife. The little one was light-skinned. When the soldier sharpshooters saw that, one of them yelled, 'Kill the squaw. She's murdering a white child!' However, before a shot could be fired, the mother, with one stroke of her knife, slashed the baby wide open. Then she drove the knife into her own breast, up to the hilt."

Custer was also mindful of the events at Sand Creek and tried to stop senseless and brutal killing of women and children wherever possible. He did not want the shame attached to Chivington's actions to tarnish his name as well. Early in the attack, when Ben Clark saw troopers firing at fleeing women and children, he asked Custer if he wanted them killed.

"No," Custer said. "Ride out there and give the officer commanding my compliments and ask him to stop it. Take them to the village and put them in a big [lodge] and station a guard around them." A short time later, Custer stopped the Osage killings of Cheyenne women, some of whom were being dragged by their ankles prior to being killed and scalped. There were many bloody acts that day along the Washita, but Custer was adamant about avoiding a repeat of Sand Creek.

Moving Behind and her aunt had remained secluded in the red grass alongside the path. She wrote:

> In this grass we lay flat, our hearts beating fast; and we were afraid to move. It was now bright daylight. It frightened us to listen to the noise and the cries of the wounded. The soldiers would pass back and forth near the spot where I lay. As I turned sideways and looked, one soldier saw us, and rode toward where we lay. He stopped his horse, and stared at us. He did not say a word, and we wondered what would happen. But he left, and no one showed up after that. I suppose he pitied us, and left us alone.*

Earlier in the morning, Major Elliott had led a group of eighteen troopers along the riverbank away from the village after some fleeing Indians. As he left he shouted to a friend, "Here goes for a brevet or a coffin"—for glory or for death. Elliott first came across twelve-year-old Little Beaver and the women and children with him. That was when he ordered Sergeant

---

*In 1937, sixty-nine years after the battle, Moving Behind told an interviewer: "A long time later, when the whites and Indians had quit fighting, George Bent asked us to go and shake hands with a soldier. We went, and he said that this was the soldier who saw us hiding, and pitied us and saved us. Of course, we shook hands with the tall soldier. I recall that he had a brown mustache and blue eyes."

Major Kennedy to take them back to the camp as prisoners. Elliott and the others rode on, chasing two Indians. They rode them down and killed them, and then heard the shots that felled Kennedy. Elliott may have lost track of the fact that they had ridden well over a mile from Black Kettle's village. The Arapaho who had gotten Kennedy were joined by five others. The group headed toward Elliott's men, cutting off their access to the camp. By then, the soldiers' horses were too weak to make a dash for it. Elliott ordered his men to dismount; one man out of every four would hold the horses while the other three took aim and fired. The Indians charged straight on, then at the last instant divided and passed the troopers on both sides.

Elliott ordered his men to move slowly toward the camp. They did not get far when the Indians attacked again. Suddenly, scores of warriors appeared, riding in circles around the soldiers and keeping up a constant heavy fire. The soldiers were trapped. There were too many Indians for them to fight their way through. Their only hope was that someone at the village would see or hear the battle and come to the rescue. No one did.

Elliott's men kept moving slowly even as the Indians surrounded them. They reached the ravine where Kennedy had been killed. All their horses had been shot or run off, so Elliott had the men form a circle in the tall grass. The warriors could not see them, but the soldiers could not see the Indians either. The troopers raised their carbines overhead and shot without being able to take aim. They hit no one, but each time a man fired he gave away his location, and the Indians would concentrate their fire on each position.

The Indian warriors did not charge through the tall grass. They did not know how many soldiers were still alive, or how many more bullets they had. Neither side was willing to make a move until Tobacco, a Cheyenne warrior, rode toward the troopers. He tore through the circle of Indians and trampled the grass as he rode on through the soldiers. A shot struck him in the chest, and he fell among them.

It was a brave feat, and now other Indians felt they had no choice but to follow Tobacco's example. The encircling warriors rushed the soldiers, and it was all over in minutes. The Indians set to work stripping the bodies and scalping and mutilating them. They fired dozens of arrows and bullets into the corpses of Elliott's men to make sure they were all dead.

FOURTEEN

THINGS
WERE GOING
TERRIBLY
WRONG

By ten o'clock that morning, the battle at Washita was over. Quiet descended on the Indian village. Custer rode off to the makeshift hospital to visit the casualties. Captain Hamilton's body had been brought in there. Captain Barnitz was alive, but the surgeon told Custer that he was not expected to survive. Tom Custer and another lieutenant were being treated for minor wounds, along with eleven enlisted men, none of whom had a life-threatening injury.

It appeared that Custer had achieved a clear, decisive victory by doing what everyone had thought impossible. He had successfully located and taken by surprise an Indian village in the dead of winter. This would be a victory to brag about, one that would wipe out any stain lingering from his court-martial. Surely it would be written up in history books for years to come. Custer had every reason to feel pleased and satisfied with what he had accomplished.

By noon, however, he was growing concerned. What he thought was a great victory might yet turn into a defeat. For some time that morning, Custer had noticed small mounted bands of Indians congregating on a knoll approximately a mile south of the village. He assumed they were warriors who had fled the camp early, managing to cull ponies from the herd.

But every time he glanced in that direction he saw more of them. Soon he counted more than one hundred. Surely not that many men could have escaped. He studied them through field glasses and was surprised to see that all were well armed, and dressed and decorated in full war regalia. No one who had escaped from Black Kettle's village could possibly have taken so much with them. These had to be warriors from another village, and one that was not so far away.

Lieutenant Edward Godfrey reported to Custer that he and his men had explored far downstream. "Peering over a ridge," Godfrey said, "I was amazed to find that as far as I could see down the well wooded tortuous valley there were tepees. Not only tepees, but mounted warriors scurrying in our direction."

Godfrey also told Custer he had heard the sounds of heavy gunfire on the side of the river where Major Elliott and his men had last been seen. He thought Elliott's detachment might have been cut off and be under attack. Custer said he did not think that was possible, but he may have been less certain than he indicated to Godfrey. Custer asked scout Ben Clark about Elliott, and Clark said he was last seen heading southeast. And now Custer was getting reports from soldiers guarding the Indian pony herd that they had seen fully dressed and armed warriors southeast of the camp. Suddenly the Indians were everywhere.

"On all sides of us the Indians could now be seen in considerable numbers," Custer wrote later, "so that from being the surrounding party, as we had been in the morning, we now found ourselves surrounded and occupying the position of defenders of the village." In an interview thirty-six years later, Clark estimated that there had been between one thousand two hundred and one thousand five hundred armed warriors. One writer concluded that Custer had "violated a fundamental military precept: He attacked an enemy of unknown strength on a battlefield of unknown terrain." But if he had conducted a thorough reconnaissance before the assault, the Indians would no doubt have discovered his troops, and the element of surprise would have been lost. Fundamental military precepts were not always appropriate in this type of warfare.

Another disturbing report came in that the soldiers were running low on ammunition. Each man had brought one hundred rounds into the battle, but there had been a great deal of indiscriminate firing during the attack. Gunfire could now be heard from the southern end of the camp, where warriors approached within shooting distance. The troopers' ammunition wagon was several miles away. If it were captured or cut off from the camp, Custer's men would run out of bullets before nightfall.

Soldiers who had been stationed north of the village to guard the overcoats and haversacks the men had left before going into battle filtered into the camp. Indians had run them off and stolen the clothing and equipment. Now they had no warm garments for nighttime and no food or coffee beyond what they might have in their pockets.

Custer had to find out the size of the Indian force and where the Indians were coming from. Taking an interpreter with him, he went to one of the lodges where the Indian women were being held. He assured them they would be treated well and would be taken to a fort. That message came as a relief; they had expected to be killed. Then one of the women told the interpreter she wanted to speak with the big chief.

Her name was Mahwissa, and she told Custer that their village chief had been Black Kettle, who was her brother, and now he was dead. Custer asked where the Indians assembling around the village were coming from. She said that Black Kettle's village was only the first in a string of Indian camps stretching ten miles along the river. They included Cheyenne, Arapaho, Comanche, Kiowa, and Apache.

"What was to be done?" Custer wrote later. "I needed no one to tell me that we were certain to be attacked, and that, too, by greatly superior numbers, just as soon as the Indians could make their arrangements to do so." But for the moment Custer was not able to do anything, because Mahwissa had other plans for him. She took him by the hand and led him to a young, pregnant woman, perhaps in her late teens. She placed the woman's hand in Custer's. He described her as

> an exceedingly comely squaw, possessing a bright, cheery face, a countenance beaming with intelligence, and a disposition more inclined to be merry than one usually finds among Indians. Added to the bright, laughing eyes, a set of pearly teeth, and a rich complexion, her well-shaped head was crowned with a luxuriant growth of the most beautiful silken tresses, rivaling in color the blackness of the raven and extending, when allowed to fall loosely over her shoulders, to below her waist. Her name was Mo-nah-se-tah, which, Anglicized, means "The young grass that shoots in the spring."*

She clearly made an impression on Custer. While he stood there holding her hand, Mahwissa spoke to them in what he described as formal, ceremonial terms. He thought perhaps she was placing a blessing on them. He listened for some time until his curiosity prompted him to question the interpreter.

"Why, she is marryin' you to that young squaw!"

---

*Monahsetah was so attractive that her husband had to pay her father the enormous sum of eleven ponies for her. The usual price for a bride was two to four ponies. Unfortunately for her husband, she was not a docile, submissive wife. She had not wanted to marry him but had no choice. Such things were arranged by a girl's father with or without her consent. When her husband took offense at her disobedient ways and sought to punish her, she shot him in the knee, crippling him for life, suitable grounds for divorce. Her father had to return the eleven ponies.

Custer politely declined what he called a "tempting alliance." He explained to Mahwissa that he already had one wife, and he knew that if he ever wanted to see Libbie again, he was going to have to get his men out of there before they were hopelessly outnumbered. A sudden movement outside caught his attention. What he saw was the answer to an unspoken prayer.

A squad of twenty-five troopers came riding hard into the camp from the north leading an ambulance and seven wagons full of supplies. The party was led by Lieutenant James Bell, the regimental quartermaster who decided on his own that Custer's men probably needed more ammunition by then. As he neared the camp, he heard shooting and sped up the wagons as fast as the mules could run. They barreled their way through the pack of Indians who had been watching the village and thus not paying attention to anything behind them. The warriors chased after the wagons, but Bell kept them going, "racing so fast that their tar-soaked wheels caught fire. In spite of that they reached the camp first, the mouths of the mules foaming with lather as they came dashing in among their cheering comrades."

After the wagons broke through, the warriors encircled the camp and began firing at the soldiers, but only when they had a target in their sights. They did not fire randomly for fear of hitting the women and children captives. They did not attack directly but dared the soldiers to come after them, shouting that the troopers were cowards for refusing to come out and fight. Some waved the overcoats and haversacks they had stolen.

The soldiers stayed in the village. For the time being, that was the safest place to be. Black Kettle had chosen his camp-site well, inside a grove of cottonwood trees, terrain that now protected the troops. Still, they knew they could not remain there long. But first they had to destroy the village, leaving behind nothing the Indians could use. Custer sent men to go through the lodges and bring out everything of value, the tribe's entire wealth and source of subsistence for the winter. The troopers stacked the supplies in huge piles. Custer then ordered that everything be inventoried so he could provide Sheridan with a detailed report on the extent of the destruction.

The next day, Custer wrote:

> We captured in good condition 24 saddles, some of very costly workmanship; 573 buffalo robes, 390 buffalo skins for lodges, 160 untanned robes, 210 axes, 140 hatchets, 35 revolvers, 47 rifles, 535 pounds of powder, 1,050 pounds of lead, 4,000 arrows and arrowheads, 75 spears, 90 bullet molds, 35 bows and quivers, 12 shields, 300 pounds of bullets, 775 lariats, 94 buckskin saddle-bags, 470 blankets, 93 coats, 700 pounds of tobacco. In addition, we captured all their winter supply of buffalo meat, all their meal, flour, and other provisions, and, in fact, everything they possessed.

The troopers also found items that had belonged to white settlers, including letters, household items, photographs, even bedding—apparently all that remained of the victims of the young warriors Black Kettle had never been able to control.

All the lodges save one, which Custer kept for himself, were set ablaze. The soldiers tossed the goods into the flames. The bright fires and towering columns of smoke enraged the warriors, and they opened fire on the troopers. Custer quickly dispatched every man he could spare to the perimeter to hold them off. Some Indians charged the soldiers, probing for gaps in the line so they could break through into the camp, but each time they were driven back.

Custer had to decide what to do with 875 captured horses and mules. He could not take them along with the army; they would slow down the march. The troopers would need to ride hard and fast to get away from the Indians who were still taking potshots at them. Yet he could not leave so many horses behind for the Indians. Horses were valuable; Indians could not make war or hunt without them. There was only one solution: the horses would have to be killed.

A few of the better horses were singled out to be given to the scouts and officers, and the women prisoners were allowed to choose the ones they wanted to ride when they left the camp. Four companies of soldiers herded the rest into an area southeast of the village. At first they tried to kill the horses by slitting their throats, but the horses went berserk at the unfamiliar smell of white men and were kicking and bucking so fiercely that the soldiers could not get near them with their knives.

While the Indians looked on in horror, Custer himself, along with his soldiers, began to shoot the horses and the scores of dogs as well. The carnage lasted for almost two hours as the horses whinnied and kicked and ran in circles until they dropped in the snow.

Moving Behind, hiding in the grass with her aunt, wrote later, "The wounded ponies passed near our hiding place, and would moan loudly, just like human beings." Another Indian woman wrote, "The ponies after being shot broke away and ran about bleeding until they dropped. In this way the snow on the whole bend of the river was made red with blood."

After the last horse had been shot, Custer decided, against all reason, that he would attack all the other Indian villages stretching ten miles down the river. He believed that since he had routed Black Kettle's village so easily, he would have no problem taking the others. Fortunately, Ben Clark had more sense and was able to talk him out of it, reminding Custer that he no longer had the advantage of surprise. Clark also told Custer that the Indians now outnumbered them, perhaps by five to one, and that they were so enraged by the destruction of the village and the horses that they would be bent on revenge. To attack other Indian camps now, Clark said, "would be little less than suicide." They would be lucky to get out of their present predicament and make it back to Camp Supply.

Cheyenne women and children taken prisoner following the attack being force-marched back to Camp Supply. (*Library of Congress*)

Finally Custer agreed with Clark and took his scout's advice. The men and horses were exhausted and needed a few hours of rest before getting under way and trying to outrun the Indians. Clark suggested they let the Indians think that the soldiers were setting up camp. That way the Indians might be caught off guard when the regiment started to leave. To further confuse them, Clark recommended that the command form up at dusk and, with great fanfare, head south as if preparing to attack the other camps. If the warriors then rushed to defend the other villages, the regiment could quickly reverse course and head north, riding as hard and as long as horses and men could stand the pace. Custer agreed.

At dusk the regiment formed a column with the prisoners in the middle. Custer's band played a rousing Civil War song, "Ain't I Glad to Get out of the Wilderness," and the 7th Cavalry headed south toward the other Indian camps. The warriors who had encircled them left quickly, riding off to defend their villages, leaving only a few behind to follow the troopers.

The soldiers rode out for about twelve miles, "following the fleeing savages," wrote the wounded Captain Barnitz. "I know this, for I was along, riding luxuriously in an ambulance with the curtains rolled up, so that I might see the painted [warriors] bedecked with war bonnets, as they made many desperate charges in efforts to stampede the mules of the ambulance train, but were, on each occasion repulsed by the countercharges of the cavalry." Once it grew dark, Custer ordered the column to reverse course.

By ten that night, the soldiers had once again reached the ruins of Black Kettle's village. After a quick stop to eat, they continued north, stopping at two in the morning. They saddled up at daybreak, and by ten o'clock had rejoined the main supply train. They pushed on again until midafternoon, when they stopped to eat and rest. Custer wrote a battle report for General Sheridan and sent "California Joe" and another courier to take it to Camp Supply. The regiment saw no more Indians for the rest of the march. Custer's luck had held again.

Black Kettle's camp was empty and desolate. The fires from the burnt lodges had melted the snow and left a bitter, acrid aroma. The soldiers were gone. A few dazed survivors tentatively emerged from their hiding places to explore the remains of their homes.

"Look, we are safe," Moving Behind's aunt said to the girl. "I can see someone walking up the hill."

The two had been hiding in the tall grass for ten hours. They stood up now when some warriors entered the camp. Among them were the aunt's husband and a young man called Crane, who was Moving Behind's future husband. He did not recognize her at first, because her face and clothing were covered with mud.

"Is this you, Moving Behind?" he asked.

"I said 'yes.' We both cried, and hugged and kissed each other."

The men had brought extra ponies in the hope of finding people still alive. Crane removed the saddle from his horse and placed it on a pony for Moving Behind.

"We all got on our ponies," she wrote, "and rode down to the river to find the spot where Black Kettle and his wife were killed. There was a sharp curve in the river where an old road crossing used to be. Indian men used to go there to water their ponies. Here we saw the bodies of Black Kettle and his wife, lying under the water. The horse they had ridden lay dead beside them.

"Clown, Afraid of Beaver, Scabby, and Roll Down got off their horses and went down to get the bodies. They were too heavy to lift, so they had to drag them in the water, then bring them up. Clown got his red and blue blanket and spread it on the ground beside a road a short distance from the river, and the bodies were laid on the blanket and covered with the same blanket. It was getting late, and we had to go, so we left the bodies of Black Kettle and his wife."*

---

*Black Kettle's body was carried to the top of a knoll and buried where the soldiers would not be able to find it or dishonor it. Magpie, the boy who shot Captain Barnitz, was among those who buried the chief. Almost seventy years later, in 1934, workers building a bridge over the Washita River found a body near the spot where Magpie said Black Kettle was buried. Jewelry found with the remains was identified as similar to what Black Kettle wore. The bones were given to the local newspaper, the *Cheyenne Star*, which put them on display in its front window, where they remained for years.

FIFTEEN

HE DIED
A SOLDIER'S
DEATH

On December 2, Custer led his men back to Camp Supply, where he soon found himself praised and reviled, hailed and condemned. Many newspapers called him the greatest Indian fighter of all time and published stories of the Washita battle focusing on his exploits, making it seem as though he had won the battle single-handed. Others claimed he was a murderer who put innocent Indians to death, and still others criticized him as a commander who deserted eighteen of his men on the battlefield, leaving their bodies to rot.

Whatever the response, his actions along the Washita were not ignored, and after too long an absence, he proudly found his name once again in headlines throughout the United States. Black Kettle's name was featured as well; the peace chief may have achieved more fame in death than in life, at least in the four years since Sand Creek.

The various judgments on Custer came within days of the battle. Indian sympathizers excoriated his actions, calling the Washita fight a massacre and comparing it to Sand Creek.

Some writers called Custer "a bloodthirsty monster" who murdered an innocent, peace-loving chief and his people. The *New York Times* quoted an anonymous 7th Cavalry officer (it was Benteen), who described Custer as "taking sadistic pleasure in slaughtering the Indian ponies and dogs," as well as killing women and children.

The commissioner of the Bureau of Indian Affairs, Thomas Murphy, was among the critics and the most strident defender of the slain Black Kettle. Murphy described Black Kettle as "one of the truest friends the whites ever had among the Indians." He wrote of how Black Kettle had consistently worked for peace and to prevent a general Indian uprising in 1867. Indian agent Albert Boone wrote that "Black Kettle was a good man; he was my friend; he was murdered." Members of the US Senate Committee on Indian Affairs charged that Washita was a repeat of the events at Sand Creek. Samuel Tappan, of the committee investigating Chivington at Sand Creek, and who also served on the Medicine Lodge Treaty Commission, wrote to condemn the army's punitive policies against peaceful Indians, which he said always led to more violence and bloodshed. Edward Wynkoop, in Philadelphia after resigning as agent to the Cheyenne and Arapaho, was devastated by the death of Black Kettle. Wynkoop eulogized him as a true "noble savage, the ruling spirit of his tribe." He argued that the government had twice betrayed Black Kettle's trust, first at Sand Creek and now at the Washita.

Custer never responded to the criticism. He didn't have to: Sheridan and Sherman did it for him. They lashed out at the "Indian lovers" back East, as well as people like Tappan who, in their view, should have known better than to believe Black Kettle wanted peace and that his was a friendly camp. In a letter to his senior officers, General Sherman urged them to ignore the newspaper furor and continue to pursue and kill the hostile Indians.

Sherman was particularly critical of Wynkoop for referring publicly to "the murdered Black Kettle." Sherman argued that if Wynkoop was so concerned about Black Kettle and his people, then he should not have left them on their own and gone "two thousand miles away to lecture on the perfidy of our people and the innocence of the Indian." Why had he not stayed with the Cheyenne he had been responsible for and continued as their agent?*

Sheridan called Black Kettle "a worn out and worthless old cypher" whose warriors had been killing and raping white settlers for years. As evidence Sheridan pointed to the incriminating items belonging to murdered whites that Custer's troops had found in the Washita lodges. The short-tempered Sheridan referred to so-called Indian sympathizers as "aiders and abettors of savages who murdered, without mercy, men, women, and children." He praised Custer for defending womanly virtue by killing "old Black Kettle and his murderers and rapers of helpless women." Referring again to people who supported the Indians, Sheridan went on, "I do not know exactly how far these humanitarians should be excused on account of their ignorance, but surely it is the only excuse that gives a shadow of justification for aiding and abetting such horrid crimes."

Custer's actions at the Washita had validated Sheridan's plan of conducting a winter campaign. It had been a risky but successful venture, and in praising Custer, Sheridan was also praising himself for having the vision and audacity to plan a campaign that was contrary to the accepted way of fighting Indians.

"Never again," Sheridan's biographer wrote, "would the Indians of the Great Plains be able to rest easy in their camps,

---

*Wynkoop remained in the East working in the family iron business until 1876, the year of Custer's death, when he went to the Black Hills of Dakota Territory to search for gold. Unsuccessful, he returned to Pennsylvania, held a series of jobs, and, in 1882, was appointed US timber agent in Santa Fe, New Mexico. He later became adjutant general of the New Mexico State Militia and warden of the state penitentiary. He died in 1891, at age fifty-five.

secure in their belief that bad weather and great distance would keep them safe from the enemy's reach. Custer's victory on the Washita, whatever its moral and tactical deficiencies, had been an enormous psychological blow to the Indians."

Custer basked in the praise from the newspapers and from Sheridan, even before he returned to Camp Supply. When Sheridan received Custer's account of the battle hand-delivered by "California Joe," he sent a congratulatory letter back with the scout. Custer was ecstatic when he read the letter from his "beloved commander," and he immediately sent it on to Libbie. "Oh," he wrote, "is it not gratifying to be so thought of by one whose opinion is above all price?"

Sheridan modified his opinion, however, when he learned about the missing Major Elliott and his men. Trying to justify his decision, Custer told Sheridan he had sent out search parties looking for Elliott, which was true, and that they had found no trace of him. Then Custer tried to persuade Sheridan that Elliott and his outfit had simply gotten lost and would find their way back soon. Sheridan did not agree, and he deemed Custer's observation unsatisfactory. The fate of Elliott and his men, Sheridan wrote, "was the only damper on our pleasure, and the only drawback to the very successful expedition." Sheridan saw the matter as a lapse of judgment on Custer's part, in leaving the scene of battle with some of his men unaccounted for. Nevertheless, Sheridan retained a high degree of confidence in Custer as a fighter. There is no evidence to suggest that Sheridan raised the matter again or used it against Custer in any way, and they continued to work closely together.

The same could not be said for Captain Benteen, who seized on the Elliott matter to malign Custer publicly. He wrote an anonymous letter to the *Saint Louis Democrat* criticizing Custer for failing to attempt to save Elliott and his men. The nature of the letter, and the details it provided, made it clear that it was written by one of Custer's officers. When a copy arrived at Camp Supply, an irate Custer summoned his officers and read the letter out loud, all the while slapping his whip against the top of his boot. He told them that if he ever found out who wrote the letter, he would horsewhip him.

Captain Benteen stepped forward. "I am the man you are after, and I am ready for the whipping promised."

Custer stammered and walked out of the tent, and apparently nothing more was said about the letter.

Not everyone blamed Custer for leaving the scene of battle without knowing what had become of Elliott's group. Most felt he made the correct decision; that he would have risked the lives of his seven hundred men had he lingered in Black Kettle's village or sent out larger patrols looking for them. So except for Benteen and a few other officers who had long hated Custer, there were no criticisms within the regiment for leaving the battlefield when he did. As one trooper put it, on reflection, "I never heard a word against General Custer for returning to Camp Supply without recovering the bodies at the time of the fight."

Even the Cheyenne who were at the Washita agreed. When interviewed years later, they said he and his command would have been killed had he stayed around to search for the missing men, who, it turned out, were already dead hours before he left.

One final point of controversy involved the number of Indians claimed to be killed. In his report to Sheridan, Custer wrote that 103 warriors had been killed, along with "some of the squaws and a few of the children." He was careful to point out that the women and children had been killed "in the excitement of the fight, as well as in self-defense." Ben Clark, the sober and reliable scout, told an interviewer twenty-one years later that approximately 150 Indians were killed at the battle, and that fully half were women and children. Another scout, James Morrison, wrote to Wynkoop that about forty women and children were killed during the battle.

These controversies and questions, which continue to occupy the interest of historians as well as Custer's partisans and opponents, had little impact on the men of the 7th Cavalry during their time at Camp Supply in early December. They were busy burying one of their own and preparing for a new campaign.

On December 3, the regiment buried Captain Louis McLane Hamilton with all the honors and rights due a fallen member. "As he died a soldier's death," Custer wrote, "so like a soldier he should be buried." The entire regiment turned out, along with the post's regular infantry garrison. Hamilton's body, draped with an American flag, was transported in an ambulance, followed by his horse with the stirrups reversed. Custer and Sheridan were among the pallbearers. The formal ceremony was a grim reminder of what could happen to any of them on their next campaign, now less than a week away.

Sheridan intended to follow up the victory at the Washita with an even greater success. He proposed to attack as many Indian villages as possible, destroy all food and supplies, and leave them so destitute they would have no choice but to go to the reservations and remain there. This time he would accompany the expedition, set to depart on December 7.

Custer's 7th Cavalry would be joined by the 19th Kansas Cavalry, a regiment of volunteers commanded by the ex-governor of Kansas, Colonel Samuel Crawford. The regiment had been formed two months before in response to a series of Indian raids in that territory. The one thousand men of the 19th were out for revenge. They were supposed to have been with Custer at the Washita but got lost in a snowstorm. They suffered terribly from cold and hunger and did not arrive at Camp Supply until after Custer had left. They were on hand to welcome him back, however, and after a few more days of rest would be ready to ride out to find Indians.

While the troopers prepared for the campaign, the Indian prisoners Custer brought back from the Washita settled into their new way of life. They were kept under heavy guard, and most expected to die at any moment. They were so afraid of the soldiers that even the wounded refused efforts to take them to the hospital tent to be treated by army surgeons. They fought any attempt to separate them from one another, although some were in danger of dying of their wounds if left untreated.

Louis McLane Hamilton. (*Library of Congress*)

They were so desperate that Mahwissa, Black Kettle's sister who had spoken to Custer back at the village, requested to see the big chief, General Sheridan. She asked him directly when the prisoners would be killed. He said they would be treated well and then sent on to another camp. Satisfied that he spoke the truth, Mahwissa returned to the prisoner enclosure and assured the women and children that they were going to be all right. Finally they were able to relax and permit the wounded among them to be helped. They even took on chores around the camp and let the children play with the soldiers. The troops were impressed by the stoicism some of the children showed while being treated for wounds. The youngsters never winced, cried, or displayed any indication of the physical pain.

"During such painful operations as probing and cleansing the wounds, the little sufferers placed their hands over their heads and closed their eyes, submitting without a murmur. One little girl with a bullet hole through the body on the left side, sat up as if in perfect health."

Mahwissa ingratiated herself with Sheridan and Custer by telling them what they wanted to hear. First, she said that the trail Custer had followed to the Washita camp had been made by a war party of Cheyenne and Arapaho recently returned from raiding in Kansas; they had with them several freshly taken white scalps. So much for the stories in the eastern newspapers about Black Kettle's village being a peaceful camp.

She also said that three white women were being held in camps downstream from Black Kettle's village. Those camps, she said, contained Cheyenne, as well as Kiowa, Arapaho, Comanche, and Apache. In the judgment of one historian, Mahwissa "was prepared to tell her captors anything that would secure their favor and save the lives of her people. She was successful in this gambit, for both Sheridan and Custer developed a high opinion of her talents, gave her special treatment, and made use of her as an emissary." Custer considered her to be "a woman of superior intelligence."

Custer's scout and interpreter, Raphael Romero, who was with Mahwissa during her conversations with Custer and Sheridan, did not believe her or trust her. "She knows they are in your power," he told Custer, "and her object is to make friends with you as far as possible. But you don't believe anything she tells you, do you? Why, give her the chance, and she'd lift your or my scalp from us and never wink."

Despite such warnings, they had confidence in Mahwissa. Custer wanted her to accompany the expedition to help him locate hostile villages and to aid in communicating with those Indians. She asked Custer if a friend—an unnamed, middle-aged woman—could also come along. Custer agreed. He also wanted a third Indian with them, Monahsetah, the young woman he had described as "exceedingly comely" and whom Mahwissa had tried to marry to Custer back at Black Kettle's village. Despite the facts that they were embarking on an arduous campaign under grueling conditions and that she was seven months pregnant, she agreed to join him.

Rumors have abounded ever since that she was Custer's mistress. One of the promoters of this intriguing tale was Benteen, who never missed an opportunity to malign Custer. However, Clark also said she was his mistress during that winter of 1868, and so did Cheyenne oral history, as later recorded by white historians and anthropologists.*

Whether or not Custer and Monahsetah were having a relationship, other officers of the regiment were having dalliances with Indian women. The interpreter Romero was in charge of the prisoners and "acted as a procurer for the officers and sent young women around to their tents at night. Among the officers of the regiment, Romero was fondly nicknamed Romeo."

Ben Clark later said that "many of the [women] captured at Washita were used by the officers. Custer picked out a fine-looking one and had her in his tent every night," Some sources also allege that during the winter of 1868–69, Custer and a number of his officers were treated for syphilis.

The temperature plunged to eighteen degrees below zero on December 10, when the expedition set up camp along the Washita, a few miles from the ruins of Black Kettle's village. The column of two thousand troops and three hundred blue-painted wagons had left Camp Supply three days before and had been battling the elements on a long, brutal march. The thermometer rarely rose above ten degrees, and it was so cold that a number of troopers succumbed to frostbite, despite their buffalo-skin boots and gloves.

*Monahsetah had a second baby in 1869. According to Cheyenne folklore, the baby had white skin and yellow hair. He was called Yellow Hair, or Yellow Bird. In one Cheyenne account, Monahsetah never married again, telling people that Custer was her husband and had promised to come back for her. She waited, so the story goes, for seven years and was at the Little Big Horn with her seven-year-old son the day Custer was killed. Other sources allege that Tom Custer was the boy's father. Libbie Custer met Monahsetah when she rejoined her husband at Fort Hays. She described her as "young and attractive, perfectly contented, and the acknowledged belle among all other Indian maidens."

On the second day, howling winds blew across the plains from the north. Horses standing still froze to death; men marched in place throughout the night to keep from a fatal chill. The Canadian River froze over, but the ice was not thick enough to support the weight of the wagons and horses, so men plunged into the water with axes to break a path to the other side. Some wagons froze in place while fording the river and had to be chopped out of the ice. It took five hours to get everyone safely to the far side. The troopers lit huge fires to help them thaw out.

Custer was the nominal commander of the expedition, with Sheridan along as "a passenger," as Custer put it. On the morning of December 11, Sheridan and Custer, along with a one-hundred-man escort, went to explore the battle site, determined to find the remains of Major Elliott and his men.

A correspondent for the *New York Herald*, DeBenneville Randolph Keim, was with them and described the scene: "Suddenly lifting from the ground could be seen thousands of ravens and crows, disturbed in their carrion feast. The dense black mass, evidently gorged, rose heavily, and passing overhead, as if to take revenge for the molestation, set up the greatest confusion of noises." A large number of wolves ran away to the top of a nearby hill where they sat on their haunches and watched the troops traverse their feasting ground. The wolves and birds had been devouring the corpses of some Indians whose remains had been left, along with the bodies of the horses Custer's men had killed.

The troopers split up into separate search parties. Sheridan, Custer, Keim, and some others headed down the Washita's south bank, the direction Elliott was last seen. Two miles downriver, they found what they were looking for.

"The bodies of Elliott and his little band," Custer wrote, "with but a single exception, were all found lying within a circle not exceeding twenty yards in diameter. We found them exactly as they fell, except that their barbarous foes had stripped and mutilated the bodies in the most savage manner."

Keim recorded his impressions:

> A scene was now witnessed sufficient to appall the
> bravest heart. Within an area not more than fifteen yards
> lay sixteen human bodies, all that remained of Elliott and
> his party. There was not a single body that did not exhib-
> it evidences of fearful mutilation. They were all lying with
> their faces down, and in close proximity to each other.
> Bullet and arrow wounds covered the back of each; the
> throats of a number were cut, and several were beheaded.
> It was with great difficulty that any of them were recog-
> nized, owing to the terrible atrocities to which they had
> been subjected.

Sheridan was livid with rage. He had seen thousands of
dead men, torn and shattered by bullet and shell in the Civil
War, but he had never seen human remains so deliberately sav-
aged by other men. He termed it barbaric and animalistic, and
vowed to have his revenge.

Other troopers found two bodies in an abandoned camp
downriver from where Black Kettle died. At first, no one knew
who they were. The young white woman had apparently been
very beautiful before a bullet tore into the middle of her forehead. The back of her skull was also crushed. A little white
boy was nearby, and he looked as if he had gone hungry for a
long time. The only mark on him was a bruise on his head,
which led the men to suspect that he had been held by his feet
and swung against a tree.

The bodies were brought back to camp and placed side by
side on a blanket in the hope that someone might recognize
them. A soldier from Kansas did; it was Clara Blinn and her
two-year-old son, Willie. They had been captured October 9
when their wagon train was attacked. Her husband had been
wounded in the raid but had escaped and was still alive. Three
weeks after her capture, she got a letter out through a trader
who passed it on to Colonel Hazen:

"My name is Clara Blinn; my little boy, Willie Blinn is two years old. Do all you can for me. Write to the peace commissioner to make peace this fall. For our sakes, do all you can and God will bless you. Goodbye. I am as well as can be expected, but my baby is very weak."

Hazen had written to Sheridan after he received the letter, saying that he was trying to arrange a trade for her release, but Sheridan refused permission for Hazen to proceed. He believed that a woman who had been captured and repeatedly raped by Indians could never be the same again and would be better off dead. Sheridan told Hazen that, after having "her own person subjected to the fearful bestiality of perhaps the whole tribe it is mock humanity to secure what is left of her for the consideration of five ponies." But confronted with the consequences, now, all Sheridan could do was see that Clara and Willie Blinn were given a decent burial.

He called for Mahwissa and asked her in which of the villages the Blinns had been held captive, and which chief had been responsible for their death. Mahwissa blamed Santanta, chief of the Kiowa. She said Clara Blinn had been his personal prisoner, "reserved to gratify the brutal lust of the chief," as Sheridan put it. Mahwissa also told Sheridan that the chief had murdered Clara and the boy with his own hand.

Sheridan vowed to hunt Santanta down and see that justice was done. He never knew, nor did Custer, that Mahwissa lied. Santanta had nothing to do with Clara Blinn. They had been captured and killed by Arapaho, long-time allies of the Cheyenne. Mahwissa lied to protect the Arapaho from retribution, and in so doing, she set the stage for another confrontation.

SIXTEEN

YOU AND YOUR SOLDIERS WILL GO TO DUST

The expedition left the Washita battle site on December 12, heading toward Fort Cobb, ready to exact revenge against Santanta and the Kiowa. Five days later, only twenty miles from the fort, scouts brought word that a party of Indians was approaching and they were carrying a white flag. The column halted, and a courier from Fort Cobb, who had been held by the Indians, was sent out to Custer and Sheridan bearing a letter from Colonel Hazen, written the day before.

"Indians have just brought in word that our troops today reached the Washita [the troops led by Custer and Sheridan]. I send this to say that all the camps this side of the point reported to have been reached are friendly, and have not been on the war path this season."

The courier told Sheridan that the Indians were detaining a second courier as hostage. They were less than a mile away and wanted to meet. The tribes were Kiowa, led by Santanta and Lone Wolf.

"This was unbelievable," Sheridan's biographer wrote. "For several grueling days Sheridan had led his men across rough terrain in vicious weather to bag these very Indians, and now that they were within his grasp, Hazen dared to throw a protective cloak around them."

Hazen had declared in his letter that Santanta and his tribe were innocent of any depredations and thus had given them immunity from attack by the soldiers. Custer was in favor of attacking the Kiowa anyway, despite Hazen's claim of innocence for them. Mahwissa insisted that Santanta had killed Clara Blinn, and perhaps Elliott and his men as well. Custer argued that Hazen had been deceived by Santanta into believing he was a friend to the whites.

Go after him now, Custer urged, but Sheridan said he could not attack Indians Hazen had declared to be friendly. Hazen had been appointed by General Sherman, who had ordered Sheridan to cooperate with him. Sheridan would not defy Sherman, despite his loathing of Santanta and his anger at Hazen.

Sheridan had no choice but to allow a parley with the chief he believed deserved to die, but his frustration was so great that he sent Custer to do the talking. Custer went out to meet the Kiowa party, accompanied by Colonel John Crosby, who was Sheridan's aide, plus several other officers, reporter Keim, and a band of scouts. As they approached the chiefs who were waiting in a narrow valley, they noticed hundreds of warriors riding back and forth on the surrounding hilltops. They had their weapons raised above their heads and were shouting war chants.

Santanta's body was painted in red, and he carried a long lance with red streamers hanging from it. A powerful, barrel-chested man of perhaps fifty years, he spoke in a booming voice as he offered to shake hands with Custer and Crosby. Both refused the gesture. Custer said he never shook hands

with anyone unless he knew for certain that he was a friend. One of the
other Indians walked up to Custer
and stroked his arm.

"Heap big nice sonabitch," he
said in a friendly tone.

Santanta was decidedly not
friendly after his handshake was
refused. He beat his chest and yelled,
"Me Kiowa!"

Custer grew concerned that he
was about to signal the warriors on
the hilltops to charge, but at that
moment, Sheridan and his entire
command of two thousand troops
came into view. Santanta calmed
down quickly when he saw them.
Custer told the chiefs he would
honor Colonel Hazen's request that

Santanta, a Kiowa chief.
(*Library of Congress*)

the Kiowa be treated as friendly Indians, but only if the entire
tribe went to Fort Cobb to show their peaceful intentions.
Santanta and Lone Wolf agreed: they and twenty of their warriors would accompany the soldiers to show good faith. The
rest of the people would take longer to reach the fort because
of the poor condition of their horses.

Neither Custer nor Sheridan believed Santanta's promise.
They were certain that the chief was feigning friendship and
accompanying the troops in order to allow the remainder of
the Kiowa to escape.

When the troopers prepared to depart for Fort Cobb the next
morning, they found that most of the Kiowa had indeed
slipped away during the night. Others disappeared during the
day, a few at a time. Finally, as the column neared Fort Cobb,
only Santanta and Lone Wolf remained with the soldiers.

Custer suspected that they would also try to leave, so he gave a prearranged signal to the officers riding with them. They drew their revolvers and took aim at the two chiefs. Custer told Romero, the interpreter, to tell them they were prisoners.

Once they reached the fort, Sheridan and Custer confronted Hazen. They blamed him for protecting the Kiowa. Sheridan and Custer knew Santanta was lying about wanting peace because Mahwissa said they were responsible for the murders of Clara and Willie Blinn, and perhaps Major Elliott as well.

Hazen said Santanta could not have been involved because he had been having breakfast with Hazen at Fort Cobb on the morning of the Washita battle. Custer and Sheridan stood their ground, insisting that Santanta was guilty and should be punished, but they knew that would not happen as long as there was the chance that the Kiowa would come to the fort for protection. Sherman had made it clear that Indians who turned themselves in would be considered peaceable and offered refuge as well as food and supplies.

The Kiowa moved closer to the fort but refused to come in. Mistrust worked both ways. Santanta's son rode as a courier between the two groups. One message he brought was a promise to come to the fort but only if Chiefs Santanta and Lone Wolf were freed and allowed to rejoin their people. That offer was refused immediately. Sheridan's patience had run out. He told Custer that Santanta and Lone Wolf were guilty of many outrages and must pay the ultimate penalty for their crimes.

"This matter has gone on long enough, and must be stopped. You can inform Lone Wolf and Santanta that we shall wait until sundown tomorrow for their tribe to come in; if by that time the village is not here, Lone Wolf and Santanta will be hung, and troops sent in pursuit of the village."

The Kiowa arrived the following evening and settled on a reservation under the watchful eye of the army, but Sheridan remained dissatisfied. "I will always regret," he wrote in his official report, "that I did not hang these Indians; they had deserved it many times."

On January 6, 1869, Custer led the 7th Cavalry forty miles south of Fort Cobb to a new post Sheridan had established. It was named Fort Sill, in honor of a West Point colleague of Sheridan's, Brigadier General Joshua Sill, killed in the Civil War. It was planned to be the new gathering point for all Plains Indian tribes to live under the control of the army. They would never again be allowed to roam free.

But there were still tribes to subdue. Sherman wrote to Sheridan that he was pleased with the results of Custer's attack at the Washita, but he wanted more. "I want you to go ahead; kill and punish the hostiles, rescue the captive white women and children, capture and destroy the ponies." Sherman favored all-out war, and Custer would continue to play the leading role.

His next expedition was to go after the remaining Cheyenne and Arapaho who had fled into the Wichita Mountains after the attack on Black Kettle's village. They were nearly destitute, low on food and forage, and Custer was so confident that he could bring them in to Fort Sill that he set out with a very small force, only forty men and some scouts. Monahsetah and her new baby went with them.

On January 26, Custer found the Arapaho camp of Little Raven, who, along with Black Kettle, had placed his mark on many treaties. Custer had no trouble persuading Little Raven that it was futile to resist the soldiers, and the Arapaho came with him peacefully. There were still Cheyenne on the loose, and Custer vowed to bring them in, too, or kill them. That was for them to decide.

He left Fort Sill again on March 2 with the 7th Cavalry and part of the 19th Kansas, now serving as infantry, since there were no longer enough horses for them all. The column contained one thousand five hundred men, and it was almost two weeks before they finally found the Cheyenne. The Indians were camped in a large village of some 260 lodges on Sweetwater Creek in Texas. Their chief was Medicine Arrows.

With Monahsetah as interpreter, Custer learned that two white women who had been captured in Kansas the previous fall were being held in the village. He knew that if he attacked, the Cheyenne would kill them. "While knowing the Cheyennes to be deserving of castigation," Custer wrote, "and feeling assured that they were almost in our power, I did not dare to imperil the lives of the two white captives by making an attack on the village, although never before or since have we seen so favorable an opportunity for administering well-merited punishment to one of the strongest and most troublesome of the hostile tribes." He decided to establish a truce first—hold a parley and then seize the advantage through more devious means.

Custer was riding out ahead of his troops, as usual, accompanied by his Osage scouts and Lieutenant William Cooke. On March 13, he spotted a group of twenty Cheyenne warriors who were watching them. Custer glanced behind to see how close his men were, but they were still more than a mile away. He rode forward on his own anyway and gestured for one of the warriors to come to meet him.

"I advanced with my revolver in my left hand," Custer wrote, "while my right hand was held aloft as a token that I was inclined to be friendly." A Cheyenne warrior rode out to him and they shook hands. Using sign language, Custer learned that Chief Medicine Arrows was among the group watching him. The Indians had slowly moved near enough to Custer to almost surround him. Apparently undisturbed by their presence, or at least not showing any sign of nervousness, he shook hands with Medicine Arrows. The chief wanted to know how many solders Custer had brought. Custer told him he had one thousand five hundred close at hand. At that moment, the head of the long, impressive column rode into view.

Medicine Arrows said that if Custer brought all those soldiers to the village, it would frighten the women and children. He suggested that Custer come alone so they could parley.

Custer agreed, certain that since Medicine Arrows knew the size of Custer's force, he would be safe. Only Cooke went with him.

Once settled in Medicine Arrows' lodge, Custer endured the long welcoming ceremony, including the traditional passing of the pipe. Then he got down to business. First Custer spoke of the need for peace between Indians and whites and said it could only come about if Medicine Arrows brought his people to live permanently near Camp Supply.

Custer knew that dealings with Indians required patience; he would not get an answer that day. He asked Medicine Arrows where his men could camp. The chief showed him to a spot about a mile from the village, and Custer left to rejoin his men.

However, the troops of the 19th Kansas were still talking about revenge for the deaths of the Blinns and the other victims of Indian raids in their territory. They were not interested in talk of making peace. They had joined up to kill Indians; they had suffered through a long winter, and now they had found some. Their officers were having difficulty keeping them in check. One shot fired, even by accident, could bring on a war. Custer issued strict orders against firing of weapons, but the Kansans obeyed only reluctantly. They cursed Custer for it, even calling him a coward and a traitor.

The situation became more dangerous when some of the Cheyenne came to Custer's camp under the guise of entertaining the soldiers with traditional songs and dances. Custer knew what they were up to. The Indians at their village planned to slip away while the troopers' attention was diverted. Custer planned to outwit them by arresting the chiefs who had come, holding them hostage to save the white women captives and bring the tribe back to Camp Supply.

He surreptitiously arranged for one hundred of his best soldiers to move into position surrounding the Indians, being careful to make it appear that they were there to enjoy the performances. At Custer's signal, they seized three of the chiefs, allowing the entertainers to flee. He sent word to Medicine Arrows that he intended to hang the chiefs unless the Cheyenne gave up their white captives and agreed to go to Camp Supply. Only then would the chiefs be released.

It was a dangerous gamble. The Indians could decide to kill the prisoners and make an attack on the soldiers, permitting their women and children to get away. After three days of posturing and negotiating with no progress, Custer had a stout rope swung across a branch of a willow tree. He tied the other end around the neck of one of the hostages. At Custer's command, soldiers pulled the rope taut and hoisted the chief to the point where only his toes touched the ground.

Then they let him down. Custer warned that he and the other two chiefs would be hauled off the ground and left hanging until death if the prisoners were not handed over "by the time the sun got within a hand's breadth of the horizon the next day." That clear message was sent by courier to Medicine Arrows.

At four o'clock the next afternoon, with the sun as close to the horizon as the breadth of a hand, the white prisoners were handed over to the soldiers. The brother of one of the women was among the soldiers. The women were described as "emaciated and swathed in stitched-together flour sacks, leggings, and moccasins. 'I never saw such heartbroken, hopeless expressions on the face of another human being,' remarked a scout." The band serenaded them by playing "Home, Sweet Home." *

---

*One of the women, nineteen-year-old Anna Brewster Morgan, gave birth to an Indian child a few months later. She never recovered from her months in captivity. "After I came back," she said, "the road seemed rough, and I often wished they had never found me." She died in an asylum in 1902. The other prisoner, twelve-year-old Sarah White, later married, had seven children, became a schoolteacher, and lived until 1939.

Custer had won again. He kept the three chiefs hostages to ensure that the Cheyenne village kept their promise to move to Camp Supply. Two weeks later, back at the camp, he wrote to Libbie, "I have been successful in my campaign against the Cheyennes. I outmarched them, outwitted them at their own game." He told a newspaper reporter, "I now hold the captive Cheyenne chiefs as hostages for the good behavior of their tribe and for the fulfillment of the promise of the latter to come in and conform to the demands of the government. This, I consider, is the end of the Indian war."

There is one final tale in the story of Custer and Black Kettle's Cheyenne nation. It occurred during Custer's initial meeting with Medicine Arrows, and the Cheyenne never forgot. They passed on the story from one generation to the next about how Medicine Arrows foretold Custer's fate if he ever made war on the Cheyenne again, as he had done at the Washita.

Custer did not understand the chief's words and would not have believed him anyway. And why should he? He was the victor at the Washita, the conqueror, head of an invincible army that had succeeded where others had failed in ending the Indian war on the Great Plains. The Cheyenne were a beaten people, no match for the Boy General.

The day Custer went to the lodge of Medicine Arrows, the chief gestured for him to sit at his right, beneath four sacred medicine arrows that hung from a forked stick. To sit in that position was to be dishonored, but Custer did not know that. The chief lit his pipe, puffed on it, and passed it to Custer, who forced himself to participate in a ritual he never liked.

Using sign language, Custer had told Medicine Arrows he had not come to make war on the Cheyenne but had come in peace. At least Custer had to pretend that he did. He later wrote, "As I knew that the captives could not be released should hostilities once occur between the troops and Indians, I became for a time an advocate of peace measures and informed the chiefs that such was my purpose." Custer told

Medicine Arrows that the only reason he had come was to persuade them to go to Camp Supply. He said nothing about the white prisoners.

Speaking in his native tongue, Medicine Arrows said that Custer was not a good man and that the Cheyenne would never forget the attack at the Washita and the death of Black Kettle. Custer, ignorant of the chief's vow, puffed on the pipe. "I was expected to make a miniature volcano of myself," he wrote. He then asked about the meaning of the pipe-smoking ceremony.

One man replied that when someone smoked the pipe before the sacred medicine arrows, he was giving his oath that he was telling the truth, that he had come only in peace and not to make war. "I will never harm the Cheyenne," Custer said, willing to tell them whatever he thought they wanted to hear if it resulted in saving the prisoners. "I will never point my gun at a Cheyenne again."

When the fire in the pipe went out, Medicine Arrows turned it upside down and tapped the ashes over Custer's boots. Custer asked what that meant.

"If you break your promise, you and your soldiers will go to dust like this."

"I will never kill another Cheyenne," Custer repeated.

Cheyenne were among the Indians Custer and the 7th Cavalry attacked seven years later at the Little Big Horn. It was June 25, 1876, the day Custer's luck ran out. After the battle, two Cheyenne women came upon his body. They had seen him before, when he had visited Medicine Arrows in his lodge. They knelt down and punctured his eardrums with a sewing awl. They did it to improve his hearing, they said, because obviously he had not heard Medicine Arrows' warning about what would happen to him if he ever made war on the Cheyenne.

EPILOGUE
AND THE BAND PLAYED "GARRY OWEN"

In 1968, the centennial commemoration of the Battle of the Washita was held in Cheyenne, Oklahoma, a town on the banks of the Washita with a population of fewer than one thousand. The town is at the western edge of the state, near the Washita Battlefield National Historic Site and the Black Kettle National Grassland. In town, a one-story brick building houses the Black Kettle Museum.

The Cheyenne who lived in the area agreed, albeit reluctantly, to the idea of a reenactment marking the brutal attack on their village on one condition: they wanted permission to bury the remains of a Cheyenne child who had been killed in the battle. The body had been on display in a local museum. Permission was granted, and the reenactment of Custer's attack on the village began.

Local whites were to play the roles of soldiers, while Cheyenne adults and children took the parts of their ancestors in a mock village of lodges reconstructed in the old style. Unfortunately, no one told the Cheyenne that another group was also joining the reenactment.

The group was known as the Grandsons of the Seventh Cavalry, but their official, if somewhat grandiose title, was U.S. Seventh Cavalry, Grand Army of the Republic, Reactivated. They showed up in authentic uniforms, just like those worn by Custer's men a century before. They charged the Cheyenne village, firing blanks from the same kinds of weapons—Spencer carbines—that Custer's troopers had used to kill the Cheyenne reenactors' ancestors. And the band

played "Garry Owen," the hated song Custer's band had started to play to signal the attack on Black Kettle's village.

It was just like old times. A bit too much like old times for
the Cheyenne, who were incensed at the blatant lack of sensi-
tivity to their tribal memories and feelings about the killings a
hundred years before. Despite their anger, which they had long
since learned to hold in check, the Cheyenne continued with
the commemoration activities.

The final event of the day was the burial of the child's
remains on the grounds of the Black Kettle Museum. A solemn
procession was led by Lawrence Hart, a Cheyenne chief who
was also a Mennonite pastor. He and the other chiefs carried
the remains in a bronze casket made for the occasion. Another
touch of authenticity was provided by the weather: snow was
falling, just as it had the day Black Kettle's village was
attacked. The chiefs chanted traditional Cheyenne burial songs
as they solemnly and sadly headed toward the museum that
honored Black Kettle's memory. Suddenly, a shout interrupted
their sacred chants.

"Present arms!"

It was the Grandsons of the Seventh Cavalry.

Pastor Hart (referring to himself in the third person) wrote:
"Emotions flared. How dare they salute someone their grand-
fathers killed, thought Hart. In the midst of the explosive
atmosphere, a Cheyenne woman, Lucille Young Bull, took off
her beautiful new woolen blanket and draped it over the coffin as the procession went by. As tradition dictated, the blanket would later be given as an honored gift."

After the burial ceremony, Pastor Hart and the chiefs met to
decide which dignitary would have the honor of receiving the
blanket. Several of the elders urged that they follow the teach-
ings of the ancient Cheyenne prophet Sweet Medicine, who
long ago foretold the coming of the whites. "They will keep
coming," he had said, "and you will all die off."

Sweet Medicine had also urged reconciliation with one's
enemies, a precept Black Kettle followed. Now the older chiefs

wanted to put that teaching into practice. They advised Hart to present the now-sacred ceremonial blanket to the leader of the Grandsons of the Seventh Cavalry, as a gesture of forgiveness and reconciliation.

Hart wondered if he could comply. His grandfather, Afraid of Beaver, had barely escaped with his life at the Washita by hiding in a snowdrift. And he had been one of the men who recovered the bodies of Black Kettle and his wife from the river after the soldiers left. But the elders were persuasive, and their view prevailed. They summoned Captain Eric Saul, the leader of the Grandsons of the Seventh Cavalry.

Saul stepped forward when his name was called and drew his saber in a smart military salute to the chiefs. Hart told him to turn around. The captain did an about-face, and Hart draped the sacred blanket over the man's shoulders, though his hands were trembling as he did so.

At the close of the burial ceremony, the Grandsons of the Seventh Cavalry fired several volleys in a salute to honor the child who was murdered by Custer's men at the Washita.

"There was not a dry eye in the audience," Pastor Hart wrote. "The grandsons followed the chiefs back to the [Black Kettle] museum. Then and there they embraced. Some cried. Some apologized. When Hart greeted the commander of the regiment, Captain Saul, the officer took the 'Garry Owen' pin from his uniform and handed it to Hart.

"Accept this on behalf of all the Cheyenne Indian people," Saul said. "Never again will you people hear 'Garry Owen.'"

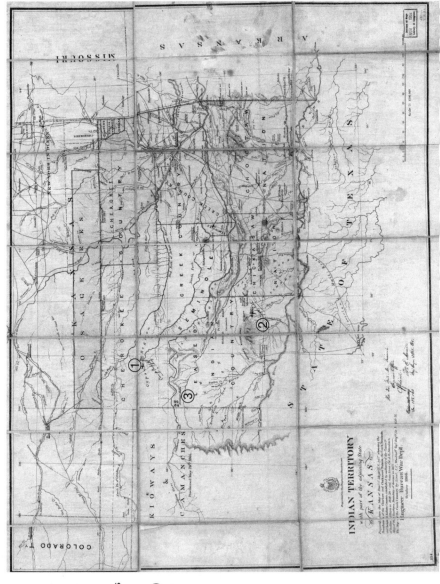

An official US military map of Indian Territory (present day Oklahoma) drawn in October 1866, with later handwritten additions showing the locations of Camp Supply (1) and Fort Sill (2). Black Kettle's encampment (3) was along the Washita River. (*Library of Congress*)

NOTES

PROLOGUE

vii "They call us Americans. We are Osages." (Keim, 122)

ix "What a pretty girl he would have made." (Ambrose, 83)

ix "In years long numbered with the past." (Schultz, *Custer*, 2)

ix "We destroyed everything of value to the Indians." (Wert, 277)

x "Emerged from the Washita campaign a new man." (Utley, *Cavalier*, 78)

x "Trampling and roar of a cavalry charge." (Hardorff, 207)

x "Garryowen" (www.us7thcavalry.com/legend.htm)

xi "The mothers had their offspring mounted behind them." (Keim, 122–123)

xiii "Made a colorful display." (Nye, 132)

xiii "General Sheridan said that the appearance of the troops." (Custer, *My Life*, 269)

CHAPTER 1: THEY WILL KEEP COMING

Sweet Medicine prophecies (Grinnell, *Cheyenne Indians*, vol. 2, 345–381)

4 "The greatest chief the Cheyenne possessed." (Brill, 49, 50)

5 "Cheyenne women ruled the camps." (Berthrong, 36)

6 "We cut off his hands." (Marquis, 12)

7 "Scalp and torture the wounded." (Longstreet, 56)

7 "A race incapable of being judged." (Custer, *My Life*, 14)

10 "If the traders occasionally had been hard to like." (Smith, 10)

11 "If I could see this thing." (Grinnell, *Cheyenne Indians*, vol. 2, 165)

12 "A smothering passion for revenge." (Lavender, 343)

CHAPTER 2: A MODEL YOUNG OFFICER

14 "He delighted in going right to the line." (Ambrose, 91)

18 "Beautiful as Absalom with his yellow curls." (Custer and Custer, 13)

18 "Pointed to him with pride as a true patriot." (Monaghan, 60)

19 "Everywhere . . . we were offered fashionable wines." (Custer and Custer, 26)

19 "I took my position in front at a slow trot." (Custer and Custer, 27)

20 "It is said . . . that there is no real or perfect happiness." (Wert, 49–50)

21 "Like a wild and untamable animal." (Connell, 109)

22 "God bless you, old boy!" (Custer and Custer, 30)

23 "He was reported to me as having accomplished an act." (Custer and Custer, 31)

23 "I have more confidence in General McClellan." (Custer and Custer, 27–28)

23 "Simply a reckless, gallant boy." (Wert, 54)

25 "I selected him as my game." (Connell, 110)

25 "Draw me not without cause." (Whittaker, 158)

26 "I must say that I shall regret to see the war end." (Wert, 59)

26 "Cousin Maggie at the piano." (Custer and Custer, 35)

28 "From my corner in our pew." (Custer and Custer, 47)

CHAPTER 3: A CIVILIZED AND ENLIGHTENED PEOPLE

32 "The chiefs who had come to the council." (Smith, 13)

34 "Old Sumner has had one good effect on us." (Utley, *Cavalier*, 125)

35 "Bear witness." (Berthrong, 139)

36 "Colonel Sumner has worked a wondrous change." (Utley, *Cavalier*, 125)

39 "It was freedom of movement." (Marshall, 14–15)

40 "If I were an Indian." (Custer, *My Life*, 22)

42 "Lofty buildings are rising." (Hafen, 197)

43 "Many a time in going about my household duties." (Ashley, 222–223)

44 "A civilized and enlightened people." (Perkin, 261)

CHAPTER 4: THE BEST CAVALRY GENERAL IN THE WORLD

46 "We have . . . onions, radishes, and ripe tomatoes." (Monaghan, 116)

47 "We have not a more gallant man in the field." (Custer and Custer, 55)

48 "I was surrounded by rebels." (Urwin, 53)

49 "How are you, General Custer?" (stories about Custer's promotion) (Monaghan, 133; Frost, *General Custer's Libbie*, 1976)

49 "The next morning [Custer] was a full-fledged Brigadier General." (Custer and Custer, 60)

50 "West Point conceit." (stories about Custer's uniform) (Wert, 85; Urwin, 66)
50 "All those little vexatious rules." (Whittaker, 172)
51 "I'll lead you this time, boys." (Monaghan, 142)
51 "The most reckless and thoughtless stunt." (Urwin, 72)
52 "So sudden and violent was the collision." (Utley, *Cavalier*, 23)
53 "I challenge the annals of warfare." (Monaghan, 149)
53 "A glorious fellow, full of energy." (Wert, 102)
53 "In years long numbered with the past." (Utley, *Cavalier*, 2)
53 "He fascinated a nation." (Wert, 178)
54 "He was clad in a suit of black velvet." (Kidd, 129)
55 "Fifteen day's leave-of-absence?" (Frost, *General Custer's Libbie*, 70).
56 "Often I think of the vast responsibility resting on me." (Custer and Custer, 65)
56 "He acted like a man who made a business of his profession." (Custer and Custer, 211)
56 "Boys of Michigan." (Monaghan, 166)
57 "I gave the command 'Forward!'" (Custer and Custer, 66)
57 "No soldier who saw him on that day." (Frost, *General Custer's Libbie*, 70)
57 "Oh, could you have but seen some of the charges." (Custer and Custer, 66)
58 "Avoid overdoing." (Wert, 137)
58 "Day by day." (Leckie, 40)
58 "Such style as we go in." (Leckie, 41)
58 "She became the leading light of the Washington social scene." (Ambrose, 197)
58 "So you are the wife of the general." (Frost, *General Custer's Libbie*, 105)
59 "He was an unimpressive little man." (Morris, 1)
60 "My sole wish was to become a soldier." (Morris, 14)
60 "Not only was he short, unattractive." (Morris, 21)
62 "Stayed with them, sitting coolly on his charger." (Urwin, 140)
62 "His headquarters flag of the gayest colors." (Urwin, 142)
62 "Custer was everywhere present." (Wert, 164; Kidd, 360)
63 "Everything except his toothbrush." (Custer and Custer, 109)
63 "When his troopers took up their proper stations." (Urwin, 199)
63 "You see that officer down there?" (Urwin, 199)
64 "Displayed the judgment of a Napoleon." (Custer and Custer, 125)

64 "Dear Friend, Thanks for setting me up." (Connell, 118)
64 "General, a gallant officer always makes gallant soldiers." (Custer and Custer, 127)
64 "His modesty was equal to his courage." (Custer and Custer, 127)
65 "By God, Phil!" (Utley, *Cavalier*, 30)
65 "Fittingly, this emblem of war's end." (Utley, *Cavalier*, 23)
66 "My dear Madam." (Custer and Custer, 159)
67 "We were massed along the sidewalk." (Custer and Custer, 166)
67 "Then . . . with his long, yellow curly hair." (Whittaker, 314)
68 "He had nothing to look forward to." (Monaghan, 251)

CHAPTER 5: WE TOOK NO PRISONERS

70 "Dispatched with a savagery rarely equaled." (Utley, 265)
73 "By the grace of God and these two revolvers." (Speer, unpaged)
76 "Does the Great Father want us to live like white men?" (MacMechen, 118)
78 "There is but one course for us to pursue." (Berthrong, 180)
79 "Though I think we have punished." (Hatch, 116)
79 "Stop the fighting!" (Hatch, 118)
81 "This Indian war is no myth." (Hoig, *Sand Creek*, 60)
81 "Dead cattle, full of arrows." (Hafen, 311)
82 "Extensive Indian depredations, with murder of families." (US Congress, *Massacre*, 65)
85 "I am young no longer." (Wynkoop, 88–89)
86 "I was bewildered with an exhibition of such patriotism." (Wynkoop, 89)
86 "If any [Indians] are caught in your vicinity." (Kraft, 98)
88 "This white man is not here to laugh at us." (Wynkoop, 92)
89 "Had been raised to kill Indians." (US Congress, *Massacre*, 77)
89 "I followed Major Wynkoop to Fort Lyon." (US Congress, *Massacre*, 87–89)
90 "I am not a big war chief." (US Congress, *Massacre*, 87–89)
91 "The Cheyenne nation." (Craig, 186–187)
92 "Scalps are what we are after." (US Congress, *Massacre*, 117)
93 "I thought it murder to jump them friendly Indians." (Kraft, 131)
94 "Damn any man who is in sympathy with an Indian!" (Hoig, *Sand Creek*, 143)
94 "Take no prisoners." (US Congress, *Sand Creek*, 68–69)
95 "Nothing lives long except the earth and the mountain." (Grinnell, *Fighting Cheyennes*, 177)
96 "I refused to fire." (Silas Soule to Ned Wynkoop, December 14, 1864, www.rebelcherokee.labdiva.com)

96 "Never saw more bravery." (Grinnell, *Fighting Cheyennes*, 172)
97 "Among the brilliant feats of arms in Indian warfare." (Gardiner, 149)

CHAPTER 6: DREAMS OF GLORY
100 "We were like children let out of school." (Wert, 231)
100 "The two veterans sat together." (Monaghan, 254)
102 "Bully for the Colorado Boys!" (Perkin, 275)
103 "Won for themselves a name." (US Congress, *Massacre*, 53)
104 "Numerous as the leaves on the trees." . . . "But what do we want to live for?" (Schultz, *Month*, 146)
105 "We found everything a hundred years behind." (Wert, 232)
105 "These rough Westerners considered him a martinet." (Monaghan, 257)
106 "Hog jowls and flour." (Leckie, 77–78)
107 "The red-faced firing squad." (Frost, *General Custer's Libbie*, 138)
107 "His word was law." (Monaghan, 258)
108 "Since this horrible massacre." (Wynkoop, 23)
109 "About one o'clock, the orgy seemed to reach its height." (Ware, 374)
111 "The temperature was about 120 degrees." (Connell, 120–121)
111 "Many a poor fellow I have seen with head shaved." (Connell, 121)
111 "That is the penalty the commanding officer generally pays." (Leckie, 78)
112 "In an admiring and sympathetic semicircle." (Connell, 121–122)
112 "Oh, I am enjoying life so thoroughly." (Wert, 238)
113 "The only way to fight Indians." (US Congress, *Massacre*, 26)
114 "I did not hear anything about that." (US Congress, *Massacre*, 26)
115 "It is difficult to believe that beings in the form of men." (US Congress, *Massacre*, iv)
115 "By such prevarication and shuffling." (US Congress, *Massacre*, iv)
115 "As to Colonel Chivington." (US Congress, *Massacre*, v)
116 "Custer! It does me good to look at you again." (Ambrose, 236)
116 "After the theater several of us went on an expedition." (Custer and Custer, 181)
117 "My costume was elegant and rich." (Custer and Custer, 181)
117 "I sat beside her on a sofa." (Frost, *General Custer's Libbie*, 148)

120 "Know Colonel Chivington? I should." (Schultz, *Month*, 178)

CHAPTER 7: WE SHALL HAVE WAR

122 "My shame is as big as the earth." (Hatch, 199)
123 "I was surrounded and greeted with the utmost kindness." (Wynkoop, 25)
123 "I once thought that I was the only man that persevered." (Wynkoop, 25)
125 "Our Great Father sent you here." (Hatch, 202)
127 "If the government is obliged to open war." (Berthrong, 261)
129 "These recruits represented almost every strata of human society." (Chandler, 2)
129 "Butchers, rampaging around the West." (Utley, *Frontier Regulars*, xii)
130 "Lunch might be Cincinnati Chicken." (Connell, 150)
130 "The spring of 1867 was the time." (Utley, *Frontier Regulars*, 87)
131 "Poor old soldiers!" (Utley, *Frontier Regulars*, 85)
131 "A medley of incongruous elements." (Utley, *Cavalier*, 46)
132 "Dominated the conversation." (Leckie, 91)
132 "Squandered every paycheck." (Monaghan, 282)
133 "Distinguished man but given at time to hellish periodical sprees." (Barnitz, 281)
133 "Great courage and enterprise." (Custer, *My Life*, 78)
134 "All of the people west of the Missouri River." (Berthrong, 267)
134 "I find the size of Indian stampedes." (Berthrong, 266)
135 "Eager to 'make coups.'" (Athearn, 98)
135 "Eyes torn out and laid on rocks." (Ambrose, 225)
136 "We must act with vindictive earnestness." (Fellman, 264)
136 "I expect to have two Indian wars on my hands." (Athearn, 100–101)
136 "I have been among them constantly." (Berthrong, 270)
137 "Our troops must get among them." (Berthrong, 272)
137 "We shall have war." (Berthrong, 273)

CHAPTER 8: HANCOCK THE SUPERB

138 "I am sorry to say that the result of the expedition is disastrous." (Kennedy, 22)
138 "It would have been for the better." (Frost, *Court-Martial*, 30)
139 "Hancock left an Indian war behind him." (Jordan, 197)
139 "He simply did not understand." (Monnett, 38)
139 "The most magnificent looking General." (Haskell, 15)

139 "His handsome face and figure." (Jordan, 10)
140 "He was always neatly dressed." (Jordan, 57)
141 "The cavalry and infantry were not ready for combat." (Nye, 68)
142 "He is a boy of extraordinary intelligence." (Stanley, 3)
143 "Proceeded to take liberties with my person." (R. Hall, 118)
143 "Within a few weeks of arriving in America." (R. Hall, 119–120)
144 "Enlisting in the Confederate service." (Bierman, 32)
144 "Littered by the forms of about a thousand dead." (Bierman, 34)
144 "Wronged children of the soil." (R. Hall, 153)
145 "He stands six feet one inch in his moccasins." (Hoig, *Peace Chiefs*, 6)
145 "A strange character." (Custer, 44)
146 "Hancock was clearly becoming edgy." (Jordan, 190)
146 "The Indians were dressed in various styles." (Stanley, 29)
148 "Now I have a great many soldiers." (Kennedy, 54–55)
148 "You sent for us; we came here." (Stanley, 31)
150 "Nature intended him for a savage state." (Custer, *My Life*, 21)
150 "How galling it must have been." (Kennedy, 58–60)

CHAPTER 9: WAR AT ITS MOST SAVAGE
151 "One of the finest and most imposing military displays." (Custer, *My Life*, 32)
152 "The wise foresight and strong love of fair play." (Custer, *My Life*, 33)
152 "Everything now looked like war." (Kennedy, 62)
152 "Here in battle array, facing each other." (Custer, *My Life*, 34)
153 "A punctual West Pointer." (Jordan, 192)
154 "He is one of the finest specimens." (Kennedy, 64)
154 "From his manner it was quite evident that he was indifferent." (Davis, 295)
155 "We don't want war." (Stanley, 38)
155 "My horses are poor." (Stanley, 38)
155 "This I communicated to General Hancock." (Jordan, 193)
155 "I am not surprised that the Indians do not wish." (Jordan, 193)
156 "You must get them back." (Grinnell, *Fighting Cheyennes*, 243)
156 "Poor Hancock." (Jordan, 183)
156 "Easily said but not so easily done." (Custer, *My Life*, 36)
156 "No sooner was our line completely formed." (Custer, *My Life*, 37–38)

157 "He enjoyed Isaac's company." (Kennedy, 69)

157 "Each one grasped his revolver." (Custer, *My Life*, 39)

158 "The Indian village consists of about three hundred hide lodges." (Stanley, 39)

158 "This looks like the commencement of war." (Utley, *Frontier Regulars*, 116)

158 "[I]n spite of the strict guard kept." (Stanley, 39)

159 "Blankets were carefully rolled." (Custer, *My Life*, 43)

159 "Oh! It was a glorious sight." (Kennedy, 75)

159 "The men in this army he found to be mostly bums." (Monaghan, 288)

160 "Encumbered by their families." (Custer, *My Life*, 46)

160 "No obstacle seemed to stand in our way." (Custer, *My Life*, 47–48)

161 "Here I was, alone in the heart of the Indian country." (Custer, *My Life*, 51)

162 "This was his first independent command." (Monaghan, 289)

163 "So mangled and burned." (Custer, *My Life*, 52)

163 "This was the first deadly work of the savage Indians." (Kennedy, 84)

163 "Lookout Station was burned." (Kennedy, 85)

164 "The following is a true list of the miscellanea." (Stanley, 46–47)

164 "The dry poles of the wigwams." (Stanley, 47)

165 "Stirred up a hornet's nest." (Monnett, 53)

166 "Now white people have taken all we had." (Grinnell, *Fighting Cheyennes*, 257)

166 "Apparently the diminutive 4-4-0 wood burner." (Monnett, 99)

166 "Plundered and burned the wrecked train." (Grinnell, *Fighting Cheyennes*, 258)

167 "The [Indians] would ride up to a station." (Nye, 83)

167 "Between Bishop's Ranch and Junction Cut Off." (Stanley, 129)

168 "Bugler Charles Clark fell." (Nye, 91)

168 "I have seen in days gone by." (Nye, 92)

169 "If fifty Indians are allowed to remain." (Berthrong, 284)

169 "The Indians are poor and proud." (Berthrong, 284)

170 "And to talk with the old ones." (Berthrong, 288)

CHAPTER 10: THE TIME HAS COME THAT I MUST GO

171 "Miserable log shanties with stone chimneys." (Monaghan, 290)

172 "Gone off armed and mounted!" (Barnitz, *Life in Custer's Cavalry*, 53)

172 "General Custer has become bilious." (Barnitz, *Life in Custer's Cavalry*, 46, 50)
173 "A halter was placed around the man's neck." (Barnard, 96)
173 "You remember how eager I was to have you for my little wife?" (Burkey, 17)
173 "Wolves, coyotes, prairie dogs." (Burkey, 21)
174 "Perfect in horsemanship." (Custer, *My Life*, 65)
175 "Referred to every object or event in his life." (Frost, *Court-Martial*, 39)
175 "Lying on knees and face." (Custer and Custer, 204–205)
177 "Custer's mistakes were overwhelming." (Ambrose, 261)
177 "His every major decision." (Utley, *Cavalier*, 51)
178 "I was never so anxious in my life." (Wert, 259)
178 "The willfulness and lack of judgment." (Monaghan, 295)
179 "Stop those men." (Monaghan, 296)
180 "A sight met our gaze." (Custer, *My Life*, 111–112)
181 "While at dinner." (Hoig, *Peace Chiefs*, 17)
181 "The clank of a saber." (Leckie, 105)
182 "There was in that summer of 1867." (Leckie, 105)
184 "When the other Cheyennes arrived." (Jones, 206)
185 "We are only revenging that one thing." (Berthrong, 294)
185 "A vast amphitheater." (Kraft, 212)
186 "Dressed in a crimson petticoat." (Monnett, 107)
186 Among the commissioners. (Connell, 144, 145)
187 "Nose was yellow." (Connell, 196)
188 "Nothing had changed." (Kraft, 216)
188 "We were once friends with the whites." (Stanley, 233–235)
189 "What we say to you may at first be unpleasant." (Stanley, 254–256)
190 "I ask the Commission." (Jones, 127)
190 "Look at the medal I wear." (Jones, 157)
191 "Only after Senator Henderson." (Hoig, *Peace Chiefs*, 90)
192 "Superstitious in regard to touching the pen." (Barnitz, *Life in Custer's Cavalry*, 115)

CHAPTER 11: WAR IS SURELY UPON US
194 "Our white brothers are pulling away." (Hatch, 235)
195 "I have the honor to inform you." (Chandler, 9)
196 "Black Kettle and the other chiefs." (Nye, 119)
197 "I can no longer have confidence." (Berthrong, 307)
198 "Murdered 117, wounded 16." (Chandler, 10)
199 "It was very hot, our meat had become putrid." (Monnett, 161, 162)

199 "At the Sioux camp." (Monnett, 148)
199 "[They] were Negroes, but boy, were we glad to see them!" (Monnett, 166)
200 "All the Cheyenne and Arapaho are now at war." (Berthrong, 309)
201 "The more we can kill this year." (Kennedy, 146)
201 "They laugh at our credulity." (Berthrong, 320)
201 "The Indian is a lazy, idle vagabond." (Monnett, 112)
202 "Let your soldiers grow long hair." (Monnett, 113)
202 "Accept the war begun by our enemies." (Moore, 353)

CHAPTER 12: THE STAR OF THE WASHITA

204 "Headquarters, Department of the Missouri." (Frost, *Court-Martial*, 266)
205 "Sheridan had seen Custer in action." (Ambrose, 286)
205 "It could hardly be said that Custer did penance." (Frost, *Court-Martial*, 265)
206 "Living in involuntary but unregretful retirement." (Custer, *My Life*, 181)
206 "Official examination of certain events." (Custer, *My Life*, 182)
206 "Now I can smoke a cigar in peace." (Morris, 310)
206 "We are all glad to see him." (Wert, 269)
207 "My official actions shall not be tarnished." (Monaghan, 307)
207 "I wish you could have been with us." (Custer, *Following the Guidon*, 7)
207 "Indignant and provoked." (Barnitz, 205)
208 "They are painted and dressed for the war-path." (Custer, *Following the Guidon*, 23)
208 "Ponderous mat of flaming red whiskers." (Keim, 111)
209 "We are going into the heart of the Indian country." (Custer, *Following the Guidon*, 13)
209 "We all went up and called on General Sheridan." (Barnitz, 209)
210 "Considerable snow fell last night." (Barnitz, 210)
210 "Everybody was in prime condition." (Chandler, 14–15)
211 "To this day I have not forgotten." (Barnard, 113)
211 "This has been a very disagreeable day." (Hardorff, 106)
211 "The trunk was burst open." (Greene, 97)
212 "Custer's rule, all through the Civil War." (Monaghan, 314)
212 "No talking [was] permitted." (Chandler, 17)
213 "What is the matter?" (Custer, *My Life*, 231)
214 "General, suppose we find more Indians." (Utley, *Cavalier*, 65)
214 "One dog in my company." (Hardorff, 190)

214 "We were obliged to sit in our saddles." (Barnard, 115)
215 "Daylight never seemed so long in coming." (Chandler, 19)

CHAPTER 13: HERE GOES FOR A BREVET OR A COFFIN

217 "I do not feel afraid to go among the white men." (Carroll, 32)
217 "I look upon you as the representative." (Carroll, 32)
218 "I am sent here to this territory as a peace chief." (Carroll, 33)
221 "I don't like this delay." (Powell, *People*, 600)
221 "Toward morning the moon disappeared." (Powell, *People*, 600)
222 "Wake up! White Men!" (Ediger, 138)
222 "We had approached so near the village." (Custer, *My Life*, 240)
222 "I rode right beside Custer." (Utley, *Cavalier*, 67)
223 "We became frightened." (Ediger, 138)
223 "One of their bullets caught [Black Kettle]." (Powell, *People*, 603)
224 "We did not show much mercy." (Kraft, 50)
224 "Hold my hand tightly." (Ediger, 139)
225 "Stood so near me that the blaze." (Barnitz, 226)
226 "In the expectation that I would very speedily die." (Barnitz, 227)
227 "We could hear the women singing." (Hardorff, 333)
228 "Not in years had [the Osage] enjoyed such a glorious opportunity." (Brill, 156)
229 "Fell upon the body." (Harrison, 13)
230 "He forgave General Custer." (Greene, 197)
231 "Now, with the other dead around her." (Powell, *People*, 606)
232 "Ride out there and give the officer." (Utley, *Cavalier*, 68)
232 "In this grass we lay flat." (Ediger, 139)
232 "A long time later." (Hardorff, 328)
232 "Here goes for a brevet or a coffin." (Kraft, 53)

CHAPTER 14: THINGS WERE GOING TERRIBLY WRONG

236 "Peering over a ridge." (Utley, *Cavalier*, 68)
236 "On all sides of us." (Custer, *My Life*, 247)
237 "Violated a fundamental military precept." (Utley, *Cavalier*, 76)
238 "What was to be done?" (Custer, *My Life*, 146)
238 "An exceedingly comely squaw." (Custer, *My Life*, 282)
238 "Why, she is marryin' you to that young squaw!" (Custer, *My Life*, 253)
239 "Racing so fast that their tar-soaked wheels." (Powell, *People*, 615)

240 "We captured in good condition 24 saddles." (Carroll, 38)
241 "The wounded ponies passed near our hiding place." (Harrison, 18)
241 "The ponies after being shot broke away." (Harrison, 18)
241 "Would be little less than suicide." (Brill, 177)
243 "Following the fleeing savages." (Hardorff, 124)
243 "Look, we are safe." (Harrison, 19)
243 "Is this you, Moving Behind?" (Harrison, 20)
244 "We all got on our ponies." (Ediger, 141)

CHAPTER 15: HE DIED A SOLDIER'S DEATH
246 "A bloodthirsty monster." (Ambrose, 294)
246 "Taking sadistic pleasure in slaughtering." (Hutton, *Sheridan*, 96)
246 "One of the truest friends." (Hutton, *Sheridan*, 95)
246 "Black Kettle was a good man." (Greene, 166)
246 "Noble savage, the ruling spirit of his tribe." (Berthrong, 331)
246 "The murdered Black Kettle." (Athearn, 275)
247 "Two thousand miles away." (Athearn, 275)
247 "A worn out and worthless old cypher." (Hutton, *Sheridan*, 97)
247 "Aiders and abettors of savages." (Hutton, *Sheridan*, 98)
247 "Old Black Kettle and his murderers." (Hutton, *Sheridan*, 98–99)
247 "Never again would the Indians of the Great Plains." (Morris, 323)
248 "Oh is it not gratifying to be so thought of." (Hutton, *Sheridan*, 69)
248 "Was the only damper on our pleasure." (Hutton, *Sheridan*, 72)
249 "I am the man you are after." (Hardorff, 175)
249 "I never heard a word against General Custer." (Wert, 279)
249 "Some of the squaws." (Chandler, 23)
250 "As he died a soldier's death." (Custer, *My Life*, 269)
251 "During such painful operations." (Keim, 125)
252 "Was prepared to tell her captors anything." (Hutton, *Sheridan*, 73)
252 "She knows they are in your power." (Hutton, *Sheridan*, 73)
253 "Acted as a procurer for the officers." (Hutton, *Sheridan*, 74)
253 "Many of the [women] captured at Washita." (Greene, 169)
253 "Young and attractive." (Custer, *Following the Guidon*, 91)
254 "Suddenly lifting from the ground could be seen." (Keim, 143)
254 "The bodies of Elliott and his little band." (Carroll, 68)
255 "A scene was now witnessed." (Keim, 145)

256 "My name is Clara Blinn." (Carroll, 51)

256 "Her own person subjected to the fearful bestiality." (Connell, 181)

256 "Reserved to gratify the brutal lust." (Morris, 319)

CHAPTER 16: YOU AND YOUR SOLDIERS WILL GO TO DUST

257 "Indians have just brought in word." (Morris, 320)

258 "This was unbelievable." (Morris, 83)

259 "Heap big nice sonabitch." (Morris, 320)

260 "This matter has gone on long enough." (Custer, *My Life*, 305)

260 "I will always regret." (Morris, 321)

261 "I want you to go ahead." (Monaghan, 327)

262 "While knowing the Cheyennes to be deserving." (Custer, *My Life*, 353)

262 "I advanced with my revolver in my left hand." (Custer, *My Life*, 354)

264 "By the time the sun got within a hand's breadth." (Moore, 14)

264 "Emaciated and swathed in stitched-together flour sacks." (Greene, 181)

264 "After I came back." (Stratton, 125)

265 "I have been successful in my campaign." (Wert, 285)

265 "As I knew that the captives could not be released." (Custer, *My Life*, 358)

266 "I was expected to make a miniature volcano of myself." (Custer, *My Life*, 358)

266 "I will never harm the Cheyenne." (Powell, *Sweet Medicine*, vol. 1, 120)

266 "If you break your promise, you and your soldiers will go to dust." (Powell, *Sweet Medicine*, vol. 1, 120)

EPILOGUE

All quotations from Lawrence Hart in Sharp, *Gathering at the Hearth*.

BIBLIOGRAPHY

Ambrose, Stephen E. *Crazy Horse and Custer*. Garden City, NY: Doubleday, 1975.

Ashley, S. R. "Reminiscences of Colorado in the Early 'Sixties." *Colorado Magazine* (November 1936): 219–230.

Athearn, Robert G. *William Tecumseh Sherman and the Settlement of the West*. Norman: University of Oklahoma Press, 1956.

Barnard, S. *Custer's First Sergeant, John Ryan*. Terre Haute, IN: AST Press, 1996.

Barnett, Louise. *Touched by Fire: The Life, Death, and Mythic Afterlife of George Armstrong Custer*. New York: Holt, 1996.

Barnitz, Albert and Jennie. *Life in Custer's Cavalry: Diaries and Letters of Albert and Jennie Barnitz, 1867–1868*. Edited by Robert M. Utley. New Haven: Yale University Press, 1977.

Berthrong, D. J. *The Southern Cheyennes*. Norman: University of Oklahoma Press, 1963.

Bierman, John. *Dark Safari: the Life behind the Legend of Henry Morton Stanley*. New York: Knopf, 1990.

Brill, Charles J. *Custer, Black Kettle, and the Fight on the Washita*. Norman: University of Oklahoma Press, 2001. Originally published 1938.

Brown, Dee. *Bury My Heart at Wounded Knee: An Indian History of the American West*. New York: Holt, 1970.

Burkey, Blaine. *Custer, Come at Once!* Hays, KS: Thomas More Prep, 1976.

Carroll, John M., ed. *General Custer and the Battle of the Washita: The Federal View*. Bryan, TX: Guidon Press, 1978.

Chandler, Melbourne C. *Of GarryOwen in Glory: The History of the Seventh United States Cavalry Regiment*. Self-published, 1960.

Connell, Evan S. *Son of the Morning Star: Custer and the Little Bighorn*. San Francisco: North Point Press, 1984.

Craig, R. S. *The Fighting Parson: The Biography of Colonel John M. Chivington*. Los Angeles: Westernlore Press, 1959.

Custer, Elizabeth B. (Libbie). *Boots and Saddles, or Life in Dakota with General Custer.* Williamstown, MA: Corner House, 1969. Originally published 1885.

———. *Following the Guidon.* Norman: University of Oklahoma Press, 1966. Originally published 1890.

Custer, George A. *My Life on the Plains.* Norman: University of Oklahoma Press, 1962. Originally published 1874.

Custer, George A., and Elizabeth B. Custer. *The Life and Intimate Letters of General George A. Custer and His Wife Elizabeth.* Edited by Marguerite Merington. New York: Devin-Adair, 1950.

Davis, Theodore R. "A Summer on the Plains." *Harper's New Monthly Magazine* 36 (February 1868): 292–307.

"Denver Ceremony Recalls Sand Creek Massacre." *Denver Post,* November 26, 2011.

Ediger, T. A., and V. Hoffman. "Some Reminiscences of the Battle of the Washita." *Chronicles of Oklahoma* 33 (1955): 137–141.

Fellman, Michael. *Citizen Sherman.* New York: Random House, 1995.

Fougera, Katherine Gibson. *With Custer's Cavalry: From the Memoirs of the Late Katherine Gibson, Widow of Captain Francis M. Gibson of the 7th Cavalry.* Lincoln: University of Nebraska Press, 1986.

Frost, Lawrence A. *The Court-Martial of General George Armstrong Custer.* Norman: University of Oklahoma Press, 1968.

———. *General Custer's Libbie.* Seattle: Superior Publishing, 1976.

Gardiner, D. *The Great Betrayal.* Garden City, NY: Doubleday, 1949.

Greene, Jerome A. *Washita: The US Army and the Southern Cheyennes, 1867–1869.* Norman: University of Oklahoma Press, 2004.

Grinnell, G. B. *The Cheyenne Indians: The History and Ways of Life.* 2 vols. New Haven: Yale University Press, 1923. Reprint, Lincoln: University of Nebraska Press, 1972.

———. *The Fighting Cheyennes.* New York: Scribner, 1915.

Hafen, L. R., ed. *Colorado and Its People.* New York: Lewis Historical Publishing, 1948.

Hall, F. *History of the State of Colorado.* Chicago: Blakely Printing, 1889.

Hall, Richard. *Stanley: An Adventurer Explored.* Boston: Houghton Mifflin, 1975.

Hardorff, Richard G. *Washita Memories.* Norman: University of Oklahoma Press, 2006.

Harrison, Peter. *The Eyes of the Sleepers: Cheyenne Accounts of the Washita Attack*. Southampton: The English Westerners' Society, 1998.

Haskell, Frank A. *The Battle of Gettysburg*. Boston: Houghton Mifflin, 1958.

Hatch, Thom. *Black Kettle*. New York: Wiley, 2004.

Hoig, Stan. *The Peace Chiefs of the Cheyennes*. Norman: University of Oklahoma Press, 1980.

———. *The Sand Creek Massacre*. Norman: University of Oklahoma Press, 1961.

Hutton, Paul A., ed. *The Custer Reader*. Lincoln: University of Nebraska Press, 1992.

———. *Phil Sheridan and His Army*. Lincoln: University of Nebraska Press, 1985.

Jones, Douglas C. *The Treaty of Medicine Lodge*. Norman: University of Oklahoma Press, 1966.

Jordan, David M. *Winfield Scott Hancock: A Soldier's Life*. Bloomington: Indiana University Press, 1988.

Keim, DeBenneville Randolph. *Sheridan's Troopers on the Borders*. Philadelphia: David McKay, 1891.

Kennedy, W. J. D. *On the Plains with Custer and Hancock: The Journal of Isaac Coates, Army Surgeon*. Boulder, CO: Johnson, 1997.

Kidd, J. H. *Personal Recollections of a Cavalryman with Custer's Michigan Cavalry Brigade in the Civil War*. Ionia, MI: Sentinel Printing, 1908.

Kraft, Louis. *Custer and the Cheyenne*. El Segundo, CA: Upton, 1995.

Lavender, D. *Bent's Fort*. Garden City, NY: Doubleday, 1954.

Lears, Jackson. *Rebirth of a Nation*. New York: HarperCollins, 2009.

Leckie, Shirley A. *Elizabeth Bacon Custer and the Making of a Myth*. Norman: University of Oklahoma Press, 1993.

Leech, Margaret. *Reveille in Washington, 1860–1865*. New York: Harper, 1941.

Longstreet, James. *From Manassas to Appomattox*. Philadelphia: Lippincott, 1895.

Lyman, [Col.] Theodore. *Meade's Headquarters 1863–1865: Letters of Colonel Theodore Lyman from The Wilderness to Appomattox*. Boston: Atlantic Monthly Press, 1922.

MacMechen, E. C. *Life of Governor Evans, Second Territorial Governor of Colorado*. Denver: Wahlgreen, 1924.

Marquis, T. B. *Wooden Leg: A Warrior Who Fought Custer.* Lincoln: University of Nebraska Press, 1931.

Marshall, S. L. A. *Crimsoned Prairie: The Indian Wars.* New York: Scribner, 1972.

Mattes, Merrill J. "The Beecher Island Battlefield Diary of Sigmund Shlesinger." *Colorado Magazine* 29, no. 3 (July 1952): 161–169.

Monaghan, Jay. *Custer.* Lincoln: University of Nebraska Press, 1959.

Monnett, John H. *The Battle of Beecher Island and the Indian War of 1867–1869.* Boulder: University Press of Colorado, 1992.

Moore, Horace L. "The Nineteenth Kansas Cavalry in the Washita Campaign." *Chronicles of Oklahoma* 2 (December 1924): 350–365.

Morris, Roy, Jr. *Sheridan.* New York: Crown, 1992.

Nye, Wilber S. *Plains Indians Raiders.* Norman: University of Oklahoma Press, 1968.

Perkin, R. R. *The First Hundred Years: An Informal History of Denver and The Rocky Mountain News.* Garden City, NY: Doubleday, 1959.

Powell, Peter John [Stone Forehead]. *People of the Sacred Mountain.* San Francisco: Harper and Row, 1981.

———. *Sweet Medicine.* 2 vols. Norman: University of Oklahoma Press, 1969.

Robbins, C. C. "Texas and New Mexico Battle over Remains of Fallen Confederate Soldiers." *New York Times,* November 29, 1987.

Sandoz, Mari. *The Buffalo Hunters.* New York: Hastings House, 1954.

Schultz, Duane. *Custer: Lessons in Leadership.* New York: Palgrave Macmillan, 2010.

———. *Month of the Freezing Moon: The Sand Creek Massacre, November 1864.* New York: St. Martin's, 1990.

Sharp, John E. *Gathering at the Hearth: Stories Mennonites Tell.* Harrisonburg, VA: Herald Press, 2001.

"Silas Soule, Assassinated." *Rocky Mountain News,* April 24, 1865.

Smith, R. A. *Moon of Popping Trees.* Lincoln: University of Nebraska Press, 1975.

Speer, J. Report to George A. Martin of Interview with Mrs. John M. Chivington. John M. Chivington Miscellaneous Papers, Manuscript Division, Kansas State Historical Society, Topeka, March 11, 1902.

Stanley, H. M. *My Early Travels and Adventures in America*. Lincoln: University of Nebraska Press, 1982. Originally published 1895.

Stratton, Joanna L. *Pioneer Women: Voices from the Kansas Frontier*. New York: Simon and Schuster, 1981.

Thetford, Francis. "Battle of the Washita Centennial, 1968." *Chronicles of Oklahoma* 46 (Winter 1968–1969): 358–361.

US Congress. *Massacre of Cheyenne Indians*. Report of the Joint Committee on the Conduct of the War, 38th Cong., 2nd sess., app. 77. Washington, DC: Government Printing Office, 1865.

———. *Sand Creek Massacre*. Report of the Secretary of War, 39th Cong., 2nd sess., Senate Executive Document 26. Washington, DC: Government Printing Office, 1867.

Urwin, Gregory. *Custer Victorious*. Lincoln: University of Nebraska Press, 1983.

Utley, Robert M. *Cavalier in Buckskin: George Armstrong Custer and the Western Military Frontier*. Norman: University of Oklahoma Press, 1988.

———. *Frontier Regulars: The United States Army and the Indian, 1866–1891*. Lincoln: University of Nebraska Press, 1984.

———. *Frontiersmen in Blue: The United States Army and the Indian, 1848–1865*. New York: Macmillan, 1967.

Ware, E. F. *The Indian War of 1864*. New York: St. Martin's, 1960. Originally published 1911.

Wert, Jeffry D. *General James Longstreet*. New York: Simon and Schuster, 1993.

Whittaker, Frederick. *A Complete Life of General George A. Custer*. Lincoln: University of Nebraska Press, 1993. Originally published 1876.

Wynkoop, Edward W. *The Tall Chief: The Unfinished Autobiography of Edward W. Wynkoop, 1856–1866*. Edited by Christopher B. Gerboth. Denver: Colorado Historical Society, 1994.

INDEX

ACKNOWLEDGMENTS

Anyone attempting to re-create events from the past owes an enormous debt of gratitude to the eyewitnesses who wrote letters and memoirs and kept diaries, as well as to the dedicated archivists who organize, maintain, and make available their extensive collections, without which books such as this would be far less complete and accurate.

My sincere thanks to the State Historical Society of Colorado, the Kansas State Historical Society, the National Archives, the United States Army Military History Institute, the Little Big Horn Battlefield National Monument, and the Washita Battlefield National Historic Site.

I am grateful to Bruce H. Franklin of Westholme Publishing for his enthusiasm and dedication to the project and for providing a genuine sense of collaboration rare in today's publishing world.

Thanks also to Robin Rue, my agent of more than twenty-five years, for her steadfast encouragement and support. I greatly appreciate the efforts of Trudi Gershenov in providing yet another striking book jacket, and of Ron Silverman for his thoughtful suggestions and meticulous editing of the manuscript. And continuing thanks to my wife, Sydney Ellen, who continues to make things better.

BOOKS BY DUANE SCHULTZ

Wake Island: The Heroic Gallant Fight

Sabers in the Wind: A Novel of World War II

Hero of Bataan: The Story of General Jonathan M. Wainwright

The Last Battle Station: The Story of the USS Houston

The Maverick War: Chennault and the Flying Tigers

The Doolittle Raid

Month of the Freezing Moon: The Sand Creek Massacre

Over the Earth I Come: The Great Sioux Uprising of 1862

Glory Enough for All: The Battle of the Crater

Quantrill's War: The Life and Times of William Clarke Quantrill

The Dahlgren Affair: Terror and Conspiracy in the Civil War

The Most Glorious Fourth: Vicksburg and Gettysburg

Into the Fire: Ploesti, the Most Fateful Mission of World War II

Crossing the Rapido: A Tragedy of World War II

Custer: Lessons in Leadership

The Fate of War: Fredericksburg, 1862